How Does Analysis Cure?

HOW DOES ANALYSIS CURE?

Heinz Kohut

Edited by Arnold Goldberg,
with the collaboration
of Paul Stepansky

The University of Chicago Press
Chicago and London

The publication of this book was assisted by contributions to the Heinz Kohut Memorial Fund.

Heinz Kohut was professorial lecturer in the Department of Psychiatry at the University of Chicago, a faculty member and training analyst at the Chicago Institute for Psychoanalysis, and visiting professor of psychoanalysis at the University of Cincinnati until his death in 1981. He is the author of *The Analysis of the Self* (1971) and *The Restoration of the Self* (1977).

The University of Chicago Press 60637
The University of Chicago Press, Ltd., London
Printed in the United States of America
93 92 91 90 89 88 87 86 85 84   5 4 3 2 1

Library of Congress Cataloging in Publication Data

Kohut, Heinz.
   How does analysis cure?

   Bibliography: p.
   Includes index.
   1. Self. 2. Psychoanalysis. I. Goldberg, Arnold,
1929-   . II. Stepansky, Paul E. III. Title. [DNLM:
1. Ego. 2. Psychoanalytic theory. 3. Psychoanalysis.
4. Self assessment (Psychology) WM 460.5.E3 K79h]
BF697.K64   1984   616.89'17   83-24090
ISBN 0-226-45034-1

To the memory of
Ernst Morawetz and Ignaz Purkhardshofer,
two teachers who decisively furthered
the development of my mind

Contents

Preface

When my husband, shortly before his death, finished writing this book, he said that he thought he had accomplished what he had set out to do for psychoanalysis and expressed the hope that his colleagues, particularly those of the younger generation, would do further research on the many questions he has raised during the course of his work. He also expressed the hope that his thoughts would stimulate them to raise questions of their own, to pursue ideas of their own in order to continue the advance of the science of psychoanalysis.

I made some revisions in Arnold Goldberg's and Paul Stepansky's editing of my husband's manuscript by including some passages from the original that I knew my husband felt were important to communicate—even to reiterate—which they had omitted for reasons of style. Although my inclusion of these passages may make the book somewhat more difficult to read, I hope that readers will have the necessary patience, for I believe they will be rewarded for their efforts by the richness of the ideas expressed and enlarged upon in this book.

I would like to express my thanks to our son, Tom, and to my husband's old friend Robert W. Wadsworth for their help to me in preparing the manuscript for publication.

Elizabeth Kohut

Introduction

This is Heinz Kohut's last book. It will not be the last book expounding his work, however, since psychoanalytic self psychology has by now achieved a momentum and a history of its own. This book is a point in that history.

It is a history that has been eventful and exciting by any standard. It is difficult to mark the beginning of this history; the story of self psychology is so integral to Heinz Kohut that its full explication must await the telling of Kohut's own life history. But one can profitably review a brief span of the intellectual life of self psychology against the backdrop of a prophecy of William James that a close friend commended to Heinz after reading the manuscript of *The Analysis of the Self*: "First they will say it is all wrong, then that it is unimportant and trivial, and finally that they knew it all along." The prediction, of course, would prove substantially true. It was revealing, as well, of the extraordinary impact of a new set of ideas on a scientific community—a story that remains to be told.

To be sure, not everyone who heard and read about Kohut's ideas on narcissism initially reacted according to that Jamesian prophecy, nor did the sequence of judgments unfold as neatly as the prophecy predicts. When Kohut first presented his paper "Forms and Transformations of Narcissism" in December 1965 (Kohut 1978*b*, vol. 1), he was at the height of his professional career within the institutional framework of psychoanalysis. His observations about narcissism provoked little dissent at the time, and even his paper "The Psychoanalytic Treatment of Narcissistic Personality Disorders," delivered two years later (Kohut 1978*b*, vol. 1), met with a generally hospitable reception. In the late 1960s, as Kohut prepared to publish *The Analysis of the Self*, he asked certain of his colleagues and students at various times to read and comment on drafts of that work. He clearly understood this first book as signaling a departure from the tradition of classical analysis, and he sought as wide a range of critical response as he could obtain prior to its publication.

Although *The Analysis of the Self* in fact received a remarkably broad and appreciative readership, it also elicited sharp negative reactions. Out of Kohut's desire for an intellectual forum and his need for a buffer against a rising tide of criticism, a group of analysts interested in his work began meeting with him regularly. It has continued to meet until the present. Over the years the self psychology study group has attracted a rich and varied membership; Michael Basch, John Gedo, David Marcus, Anna Ornstein, Paul Ornstein, Marian Tolpin, Paul Tolpin, and Ernest Wolf have all belonged to the group at one time or another. More recent members have included Bernard Brandchaft, Arthur Malin, Evelyne Schwaber, Estelle Shane, Morton Shane, and Robert Stolorow. Out of the expanding interest in Kohut's work, a larger group with some fifty members eventually supplanted the original study group. Although the majority of our meetings dealt with the ideas involved in self psychology, we occasionally proceeded with projects such as the collaborative publication of *The Psychology of the Self: A Casebook* (Goldberg 1978) along with the organization of self psychology conferences.

I can think of no more heated discussions of self psychology than those that began in the study group and continue even today. We have, all of us, wrestled with almost every criticism that has been leveled at self psychology, although we undertook our discussions not in the spirit of realizing James's prediction, but rather to make sense of what we were struggling to understand. I do not think it hyperbole to suggest that we rarely hear a criticism that we have not already grappled with and satisfactorily answered within the study group. To be sure, we continue to live with many criticisms of our own that are as yet unanswered, but, surely, this is characteristic of all sciences.

The present book is a chapter in the evolution of psychoanalytic ideas; it testifies to the evolving status of the concepts of psychoanalytic self psychology. It grew out of many group discussions with Kohut and it represents, in part, his attempt to answer certain questions that followed the publication of *The Restoration of the Self*. It is not, however, restricted to a commentary on this latter volume, because the very questions that Kohut addresses directed him to a set of hypotheses about the nature of the analytic cure that are fundamentally different from his previous ideas about cure; along with this theoretical advance, Kohut offers substantive elaboration of the concept of empathy, the status of the Oedipus complex, the nature of defenses and resistances, and the variety of selfobject transferences—among the many topics covered in the volume. One of the most significant aspects of the book is Kohut's cogent articulation of the many problems in self psychology that remain to be studied and ultimately solved.

Anyone who has participated in the history of self psychology can offer a ready response to the elements of the Jamesian prophecy invoked by Heinz's friend. Kohut's ideas and theories are not "wrong" because such new ideas and new theories can never be summarily labeled right or wrong. Rather, we have a pragmatic criterion by which to judge them: we must ask just how worthwhile these ideas are in the conduct of clinical analyses. There can be no question that Kohut's ideas are important and deserving of further study and debate, but these activities must be undertaken less in a spirit of dissent than in a spirit of exploration: to find out whether they allow us to see more than we saw before. Kohut's ideas are hardly "trivial": too many analysts have been able to make significant clinical and theoretical use of them to allow self psychology to be dismissed as unimportant. The last element of the prophecy forces us to ask whether analysts have, in fact, been utilizing self psychological ideas all along. Not surprisingly, it is a question that is answered in the course of this book, and the reader can look forward to Kohut's insightful perspective on this issue in the pages ahead.

This present book was edited by Paul Stepansky and me from a manuscript left by Heinz Kohut. I think it is fair to say that we have neither added to nor subtracted from his ideas but have undertaken our work mainly with an eye toward clarity of expression. The bulk of this effort was Stepansky's, and I am sure this task could never have been completed without his collaboration. I can take responsibility for the accuracy or inaccuracy of his rendering of Kohut's ideas, but I am confident that we have here a faithful version of what he intended to say.

Arnold Goldberg, M.D.
Chicago

Part One
The Restoration of the Self: Responses and Afterthoughts

Not surprisingly, some of the ideas contained in my recent book *The Restoration of the Self* (1977) have evoked a variety of responses from colleagues. On many occasions, in consultative sessions, seminars, and correspondence, I have been asked to clarify certain thoughts that I had apparently not elaborated sufficiently in my book. In addition to this external stimulation from the side of colleagues and friends, I have continued to pursue certain lines of thought a bit further and have arrived at new insights that I would like to communicate. Although the various topics that I wish to take up in Part I are to a certain extent interconnected, they do not form a truly cohesive whole. They belong together mainly insofar as they are all responses and afterthoughts to *The Restoration of the Self*.

1
Analyzability in the Light of Self Psychology

Should Some Analyses of Severe Personality and Behavior Disorders Remain Incomplete?

Although the majority of comments elicited by *The Restoration of the Self* (1977) have been supportive of the psychoanalytic psychology of the self set forth in that work, one aspect of my presentation that seems to require further discussion has been constructively brought to my attention by a colleague. In a letter that was favorably disposed toward self psychology in general and warmly approving of *The Restoration of the Self* in particular, this colleague took exception to what he understood to be one implication of my recent work. Specifically, he believed I advocate "that one will have to break off treatment before the analysand gets into too disturbing material." While conceding that "a regression can be in certain cases difficult to control," he voiced the opinion, which he felt was in opposition to my view, that "slow and cautious work and especially the ability to verbalize the experiences" would counteract the danger sufficiently. These statements disturbed me. I had not realized that my views concerning this issue, particularly as they were presented in *The Restoration of the Self*, would be interpreted in the way in which my friendly colleague had. And there are undoubtedly other readers who similarly misunderstood my therapeutic attitude toward those conditions which the colleague in question characterized as "real deficiencies of the self." In the following I will try to explain my actual position.

The essential therapeutic conclusion of all my contributions to the understanding of the self and its development can be formulated as follows: it is the defect in the self that brings about and maintains a patient's selfobject (narcissistic) transference, and it is the working through of this transference which, via transmuting internalization, that is, via a wholesome psychic activity that has been thwarted in childhood, lays down the structures needed to fill the defect in the self. Indeed, I take the emergence of this process, and especially its persistent engagement, as evidence that the treatment situation has reactivated the developmental potential of the defective self. This central hypothesis, clearly set forth in *The Analysis of the Self* (1971) and many other publications, was not contradicted by my presentation in *The Restoration of the Self*.

The misunderstanding that I am advocating incomplete analyses for analyzable disorders of the self, that, in particular, I am advising that certain structural defects in the self should in such cases be allowed to remain unhealed, stems perhaps from the fact that I did not succeed in impressing upon some readers the significance of certain theoretical refinements concerning the development of the self in childhood and the significance of certain correlated shifts in the definition of psychological health and psychoanalytic cure that now supplement my earlier hypotheses.

But I must proceed slowly and present my views concerning early development, mental health, and cure not in isolation but within the fundamental context from which all explanations derive: the empathic observation of the experiences of my analysands in the analytic situation. I will start by affirming once more my central claim with regard to the cure of the self: in the analysis of narcissistic personality disturbances all existing defects in the self become spontaneously mobilized as selfobject (narcissistic) transferences. And I will only add, to prevent a possible misunderstanding, that when I speak of the spontaneous mobilization of the transference in this context, I am fully aware of the fact that transference resistances which oppose this development exist and must be recognized and then dealt with by interpretation (see Kohut 1978*b*, 2:547–61). But acknowledgment of the existence of forces that oppose the unfolding of these transferences does not contradict my central claim that, given the actuating matrix of the psychoanalytic situation, the defective self of the patient with a narcissistic personality disturbance will mobilize its striving to complete its development, that is, that it will try again to establish an uninterrupted tension arc from basic ambitions, via basic talents and skills, toward basic ideals. This tension arc is the dynamic essence of the complete, nondefective self; it is a conceptualization of the structure whose establishment makes possible a creative-productive, fulfilling life.

If a self has attained such nondefective structural completeness but is still unable to enact its intrinsic program because its energies are consumed by unresolved oedipal conflicts, then oedipal conflicts will be mobilized in the psychoanalytic situation, and an oedipal transference will offer itself to be worked through. The self psychological approach to those psychic disturbances that Freud called the "transference neuroses" is, prima facie, the same as that advocated by traditional analysis: the facilitation of the unfolding oedipal transference via systematic defense-analysis and the avoidance of premature transference interpretations (see Kohut 1971, p. 266) followed by a protracted phase of interpretation and working through. The differences between the traditional and the self psychologically informed therapeutic approaches to the classical transference neuroses relate to their different conceptions of the basic pathogenesis. The classical position maintains that we have arrived at the deepest level when we have reached the patient's experience of his impulses, wishes, and drives, that is, when the patient has become aware of his archaic sexual lust and hostility. The self psychologically informed analyst, however, will be open to the fact that the pathogenic Oedipus complex is embedded in an oedipal self-selfobject disturbance, that beneath lust and hostility there is a layer of depression and of diffuse narcissistic rage. The analytic process will, therefore, not only deal with the oedipal conflicts per se but also, in a subsequent phase or, more frequently, more or less simultaneously (though even then with gradually increasing emphasis), focus on the underlying depression and the recognition of the failures of the child's oedipal selfobjects. In view of the fact that the flawed selfobject matrix that is the breeding ground for the pathogenic Oedipus complex in childhood will be extensively discussed later in the present work, I will now leave the topic of the analysis of the oedipal neuroses and turn to the analyzable self disorders in the narrow sense of this term, that is, to the narcissistic personality and behavior disorders.

With regard to the analysis of narcissistic personality disturbances in the narrow sense, I want to emphasize the essential importance of such patients reexperiencing and working through the lethargies, depressions, and rages of early life via the reactivation and analysis of their archaic traumatic self-selfobject relationships in the transference. While, as I noted above, all properly conducted analyses of oedipal neuroses will eventually reveal a layer of depression and diffuse rage concerning the failures of the selfobjects of the oedipal period, with the narcissistic personality disorders the remobilization of the analogous experiences of early and earliest childhood must occupy the center of the analytic stage for prolonged periods. If, that is, the insufficiently coherent or enfeeblement-prone self of the analysand suffering from a severe narcissistic personality disorder requires the working through of the lethargies and rages of earliest infancy on the way toward its rehabilitation, then these archaic experiences will be mobilized in the psychoanalytic situation and worked through. I might add here that these primeval experiences usually manifest themselves in the transference via the "telescoping" of archaic needs and archaic responses to their frustration on the one hand (such as the need for a primitive merger and primitive forms of rage and lethargy), with analogous needs and frustration-responses of later developmental stages on the other (such as the wish for closeness via perfect empathy and the feeling of disappointment when the empathic response is imperfect).

Having now corrected with, I hope, unmistakable clarity the misunderstanding to which I initially referred—I do not, in other words, advocate "that one will have to break off treatment before the analysand gets into too disturbing material"—it behooves me also to clarify the point made in *The Restoration of the Self* that led my friendly critic astray. The crucial point that I stressed in that work but apparently did not succeed in illuminating sufficiently was this: If during its development in early childhood the self succeeds in disentangling itself from a seriously pathogenic selfobject and creates a new pattern for itself via a new developmental route, nearly reaches its goal in this second attempt at taking shape but ultimately fails again, though not by as wide a margin, then given the renewed chance for further self development in adult life made possible by psychoanalysis, the spontaneously unrolling sequence of transferences will ultimately come to rest at the point at which those needs begin to be remobilized that had not been responded to in the child's second and more promising attempt to build up its self. It is in the analyses of these cases—and of these cases only, I will stress—that the transference, after briefly touching early depressions and rages, will spontaneously move on and settle at a different, later point in development. And it is in the analyses of these cases—and of these cases only, I reiterate (see in this connection my discussions of Mr. X. in Kohut [1977, pp. 199–219] and of Mr. Z. [1979])—that experience has taught me that it is an error to attempt to guide the patient to the analysis of archaic traumata. It is the pivotal point in later development when for the second time the self sought the cohesion-firming responses of a selfobject that is revived in the crucial transferences of such analyses. And the working-through processes that are then set in motion will ultimately bring about a true cure of the disease of such a self, that is, they will establish a structurally complete self. I will only add that when I speak of the "cure" of the self in this context, my statement is in harmony with my conviction that the psychological health of this core of the personality is always best defined in terms of structural completeness, that is, that we should speak of having achieved a cure when an energic continuum in the center of the personality has been established and the unfolding of a productive life has thus become a realizable possibility.

The healthy self that may ultimately establish itself may deviate from norms derived from the assumption that every analytic cure is defined either—according to the traditional Freudian outlook—by the engagement and ultimate resolution of oedipal conflicts or—according to the Kleinian view—by the reexperiencing and ultimate overcoming of the most archaic layers of depression, suspicion, and rage. However rough-hewn the definition of mental health on the basis of the structural and functional completeness of a sector of the self may be, I believe it is not only more meaningfully applicable to human life in general, but more specifically relevant to the psychic disturbances that are prevalent today than definitions which, following the traditional Freudian and Kleinian norms, equate mental health with the attainment of a specific psychological task of early development: the attainment of postoedipal genitality, of the capacity for post-paranoid-depressive object love, of object constancy, or of any other number of specific developmental successes that are deemed to be crucial. I am opposed to these definitions neither because of their perfectionism—all standards are ideals—nor because to a certain extent they set up self-fulfilling prophecies—all value judgments share this limitation—but because I believe they are in error. Although the attainment of genitality and the capacity for unambivalent object love have been features of many, perhaps most, satisfying and significant lives, there are many other good lives, including some of the greatest and most fulfilling lives recorded in history, that were not lived by individuals whose psychosexual organization was heterosexual-genital or whose major commitment was to unambivalent object love.[1]

All in all, then, I am fighting two orthodoxies: one decrees that every cure rests on the analysis of the Oedipus complex, the other legislates that every cure rests on the analysis of the depressions and rages of earliest infancy. Furthermore, I must emphasize at this point that I am not fighting these orthodoxies on the basis of considerations that spurn idealistic perfectionism in therapy and advocate the need for compromise.

In fact, I am not disregarding the necessity for making compromises with regard to the goals of the psychoanalytic practitioner. I fully acknowledge that disorders that are in principle analyzable are encountered, though not as frequently as some believe; I tend to be on the side of courage here and find that, with caution and patience, it will be rewarded by success—in which analyst and analysand will rightly decide to let sleeping dogs lie—even though the decision means that the analysis remains incomplete, that areas will be avoided which would have to be activated and examined in order to heal the essential defect in the self. But these issues are irrelevant in the present context, and they were similarly irrelevant in the context in which I contemplated them in *The Restoration of the Self* (1977). The basis on which my therapeutic conclusions rest is not expediency, however laudable, in instances carefully selected by the seasoned clinician, but a new definition of the essence of the self and a new conceptualization of its structural development.

I will now, at the risk of appearing pedantic, present a schematic survey of the therapeutic possibilities vis-à-vis each of the three genetic-structurally defined classes of disorders—the psychoses, the narcissistic personality disturbances, the classical transference neuroses—in which the functional freedom of the self is impaired.

The Three Classes of Psychic Disorder and Their Analyzability

The Psychoses

In the psychoses, including those covertly psychotic personality organizations (central hollowness, but a well-developed peripheral layer of defensive structures) for which I reserve the term borderline states, a nuclear self has not been shaped in early development.[2] Although my analytic experience with such patients is very limited, I have reached the conclusion that in these cases the psychoanalytic situation does not bring about the long-term activation of the central chaos of the self within a workable transference that is a precondition for setting in motion the processes that would lead to the creation, de novo, of a nuclear self. In order to lead to a causal cure, the therapeutic process would have to penetrate beneath the organized layers—the defensive structures—of the patient's self and permit the prolonged reexperience of oscillations between prepsychological chaos and the security provided by primitive merger with an archaic selfobject. It is certainly imaginable that, even in adult life, the repeated experience of optimal frustration in an archaic homeostatic selfobject environment brought about in the analytic situation would lead, as in earliest infancy, to the birth of a nuclear self. But I cannot imagine that an individual would submit himself to the dissolution of defensive structures that have protected him for a lifetime and voluntarily accept the unspeakable anxieties accompanying what must seem to him to be the task of facing a prepsychological state that had remained chaotic because the selfobject milieu in early life lacked the empathic responsiveness that would have organized the child's world and maintained his innate self-confidence. I am aware of the fact that I may simply be describing my personal limits as a psychoanalyst and thus my acceptance of the existence of psychoses and borderline conditions. (I am a diagnostic relativist here: to my mind the terms "psychosis" and "borderline state" simply refer to the fact that we are dealing with states of pre-psychological chaos which the empathic instrument of the observer is unable to comprehend.) Be that as it may, however, my clinical experience suggests that the analytic dissolution of defensive structures that have formed around a persisting hollowness in the center of the patient's self cannot be achieved—even in cases where this central hollowness is experienced as painful by a would-be analysand. Perhaps the basis of my conviction, as I implied before, is the feeling that I would not be able to maintain a reliable empathic bond with the patient when, at the end of his journey toward the basic transference, he would have to tolerate the protracted experience of prepsychological chaos and, not just temporarily but for long periods, borrow the analyst's personality organization in order to survive. Of course, the fact that a therapist cannot accompany his patient into the lands of prepsychological chaos does not mean that he cannot be of help to him. While a nuclear self cannot be created by the therapy, the patient can still use the therapist as a selfobject to build up new defensive structures and, especially, to firm already existing defensive structures. A selfobject transference establishes itself, in other words, in which the threatened *defensive* structures are offered to the selfobject therapist for his mirroring approval, or in which the selfobject therapist's personality is used, via a twinship merger or goal-setting idealizations, to strengthen the patient's defensive structures. As the result of straightforward educational activities from the side of the therapist, moreover, the patient can learn how to manage his defensive structures to his best advantage.

The Narcissistic Personality and Behavior Disturbances

In the narcissistic personality and behavior disturbances, in contradistinction to the psychoses and borderline states, the outlines of a specific nuclear self *have* been established in early development. The structuralization of the pattern of the self has remained incomplete, however, with the result that the self reacts to narcissistic injuries with temporary break-up, enfeeblement, or disharmony (see Kohut and Wolf 1978). In contrast to the psychoses, however, the psychoanalytic situation here does provide a matrix in which the defects in the structure of the self—even severe defects that lead to the temporary appearance of serious, quasi-psychotic symptoms—are filled in via reactivation of the needs for narcissistic sustenance (i.e., the need for mirroring and the need to merge with an ideal) that had not been provided in childhood.

The Structural-Conflict Neuroses

With regard to the psychoses and narcissistic personality disturbances, a definition of the essence of the disorder and of the correlated therapeutic approach could be stated unambiguously. With regard to the structural neuroses, however, we unfortunately cannot be equally positive at this time. If we had to formulate the traditional outlook on the structural neuroses in self psychological terms, we would simply say that in the structural neuroses a nuclear self has become more or less firmly established in early childhood but that the self is ultimately unable to realize its creative-productive potential (its nuclear program of action) because its energies are absorbed by the conflicts to which it became exposed in later childhood (the Oedipus complex). In these cases, we would say, the psychoanalytic situation becomes the milieu in which the unresolved conflicts of later childhood are reactivated in the transference, made conscious and worked through, and ultimately settled, with the result that the self can turn to its essential goals.

The preceding formulation is immediately appealing because of its reasonableness and simplicity. Closer scrutiny, however, reveals that it leaves unanswered a number of questions including not only the therapeutic approach to the structural neuroses but also, and especially, the position of the structural neuroses within the framework of psychoanalytic self psychology. How, to turn to the decisive theoretical issue first, does the statement made above that "in the structural neuroses a nuclear self has become more or less firmly established" jibe with the theory (Kohut 1977, pp. 246–48) that the normal oedipal phase is not pathogenic or, in the obverse, that the pathogenic Oedipus complex that we uncover as we analyze a classical transference neurosis is a disintegration product which assumes the presence of a noncohesive or at least enfeebled self? It seems that our task is to reconcile two contradictory hypotheses: that the self in true oedipal neuroses (with regard to *pseudo*transference neuroses, see Kohut 1978*b*, 2:624–28) is basically cohesive and firm and only becomes enfeebled in consequence of oedipal conflicts, in particular because of its persistent entanglement with the oedipal imagoes; and that the self in true oedipal neuroses is basically fragmented and weak because only a fragmented and weak self, unsupported by oedipal selfobjects, would react to the experiences of the oedipal phase with the intense sexual and hostile-aggressive responses that are reactivated during the analysis of these cases and subsequently uncovered (made conscious) by the analytic work.

Will this paradox be resolved by our ultimately reaching the conclusion that true transference neuroses in the classical sense do not exist, that the classical hysterias, the phobias, and the phobic nucleus of compulsion neuroses are in fact only variants of narcissistic personality disorders? I do not think so. I rather believe that the answer to the puzzling question I posed will have to come from a more exact differentiation between the structural weaknesses of the self and the developmental failures leading to those weaknesses. We need a more exact differentiation between (a) those self weaknesses that lead to the drive phenomena encountered in narcissistic personality disorders (e.g., those encountered in the great majority of the perversions and in the overwhelming majority of the addictions) and (b) those self weaknesses that lead to the intensification and isolation of drives that underlie the classical oedipal neuroses. Second, we require a more exact differentiation—a differentiation, in other words, that provides more than the specific psychosexual stage of the child's development at which these failures occur—between (a) those selfobject failures that lead to narcissistic personality disorders and (b) those selfobject failures that lead to oedipal neuroses. We do not yet have clear-cut answers to these questions and only further empirical data obtained during the analyses of cases of classical transference neuroses by observers familiar with the psychology of the self will ultimately enlighten us here. At this point I can do no more than give voice to my impression that the changes in the self in classical neuroses are not only in general less severe than those in the narcissistic personality disorders but that they are also qualitatively different. Could it be that this qualitative difference is due to the fact that the empathy failure from the side of the selfobjects of childhood was different in the two classes of psychopathology? That, as I suggested earlier (1977, pp. 267–80), we are seeing the difference between distant, understimulating parental selfobjects whose children[3] will later suffer from narcissistic personality disorders and excessively close, overstimulating selfobjects whose children will later suffer from classical transference neuroses? If this should indeed prove to be the case, then we could say that after an eighty-year-long detour, we are returning to Freud's original seduction theory—though not in the form in which Freud had entertained it. The seduction that we have in mind relates not to overt sexual activities of the adult selfobjects—although such behavior would have to be included—but to the fact that the selfobjects' empathy is distorted in a specific way. Instead of responding to the child's total oedipal self (the child's affection and assertiveness), they respond to fragments of the child's oedipal self (the child's sexual and aggressive drives). In view of the fact that I have already explained my views (see Kohut 1977, 1978*b*, 2:783–92) concerning the psychological primacy of phenomena (affection and assertiveness) that are traditionally considered secondary (that is, that are considered sublimated drives) and of the secondary nature of phenomena (lust and destructiveness) that are traditionally considered primary (that is, that are considered unsublimated drives), I do not need to set forth my arguments here. Instead I will focus in the next chapter on one specific issue, the role of castration anxiety, which I have not discussed extensively in the past despite the central position assigned to this emotion in the structure of the oedipal neuroses as traditionally conceived.[4]

2

A Reexamination of
Castration Anxiety

At first sight the self psychological evaluation of the position and significance of castration anxiety as it contrasts with the traditional psychoanalytic evaluation would seem clear-cut: in contrast to the customary analytic formulation which assigns a causal-motivational role to castration anxiety in its explanatory schema of the neuroses, the simple statement expected from us is that self psychology considers castration anxiety a secondary phenomenon, that is, a symptom. The web of causal-motivational factors, however, is more complex. The relation between oedipal neuroses and castration anxiety as understood by self psychology, in other words, is not adequately described by saying that it is not castration anxiety that causes the neurosis but a disorder of the self—the basic disease—that causes the castration anxiety. In order to understand the role of castration anxiety in the neuroses, we must examine the significance of this emotion not only in the life of the older child, the adolescent, and the adult, but also, and especially, in earlier childhood, that is, in the oedipal situation where it was first experienced or at least first discovered.

If we examine the genetic and causal circumstances at the point when, in accordance with the traditional view, castration anxiety is first experienced in childhood or when, to be more exact, castration anxiety first attains that pivotal significance in neurosogenesis traditionally assigned to it by analysis, we can discern a sequence of events with which we have become familiar through our past investigations of the disorders of the self via the scrutiny of the selfobject transference. We discover, in short, the cause-and-effect sequence of selfobject failure and defect in the structure of the self. Disregarding the innate element (i.e., the individual child's greater or lesser yet never absent survival-related capacity to *respond* with anxiety to danger or threat), the self psychological observer, focusing not only on the phenomenon but also on the milieu (i.e., the child's selfobject milieu) in which the phenomenon arose, will not view castration anxiety as a feature of the oedipal phase of the healthy child of healthy parents.

I will add that the maxim that castration anxiety in childhood should be considered pathological does not imply per se that castration anxiety occurs infrequently during this period of life. But even if one maintains that it is, in fact, ubiquitous, I would reply that frequency of occurrence implies no judgment with regard to health. Dental caries is ubiquitous, and yet it is not constitutive of dental health.[1] Still, moving from the question of definition to the issue of ascertainable fact, I will give voice to my impression that significant childhood castration anxiety is present less frequently than psychoanalysts believe. If, conforming now to the established analytic custom ushered in by Freud, we focus for comparison's sake on the little boy rather than the little girl, we can say that a boy who is exposed to the responses of psychologically healthy parents does not experience a significant degree of castration anxiety during the oedipal phase. This conclusion follows from the scrutiny of certain transference phenomena from analyses of patients with narcissistic personality disorders that tended to be taken as evidence of the reactivation of castration anxiety (see Kohut 1979) and, especially, on the basis of evidence obtained from the scrutiny of the transferences in the late stages of analyses with such patients (see Kohut 1978b, 1:228–29). Extrapolating from the evidence of the latter sort, I said (1977, pp. 245–48) that the healthy child of healthy parents enters the oedipal phase joyfully. The joy he experiences is due not only to the fact that he himself responds with pride to a developmental achievement, that is, to a new and expanding capacity for affection and assertiveness, but also to the fact that this achievement elicits a glow of empathic joy and pride from the side of the oedipal-phase selfobjects.[2] Owing to this joy and pride of achievement, the boy's affectionate attitude does not disintegrate into fragmented sexual impulses, his assertiveness is not transformed into destructive hostility, and he is not intensely afraid of his parents. Only if his parents do not function appropriately as oedipal selfobjects will the child experience high degrees of anxiety.

I am familiar with the traditional psychoanalytic tenet that the most paralyzing forms of castration anxiety (and at a later developmental stage the most paralyzing forms of superego anxiety) supervene in just those instances where the child's parents are unusually kind whereas anxiety-proneness in later life is diminished when the parents' openly expressed disapproval and consistently applied punishment succeed in creating a well-functioning internal system of drive-control. Although these statements are valuable up to a point, correctly describing the result of certain types of parental behavior, they are misleading with regard to the crucial issue at hand. We are not narrowly focusing on a particular aspect of parental behavior that can be characterized in terms of kindness or strictness, but are investigating the whole emotional ambience that characterizes the self-selfobject matrix during the oedipal phase. In doing so, we should be guided by the maxim that, with reference to the investigation of the parental role during certain crucial phases of the child's development (and the oedipal phase is to be evaluated par excellence as a developmental phase), it is, as I once put it, "less important to determine what the parents *do* than what they *are*." True enough, what the parents are— for example, the ways in which their personalities enhance, restrict, or distort their functions as the selfobjects of the oedipal child—will have to be investigated via their behavior. But the crucial differentiation between adequate and inadequate parental selfobjects will in some instances, perhaps in most, not pertain to such gross empathy failures as overtly sexual or sadistic responses, but to subtly expressed yet repeatedly deleterious responses. Is it really necessary to explain to analysts that, on the one hand, behavior cannot be taken at face value, that overt kindness may be experienced by the child—and rightly so— as stifling, as cruel (without providing even the chance for reactive anger), or simply as distant, disinterested, uninvolved? And will it come as a surprise when I along with many others say, conversely, that parental strictness may be experienced by the child—and, again, rightly so—as a development-enhancing, mastery-increasing gift from parents who allow with appropriate tolerance, indeed with pride,[3] the child's brief expression of anger when the wish is not fulfilled? All in all it is often by focusing our attention not on the content but on the form of parental behavior that we can best answer the decisive question of whether the behavior in question will create a traumatic or a wholesome atmosphere with regard to the development of the child— in the sphere of affection, sexual love, and sexual drivenness, as well as in the sphere of assertiveness, aggression, and destructive hostility.

Must we then expect parents to be near-perfect if they are not to hamper their children's emotional growth? Certainly not. The emotional health of the oedipal child is not dependent on the presence of parents who *never* feel envious of the younger generation or who *never* during periods of temporary self disturbance respond with a degree of sexuality to their child's affection. As long as these flawed responses constitute only the occasional disturbances of a basic attitude of appropriate empathic affection and pride, they can be counted as belonging to the optimal failures, which—like the analyst's analogous failures in therapy—bring about internalizations and structure-building. If the failures of the oedipal selfobjects are chronic, however, if they proceed not from the occasional emotional imbalance of a parent but from serious self pathology, then the child will indeed experience undue anxiety during the period under scrutiny.

This pathologic anxiety appears in two forms: as primary and as secondary oedipal anxiety. The primary anxiety of the oedipal period, which I consider to be the more basic of the two types, arises in response to the defective empathy of the child's parents, that is, in response to the flaws in a selfobject matrix that does not sustain the child. The secondary anxiety of the oedipal period, which often presents more conspicuous manifestations despite its derivative quality, arises in the child when, after the disintegration of the healthy oedipal self, characterized by affectionate and assertive attitudes, the fragmented oedipal self, characterized by sexual and destructive fantasies and impulses, takes over.

Let us now focus on the primary anxiety of the oedipal child. In the most general terms, such anxiety is simply one special and specific instance of the type of basic anxiety that I have characterized in recent years (Kohut 1977, pp. 104–5) as "disintegration anxiety." It is the deepest anxiety man can experience,[4] and none of the forms of anxiety described by Freud (1926, 1953, 20:87–157) are equivalent to it, in particular with regard to the basic content of the experience of the disintegration anxiety posited by self psychology.[5] Although disintegration anxiety is in essence different from what is usually called fear of death, the fear of death as it is strongly experienced by certain individuals is not unrelated to disintegration anxiety. What is feared in the latter case is not physical extinction but loss of humanness: psychological death. Clearly, the attempt to describe disintegration anxiety is the attempt to describe the indescribable. But since it is a profound human experience, it is not an exact verbal definition that is called for, but rather an attempt to evoke a taste of the experience in question. I will first attempt to do this by recounting two clinical episodes. Both center around dreams, the scrutiny of which may assist us in circumscribing the nature of disintegration anxiety.

The first of these dreams, which I have described in some detail before (Kohut 1979, pp. 19–20), is Mr. Z.'s dream of seeing his mother from the back.[6] Briefly stated, Mr. Z.'s anxiety at the point of his analysis when the dream occurred related to his relinquishment of a selfobject. More specifically, the anxiety related to the relinquishment of the selfobject functions of the mother whose own needs for a selfobject had up to that point prevented Mr. Z. from disentangling his personality from hers. By accepting this enslavement, he had, up to this time, retained the hope that his tentative moves toward independent maleness would ultimately elicit an accepting-approving smile from her that would consolidate his self. By rejecting the enslavement, as he was in the process of doing with a father-analyst, Mr. Z. gave up this hope, confronting for a last time the horrible fear that he could never again elicit his mother's smile. The mother had become faceless.

The second clinical vignette concerns an analogous moment during the analysis of Mr. U.[7] It occurred about one year before this analysis ended, a point in time that is noteworthy because of the emotional significance of this particular juncture of the treatment. What the patient experienced at the time—I feel certain of my interpretation of the significance of that moment only in retrospect, for at the time I had not yet been able to grasp it fully—was the first inkling of the fact that he would have to relinquish the emotional sustenance he had been receiving from the analyst and, not being a young man anymore, would have to face life on his own with the support of selfobjects he would have to find through his own active efforts. In childhood he turned from the unreliable selfobject support of the mother-grandmother couple to a fetish, and the fetish had supported him throughout his life, providing him with a reliable source of pleasure and a modicum of soothing. It was only during the analysis with me that he finally began seriously to contemplate life without the fetish, but he was able to tolerate this idea only as long as he was supported by the father-analyst ideal.[8] But now the impermanence of this particular selfobject support had to be accepted. At this moment—at the very point when, for the first time in analysis, he began to contemplate preconsciously that he could not retain my selfobject support forever, that the support of the idealized father imago would have to be maintained without my presence—the anxiety dream occurred.

In the dream the patient found himself in an ice tunnel whose walls were not smooth. Instead large strands of glistening ice emanated from them, going up to the ceiling or down to the floor (in accordance with his associations: as in the giant model of the human heart into which the visitor can walk in one of the well-known local museums that the patient often visited). As he was walking inside this cold, icy heart, he experienced great apprehension, the foreboding of some great yet nameless danger to which he was exposed. He tried to appeal to someone, a shadowy figure, to help him, but the appeal was of no avail. Suddenly he was pulled through a crack in the wall and found himself in a blinding bright landscape. Despite the fact that this landscape looked in all details like a usual cityscape, with many people present and all kinds of busy activities going on, it was unreal and the people in it were unapproachable. In the patient's words, it was a "stainless steel world." Whereas in the world of the cold heart he could still at least appeal for help, now even such appeal was out of the question. The workmen and passersby were completely—in principle as it were, not because of their coldheartedness—unreachable. No communication with them was thinkable; the patient was trapped forever without escape. It was at this moment, on realizing that he was caught in a science fiction world from which there was no return, that he woke up. The intense anxiety he had increasingly experienced during the dream continued for some minutes after he had become fully awake.

It must be clear now that the horror experiences of Mr. Z. and Mr. U. relate to the loss of the selfobject without which the self cannot continue to exist, without which it either disintegrates or is changed so profoundly (ceasing to be a human self, we might say) that its altered state is equivalent to disintegration. It makes no difference whether we experience this fear as the permanent loss of the responses of all present and potential selfobjects as was portrayed in Mr. U.'s dream of the stainless steel world, or whether we experience it as the irrecoverable loss of the single archaic selfobject that had sustained our self before we knew of substitutes, as portrayed in Mr. Z.'s dream. What is feared in both instances is the destruction of one's human self because of the unavailability of the psychological oxygen, the response of the empathic selfobject without which we cannot psychologically survive. It is not fear of loss of love that is at stake here. As I explained elsewhere (Kohut 1980, pp. 482–88), even hatred—that is, human hatred which confirms the victim's humanness—is sustaining. What leads to the human self's destruction, however, is its exposure to the coldness, the indifference of the nonhuman, the nonempathically responding world. It is in this sense, and in this sense only, that we may say that disintegration anxiety is closer to what people call fear of death than to what Freud designated the fear of loss of love. It is not physical extinction that is feared, however, but the ascendancy of a nonhuman environment (e.g., of an inorganic surrounding) in which our humanness would permanently come to an end. A human death can be and, I will affirm, should be an experience that, however deeply melancholy, is comparable to a fulfilled parting—it should have no significant admixture of disintegration anxiety. It must be stressed, however, that in order to enable the dying person to retain a modicum of the cohesion, firmness, and harmony of the self, his surroundings must not withdraw their selfobject functions at the last moment of his conscious participation in the world.

Not only the fear of loss of love, or the fear of death, but also the fear of a loss of contact with reality or the fear of psychosis can be compared with the feeling of horror that self psychology understands as disintegration anxiety. And again, as with the acceptations of "fear of loss of love" and "fear of death," there is some conceptual overlap. But the concept of a "loss of contact" has many shades of meaning, some clearly unrelated to the experience of disintegration anxiety. Even where "loss of contact" does convey a cognate meaning, moreover, its traditional usage leaves us in the dark about the crucial issue that the term "disintegration anxiety" is meant to evoke in us: namely, that it is a specific loss, the threatened loss of the self-cohesion-maintaining responses of the empathic selfobject, not the loss of contact with "reality" in general.

Going to sleep, after all, while clearly a relinquishment of a broad sector of reality, is not feared but, on the contrary, a joyful experience for most people. Indeed, I believe that an examination of the psychopathology of going to sleep—its experience-near substance is, in general, the *fear* of falling asleep—would not only help us understand certain forms of insomnia, but also the psychopathology of dying. Insomnia is often characterized by the fact that the afflicted individual tries to avoid altogether the transitional psychic stages of the gradual passage toward sleep by moving abruptly from wakefulness to sleep, or tries shortening the transitional period either with the aid of drugs or by producing states of extreme overtiredness. Babies and children retain the original capacity to fall asleep without anxiety because they are never—or only infrequently—deprived of the presence of an empathically responsive selfobject while they relinquish contact with reality in going to sleep. Similarly, as I noted above, one of the conditions for the maintenance of a cohesive self as one faces death is the actual or at least vividly imagined presence of empathically responsive selfobjects.

In harmony with this viewpoint, the cure of certain sleep disturbances is brought about by the patient's (re-)establishing the sense that selfobject support is not being withdrawn from him while he is going to sleep, that it continues while he is asleep, and that it will continue to be available after he wakes up. Otto von Bismarck's severe and chronic insomnia, for example, was cured by Schweninger, a physician who, because of his unorthodox methods, was considered a quack by the German medical profession of his day. Schweninger, whose intuitive grasp of the nature of Bismarck's sleep disturbance anticipated some of the essential insights of psychoanalytic self psychology, came to Bismarck's house at bedtime one evening and sat next to the statesman's bed until he had fallen asleep. When Bismarck awakened the next morning, after a full night's sleep, Schweninger was still sitting at his bedside, welcoming him, as it were, into the new day. I believe it would be difficult to find a more striking clinical instance demonstrating how, via a transference enactment, the fulfillment of a patient's need for an empathically responsive selfobject can restore the patient's ability to fall asleep. (To be completely accurate, I should say that with the aid of the responsive selfobject the patient's innate capacity to fall asleep is reestablished.)

I cannot resist the temptation, even though I will for a minute stray from the topic of our present concern, of referring to two other lessons that can be derived from the curative results of Schweninger's therapeutic activities with Bismarck. The first of these two lessons is that enactments like the one brought about by Schweninger's responsiveness to Bismarck's need for a soothing idealized selfobject lead to psychotherapeutic but not psychoanalytic results unless the transference is interpreted and analytically worked through (see chap. 7, below). To be specific: after the night at Bismarck's bedside, Schweninger became an indispensable member of the Bismarck entourage, indeed a member of his family. He continued, in other words, to serve as Bismarck's selfobject instead of bringing about that increase of the new or reinforced psychic structure that would have given Bismarck the ability to soothe himself into falling asleep with the aid of other selfobjects he would have to provide for himself.

The second lesson to be learned from the therapeutic selfobject transference that Bismarck established with Dr. Schweninger concerns the significance of oral cravings which often assert themselves beyond control in psychoanalytic patients whose ability to go to sleep is disturbed. Clearly, the ascendancy of oral cravings in such instances— their independent pursuit of their aim, in a word, their taking on the character of a "drive"—occurs, like the sleep disturbances discussed in the foregoing, when selfobject failures of a traumatic degree lead to the disintegration of (certain sections of) the self. Bismarck, at any rate, had been very obese up to the point when his therapeutic relationship with Schweninger began. From that point on, however, he lost weight steadily, demonstrating that, in the presence of the sustaining selfobject represented by Schweninger, Bismarck's need for an empathic selfobject was responded to and his essentially ineffectual attempt to replace the selfobject (and the transmuting internalizations it provides) with food (and the activity of eating) could be abandoned.[9]

But let us now turn, or rather return, to a consideration of the fear of psychosis. This fear is encountered not infrequently during analysis, even during the analyses of patients who, as far as can be judged, are not threatened by serious, protracted, psychic disintegration. Certainly, an anxiety experience such as that contained in Mr. U.'s dream of the stainless steel world could be taken as the expression of a fear of psychosis. But many people in addition to those who have suffered psychotic illness in the past or who have psychotic parents or relations know what it means to be afraid of becoming psychotic. In any analytic situation, the patient's associations to such fears always lead to the fear of losing the empathic selfobject and, as a result, of losing one's human self.[10]

It might well be that, on considering the preceding reflections, even some well-disposed readers might chide me for dwelling on experience-near levels of psychological life rather than penetrating beneath them, for being expansive and evocative rather than scientifically terse and explanatory. I believe, however, that I have a good defense against such accusations. I need merely underline the concrete context—developmental and clinical—of the foregoing considerations and the specific purpose which they are to serve. Simply put, I want to demonstrate that, behind the noisy manifestations of castration anxiety which lie near the psychological surface and are easily discerned, there is another deeper anxiety that is not so easily identified; that, behind the fear of castration which occurs only during a specific developmental period—albeit the oedipal period traditionally felt to play a crucial role in the pathogenesis of psychic disturbances—there is another more pervasive fear of the disintegration of the self. This latter fear is present during all stages of psychosexual development—including the oedipal stage—and it plays a vastly more significant role in the pathogenesis of psychic disturbances than the first type of anxiety.

From a different perspective, I might say that I am continuing to investigate a question that I first treated some years ago in a brief essay on female sexuality (Kohut 1978b, 2:783–92). There I noted that the girl's rejection of femininity, her feeling of being castrated and inferior, and her intense wish for a penis arise not because the male sex organs are psychobiologically more desirable than the female ones,[11] but because the little girl's selfobjects failed to respond to her with appropriate mirroring, since either no idealizable female parental imago was available to her, or that no alter ego gave her support during the childhood years when a proud feminine self should have established itself. Furthermore, I said that the little boy's manifest horror at the sight of the female genitals is not the deepest layer of this experience but that behind it and covered by it lies a deeper and even more dreadful experience—the experience of the faceless mother, that is, the mother whose face does not light up at the sight of her child (see Kohut 1979, pp. 19–20). This is the experience, once more, of the absence of that responsive selfobject milieu without which human life cannot be sustained.

Let me then, on the basis of the preceding reflections on disintegration anxiety—in particular its relationship to fear of death and fear of psychosis—as well as my comments on female sexuality, return to the anxieties of the oedipal period and my reevaluation of castration anxiety. To begin with I will stress that the developmental theories I am presenting are not the result of armchair speculation.[12] While my practice in recent years has not given me the opportunity to study many cases that could properly be called "oedipal neuroses," I still occasionally treat (or supervise the analysis of) a patient who suffers from a disturbance which, although hardly ever pure, still deserves to be termed a transference neurosis (in the classical sense of Freud's term) or an oedipal neurosis.

The theory that I now present rests, therefore, on clinical observations. Specifically, it is derived from observations regarding the sequence of various transferences and other experiential contents that more or less regularly unroll in the clinical situation. I have made only one theoretical assumption which, like all such principles, must be judiciously applied: that the process of analysis generally leads from the surface to the depth, and correspondingly, that transference sequences generally repeat developmental sequences *in the reverse order.*

What is the crucial transference sequence that leads us to reevaluate the basic significance—though not, as we cannot stress sufficiently, the importance—of castration anxiety and thus of the oedipal experience as a whole? To put my message in a nutshell: I believe that we can, under favorable circumstances, observe a three-stage sequence of transferences or, to be more exact, a three-stage sequence of transferences, each of which is preceded by a stage of more or less severe resistances (see chap. 7, below). Schematically, then, we have (1) a phase of generally severe resistances; (2) a phase of oedipal experiences in the traditional sense dominated by the experience of severe castration anxiety—let us refer to it as the Oedipus *complex,* the time-honored term that has fallen into some disuse but which for purposes of clearly differentiating this third stage from the fifth stage in the sequence of transferences, I would like to rescue from obsolescence; (3) a phase of very severe resistances (for example, see Kohut 1979, pp. 12–20); (4) a phase of disintegration anxiety (see Kohut 1979, pp. 19–20); (5) a phase of generally mild anxiety, alternating with joyous anticipation; and finally (6) a phase for which I reserve the term oedipal stage[13] in order to indicate its significance as a healthy, joyfully undertaken developmental step, the beginning of a gender-differentiated firm self that points to a fulfilling creative-productive future (cf. Kohut 1977, pp. 228–29 and 235–36).

It is often not difficult to reconstruct the temporal sequence of childhood events that led to the child's Oedipus complex, that is, that transformed the experiences of a healthy step of early development into pathological and potentially pathogenic ones. Specifically, we will proceed on the basis of the aforementioned theoretical assumption that the sequence of the unrolling of the transference during analysis tells us the childhood story in the reverse order and make the following reconstruction. The child, we will conclude, must have entered the oedipal phase joyfully, that is, on the whole with the exhilarating feeling that accompanies a forward step in maturation and development, responding to the awareness of a new set of experiences, however hazy it might be, characterized by a qualitatively altered and intensified affectionateness and assertiveness. We will further conclude from the foregoing reconstruction (extrapolated from the occurrence of stage six of the aforementioned sequence of transferences) that the child's self had on the whole been formed in response to optimally frustrating selfobjects up to this point in development, that it had not been exposed to traumatically disruptive rejections of its need to be confirmed in its vitality and assertiveness by the mirroring selfobject, to be calmed and uplifted by the idealized imago, or to be surrounded by the quietly sustaining presence of alter egos. The least one can conclude from the occurrence of stage six of our transference sequence is that the child must have entered the oedipal stage with the expectation, however short-lived, that the selfobjects would again respond to this great forward move in development with the sustaining responses they had provided in the preceding stages. Although one instance is exactly like another, the fact is that the specific experiences of the analysand who has reached this final stage of the analysis (in particular, his experiences of mature affection toward, and mature competitive-assertiveness with, the analyst) are undoubtedly healthy aspects of his oedipal stage at least as it attempted to unfold at its very beginning before the traumatic responses of the oedipal selfobjects began to shatter the strength, cohesion, and harmony of the barely established oedipal self.

Since I have written on earlier occasions about the specific parental psychopathology which, as I see it, leads to the replacement of the normal oedipal stage by the pathology I now refer to as the Oedipus complex (Kohut 1977, pp. 223–48 and 269–73) or which, to say the least, makes a decisive contribution to this deleterious change, and since, furthermore, I will speak about this specific parental psychopathology later in this work in the context of a broadly based self psychological discussion of the therapeutic action of psychoanalysis,[14] and last but not least, since the gap in our knowledge here can only be filled by extensive clinical reports concerning analyses of cases suffering from structural neuroses treated by self psychologically informed analysts, I will not go into the detailed reconstructions that can be extrapolated from the examinations of the other stages in the sequence of transferences and transference resistances. Suffice it to reiterate that the strong, cohesive, harmonious self of the oedipal child—the normal oedipal self that should be a center of independent affectionate and assertive initiative—will break into fragments and become weakened and disharmonious if its affection and assertiveness do not elicit the parents' proud mirroring responses (and various other empathically affirmative reactions) but eventuate instead in the parents' (preconscious) stimulation and (preconscious) hostile competitiveness. These flawed parental responses may occur via open and direct actions. They may be expressed verbally (which is rare) or may manifest themselves indirectly via prohibitive-rejecting responses or withdrawal (the more usual way in which the pathology of the self-object adult milieu surrounding the oedipal child expresses itself). At any rate, whether the parental pathology is expressed openly or covertly, the child's self becomes fragmented, weakened, and disharmonious and his normal nonsexual affection and normal nonhostile, nondestructive assertiveness become grossly sexual and hostile. While the sexual and destructive aims that arise in the child after the breakup of the healthy oedipal self can also be viewed as an attempt to organize the fragments of the self (for an example of this approach see Kohut 1980, pp. 521–27), the final outcome, that is, the pathological Oedipus complex, forms the nucleus for the pathological development that culminates in the manifestations of what we have traditionally referred to as the oedipal neurosis, classical transference neurosis, or structural neurosis.

Putting these insights into concrete terms and thereby returning to our starting point, that is, the differentiation between the two sets of fears that may occur during the oedipal period, we may say that the girl's *primary* oedipal fears are of being confronted by a nonempathically sexually seductive rather than affection-accepting paternal self-object or by a competitive-hostile rather than pridefully pleased maternal one. The boy's primary oedipal fears, on the other hand, are of being confronted by a nonempathic sexually seductive rather than affection-accepting maternal selfobject or by a competitive-hostile rather than pridefully pleased paternal one. The secondary fears occur subsequent to the child's shift of focus from its deeper concerns about the absence of a life-sustaining parental selfobject matrix to its concern with psychosocial tensions, however elaborated by fantasies the child's apprehensions may be. These tensions occur when, following the breakup of its affectionate and assertive attitudes, the child experiences the pathological sexual drivenness and destructive hostility which arise pari passu with the fragmentation or enfeeblement of its self. Subsequent to an oedipal phase that is marred by the failure of the parents to respond healthily to their child, a defect in the child's self is set up. Instead of the further development of a firmly cohesive self able to feel the glow of healthy pleasure in its affectionate and phase-appropriate sexual functioning and able to employ self-confident assertiveness in the pursuit of goals, we find throughout life a continuing propensity to experience the fragments of love (sexual phantasies) rather than love and the fragments of assertiveness (hostile fantasies) rather than assertiveness and to respond to these experiences—which always include the revival of the unhealthy selfobject experiences of childhood—with anxiety.

Am I putting all the blame for a person's later psychopathology and characterological shortcomings on his parents? Am I taking him off the hook, so to say, and in particular, am I the credulous victim of those of my patients who do not want to shoulder the responsibility for their symptoms, actions, and attitudes but waste their time accusing others, including and par excellence their parents? No, I do not believe that I have committed any of these errors, and I am not simply falling in with the accusations my analysands may level against their parents even though I may listen to them respectfully for a long time without contradicting them. First and most important: the self psychologically informed psychoanalyst blames no one, neither the patient nor his parents. He identifies causal sequences, he shows the patient that his feelings and reactions are explained by his experiences in early life, and he points out that, ultimately, his parents are not to blame since they were what they were because of the backgrounds that determined their own personalities. The self psychologically informed psychoanalyst, therefore, with all the human warmth he may display, always remains a scientifically objective observer. It follows that at the appropriate point (usually late) in the analysis, he will demonstrate to the analysand (if, indeed, the analysand has not come to this conclusion on his own) that when the oedipal self began to crumble and lust and destructiveness began to rise in consequence of the fragmentation of the oedipal self, the analysand's perception, too, began to be impaired. Thus, in response to not being experienced in toto by the parents, who saw not the child but his "drives," the analysand, too, may have seen the parents as less human and whole than they were. As a result, he may have experienced them as seductive or hostile-competitive at times when, indeed, they had acted with warmth and tried to offer empathic parental responses to their child.

I will add here for completeness's sake that these considerations are of great importance in the psychoanalytic situation because they bear on the way in which the analyst both responds to the transference and interprets vis-à-vis the patient's childhood memories about his parents. It follows from the preceding remarks that the analyst will encourage the full unfolding of the patient's reproaches and will, in particular, admit his own inevitable shortcomings to the analysand who, in the transference, feels unempathically misunderstood. As I have said before (Kohut 1977, p. 88), some patients, though by no means all, require that this phase of *only* understanding last a long time—the explanation phase must wait. Even with such patients, however, things eventually do begin to be seen in a new light. The patient, in other words, alone or with the help of the analyst, comes to recognize that he, too, has distorted reality—that while his parents always seemed to have acted hostile or sexually seductive and while he may have felt the same way about important people in his present surroundings (including and par excellence the analyst), he misperceived the selfobjects' shortcomings at times and even provoked them by the intensity of his demands that followed his traumatization. Since all these considerations will be clear to every experienced analyst and easily substantiated with the aid of everyday clinical experience, I will not pursue this issue any further here.

Two questions, however—really two variants of the same question— must yet be faced as we come to the end of these reflections on the Oedipus complex in general and on one of its most prominent experiential contents, castration anxiety (and its variants), in particular: (1) How frequently do the Oedipus complex and castration anxiety occur? And (2) are the Oedipus complex and castration anxiety ubiquitous, and if so, are not all the considerations presented in this discussion simply an empty exercise, a verbal game that can be disregarded by both the clinician and the theorist?

I have no trouble responding to these questions, even though I cannot supply clear-cut answers to both of them. First of all I will stress again that great frequency of occurrence—even ubiquity—does not connote normality, let alone health. Keeping this tenet in mind, we can focus on these two important questions. Does the Oedipus complex occur frequently? Is it ubiquitous? Strangely enough—and at first sight incongruously—I am inclined to reply to the first question by saying "not as frequently as it was once believed to occur" or "not as frequently now as it may have occurred a hundred years ago," while, at the same time, I would tend to affirm that it is ubiquitous. On the face of it the two replies contradict each other. But the seeming contradiction resolves itself completely as soon as we consider the fact that my remarks about the lesser frequency of occurrence are aimed at the full-blown complex that later comes to constitute the center of serious manifest psychopathology in the adult, while my remark concerning its ubiquity points to the fact that traces of it are indeed discernible in every human being.

It is the reply to the second half of the question that I consider to be of greater significance by far. Should it be at all surprising if traces of an Oedipus complex can be found in every person? I think not. The oedipal selfobjects are imperfect, just as they were imperfect before the oedipal period. And our selfobjects will remain imperfect throughout the whole span of our lives, including their responses to us at the time we die. But the confrontations with such limited failures are part of the essence of life, I affirm, since we are in fact equipped to deal with the limited shortcomings of the matrix that sustains our humanness. Indeed, we are equipped to respond to these shortcomings with the most valuable possession of human beings, the capacity to respond to optimal frustrations via transmuting internalizations and creative change.[15]

But still, even though I am certain that nonpathogenic traces of an Oedipus complex and of castration anxiety can be found in every human being, just as nonpathogenic traces of other syndromes (such as minor and/or fleeting addictive, perverse, or delinquent behavior) can be found in every human being, I would insist that, despite their ubiquity, neither the Oedipus complex nor the traces of these other clusters of pathological experience and behavior that occur because a breakup of the self isolates the drives should be designated as "normal." To make my point via analogy and in reverse: a textbook of normal anatomy, let us say, or of normal physiology, describes conditions that could not be found to exist in any individual who ever lived. Still, even though the standards outlined in such treatises are only approximated by reality, they give us a baseline we refer to as "normal." There is no individual who is totally free of addictive features, whose sexuality is totally free of perverse interests, who is always incorruptibly nondelinquent. Similarly, there is no individual who does not have traces of oedipal lust, hostility, guilt, and fear. Despite the ubiquity of these traces, however, none of these drive-dominated modes of behavior and experiences should be designated as normal.

The foregoing examination of the significance of certain aspects of the oedipal period in the light of psychoanalytic self psychology is not only of theoretical interest but has important consequences for our therapeutic outlook as well.[16] Issues that are traditionally considered genetically primary and structurally central in the neuroses (the *content* of the Oedipus situation, the *conflicts* of the child) are now, without denying their importance, considered secondary and peripheral; on the other hand, issues that are traditionally considered secondary and peripheral (the propensity toward the spreading of anxiety, the patient's moves to protect himself against anxiety by various maneuvers) are now considered primary and central. Let us, by way of illustrating my meaning, look at the syndrome of phobias, specifically the so-called agoraphobias.

A Reexamination of Agoraphobia

According to the traditional psychoanalytic view—a view that decisively influences the ambience of the analysis and the analyst's therapeutic strategy—the (female) patient's anxiety when unaccompanied in the street is the secondary, overt (conscious) manifestation of a specific underlying (unconscious) disturbance which is deemed primary. Namely, the patient's paralyzing fear arises in reaction to the mobilization of oedipal sexual wishes toward her father, as displaced upon the men whom she encounters in the street. The patient's panic—again in accordance with the traditional view—is no more than a symptom, and the relief the patient experiences when she is accompanied by a woman, in particular an older woman, is no more than a defensive maneuver. This maneuver is understandable as an enactment of the mother's presence which, by making the fulfillment of the oedipal desires impossible, short-circuits the fantasy and forestalls the outbreak of anxiety. Expressed most tersely in terms of Freud's earlier theories: the phobia is a symptom of an underlying anxiety hysteria in which libido is transformed into anxiety. Expressed most tersely in terms of the ego-psychological transformation of Freud's earlier theories: the ego reacts with panic and regressive infantilism to the mobilization of incestuous oedipal wishes.

Before proceeding to outline the self psychological evaluation of the syndrome of agoraphobia, I will first respond to a question that may well arise in many minds at this point. Why, it may be asked, do I choose agoraphobia as my sample of classical psychopathology, as the prototype of oedipal pathology or structural neurosis? Agoraphobia, after all, has for a long time been recognized as significantly interpenetrated by preoedipal pathology and thus should not be made to serve as a prototypical example of oedipal pathology.

I fully recognize the validity of the foregoing argument as far as agoraphobia per se is concerned, but I would be inclined to extend the same reasoning to all other forms of so-called oedipal pathology. Even in terms of ego psychology, in other words, pure oedipal neuroses are no longer encountered, or, to say the least, they must be considered a great rarity. But my present efforts should not be understood as an attempt to demonstrate that *pure* oedipal pathology is pratically nonexistent; that could indeed be carrying coals to Newcastle. What I will try to illustrate, using the well-known syndrome of agoraphobia as an example, is the different viewpoint adopted by self psychology as it evaluates the significance of the clinical phenomena.

I thus insist on the fact that, traditionally, the pregenital elements, however prominent in the layering of the clinical phenomena, have in essence been seen as regressive evasions, as secondary to the primary oedipal conflict that must ultimately emerge and be confronted in any successful, complete analysis. Fenichel's beautiful chapter on anxiety hysteria (1945, pp. 193–215) is still unsurpassed in describing these complexities from the ego psychological point of view and remains as impressive as ever; I cannot recommend it too highly to anyone who wants to get an encompassing picture of the traditional view.

I will add, furthermore, that I could easily have chosen any other of the classical syndromes, such as animal phobia, for my comparison.[17] I have selected agoraphobia mainly for historical reasons, that is, in deference to the fact that agoraphobia came to play a prototypical role in Freud's writings and that it has served the same function for many generations of psychoanalytic instructors and students. But let us now return to the task we have set ourselves.

How does self psychology look at the phenomena presented by agoraphobia? The answer to this question is as simple as it is significant. As I said before: what traditional analysis looked upon as secondary and peripheral self psychology sees as primary and central. This follows from the fact that self psychology considers the structural and functional deficiencies of the patient's self as the primary disorder and focuses its attention on them, whereas traditional analysis saw the content of conflicts as the primary disorder and focused on it. We believe, to return to our example, that the agoraphobic woman's essential illness is not defined by her unconscious wish for incestuous relations with her father and by her unconscious conflicts over them, but by the fact that she suffers from a structural deficiency of the self.

The causal role played by the oedipal selfobjects in bringing about the pathogenic Oedipus complex has already been discussed at length and I will, therefore, only briefly repeat that when the little girl reached the oedipal stage, her phase-appropriate affection and assertive behavior did not elicit affectionate pride from her oedipal selfobjects. Instead, they were (preconsciously) stimulated and competitive, for they displayed guilt-inducing prohibitive attitudes, for example, via overt censure or emotional withdrawal. As a result, the child's unsupported oedipal self began to fragment, and isolated drive experiences and conflicts about them replaced the primary joyful experiences of the phase-appropriate affectionate and assertive whole self. These are the conditions which, I believe, prevail in all instances of subsequent pathology that arise on the basis of an Oedipus complex. The situation in the case of agoraphobia, however, has certain specific features to which I will now turn.[18]

Although the breakup of the self accounts for both the disintegration of the agoraphobic woman's affectionate attitude toward the father in childhood (with pathogenic sexual fantasies replacing the former joyful warmth) and the tendency toward the spreading of anxiety and development of paralyzing panic, it is the faultily responsive *paternal* selfobject that accounts for the first aspect of the structural disease of the self (i.e., the ascendancy of an Oedipus complex) and the faultily responsive *maternal* selfobject that accounts for the second aspect (i.e., the patient's tendency to become overwhelmed by panic rather than being able to control her anxiety so that it can serve as a signal [Freud 1926, 1953, 20:87–157]). The mother, in other words, was apparently not able to provide a calming selfobject milieu for the little girl which, via optimal failures, would have been transmuted into self-soothing structures capable of preventing the spread of anxiety. It is this structural deficit, the deficiency in calming structures—a defect in the soothing functions of the idealized pole of the self—that necessitates the presence of a companion (a maternal woman who temporarily replaces the missing structure and its functions) to forestall the outbreak of anxiety. It was the nonempathic selfobject milieu of the oedipal phase, in other words, that both brought about the deleterious transformation of the little girl's originally affectionate attitudes into sexual drivenness and failed to provide the necessary conditions for the gradual internalization of those self structures that would have given self-confidence to the little girl and enabled her to remain calm despite conflict and tension.[19]

To summarize: self psychology sees the failure of the oedipal selfobject milieu as the essential genetic factor in agoraphobia. It considers the pathological oedipal fantasies as a symptomatic consequence of the flawed selfobject response. Finally, it believes that in the adult symptomatology the addictionlike need for an accompanying woman is not to be viewed as a defensive maneuver but as a manifestation of the primary disorder: the structural defect of which both the unconscious oedipal fantasy and the conscious need for a female companion are symptoms. The fact that the sexual wish for the father can be kept outside of awareness ("repressed") while the reliance on the selfobject mother to curb the anxiety is conscious does not mean that the first is the dynamic source (the cause) of the patient's psychological illness and that the second arises in consequence of the first. The sexual wish for the father, in other words, despite being unconscious, is not "deeper" than the need for the selfobject mother.[20] The dynamic prime mover (the cause) of the disturbance and the "deepest" layer of the disease, as far as we can determine at this time, is the flawed self-selfobject relationship that transformed the positive experience of the oedipal stage, an upsurge of affectionate and assertive feelings, into the potentially pathogenic Oedipus complex. Vastly more important than the agoraphobic woman's subsequent exposure to the unconscious incestuous desires of the Oedipus complex, however, is the structural defect that followed from the failure of the idealized maternal selfobject to provide the child with the idealized omnipotent calmness which, via transmuting internalization, should have become self-soothing, anxiety-curbing psychic structure.

Is this lack of anxiety-curbing structure specific and circumscribed or general and diffuse? Did the selfobject milieu, in other words, provide the child with sufficient opportunities of merging with a calm idealized parent imago early in life and fail only vis-à-vis the specific anxieties surrounding the new experiences of the oedipal stage? Turning to the overt manifestations of the illness, is the agoraphobic's anxiety restricted to the pathological incestuous and competitive-destructive drive fragments or is it more widespread, is there a more general propensity to respond with panic vis-à-vis those various inner and outer circumstances that would be responded to with limited fear, that is, by the appearance of an anxiety signal and secondarily with appropriate action, in those whose wholesome development had provided them with adequate psychic structures?

Clinical experience, not speculation, must provide the answers to these questions. We know clinically that there are various kinds of phobias, that phobias occur in a spectrum that extends from those instances—now very rare but perhaps formerly much more frequent—in which the panic is restricted to the mobilization of the Oedipus complex to those instances—now clearly the vast majority—in which the agoraphobic symptom is only one of many manifestations of a widespread and nonspecific propensity to become anxious to the point of panic states, disorganized action, or paralysis of all initiative. In the former instances, the responses of the early selfobjects to the "preoedipal" child's anxieties must have been adequate; in the latter instances the responses of the selfobjects must have been faulty all along, beginning in early life. Still, for the sake of completeness, we must add that, even when the anxiety tendency is more diffuse, the uncovering of a concentration of unconscious oedipal strivings in the transference before the earlier selfobject failures begin to occupy center stage testifies to the fact that the deleterious responses of the selfobject intensified at the very point when the child reached the oedipal stage.

The most general statement that can be made about the pathogenic defect of the idealized selfobject in these phobias may be the following. Because the parental figure with whose power and calmness the child's self needs to merge has herself a self defect—I say "herself" because in the case of the agoraphobic woman it is the mother, whereas in other forms of psychopathology, whether oedipal or preoedipal, it is the father—she experiences the child's developmental progress (his emotionally moving away from her) as a threat to her cohesion. She therefore fails to respond with mirroring pride or with other appropriate reactions that the child needs in order to maintain his self-esteem and ensure his self-cohesion. Moreover, this parental failure comes at a moment when the child's self, in the midst of a pivotal forward move, is only precariously established and thus especially vulnerable.

Am I, it may be asked, despite all my excessive care to illuminate the problem of phobias from all possible sides, disregarding a factor which for Freud was potentially more important than childhood experience, namely, the biological factor, in Freud's early terms: the strength of the drive, in later terms: a congenital inherited possible weakness of the ego? Is the phobia not also, to a greater or lesser extent, due to the fact that the infantile sexual demands are, ab initio, especially great in some children and/or the defensive and sublimatory powers of the ego are, ab initio, especially weak? Should we not say, with Freud, that it is faulty biological equipment which we may ulti- mately have to hold responsible for both the oedipal phobias and the diffuse propensity to experience excessive anxiety?

This is not the place to explain my position vis-à-vis the so-called psychobiological attitude. As I have stated repeatedly since 1959 when I first clarified my operational position, I do not believe we are dealing with separate biological and psychological universes, but with two approaches to reality. When science approaches reality via extrospection (and vicarious extrospection), we call it physics or biology; when it approaches it via introspection (and empathy), we call it psychology. Both instruments of observation have limits. Only a specific, strictly delimited part of reality can be approached via introspection and empathy: our own inner life and the inner life of others. Our inner lives, moreover, are not graspable via extrospection, even though the possibility cannot be dismissed that some day even the nuances of our experiences (thought contents) may become decipherable via physical data such as electromagnetic tracings of the activity of our brains. At present, however, the psychological approach, with all its limitations, is the only useful one for investigating the inner life of man, including his psychopathology.

Still, even though at present we have, outside of the area of organic disturbances extensive enough to lead to "organic" psychopathology, no clear-cut proof that variations in biological equipment contribute to the fact that some individuals experience drive-wishes with greater intensity than others, or are less able to transform primitive urges into socially acceptable actions than others, and that some individuals cannot curb the spreading of their emotions and develop panic states or depression and/or elation, it stands to reason that our biological inheritance should influence these psychological functions. In practice, analysts do not need to be told that these considerations should in clinical work only be an explanation of last resort, that the search for psychological causes must remain paramount. But there is another set of factors that must not be neglected in this context. Granted that variations in congenital equipment exist, the response of the selfobject milieu to congenital shortcomings must by all means be taken into consideration, and any resulting psychopathology—for example, an excessive tendency to develop panic states or an inability to curb anxiety—must be explained not only in terms of the congenital defect, but also with regard to the failure of the selfobjects to respond adequately to an especially trying situation. Specifically, we must ask whether the parents were able to fill the specific or excessive needs of certain children, and, if not, why they were unable to do so and how specifically they failed. The capacity of a parent to respond empathically to the unusually great or highly specific selfobject need of a child is, in the last analysis, a function of the firmness of the cohesion of the parent's self. Certainly neither in such cases nor, indeed, in the case of any selfobject failure do we judge the selfobject's shortcomings from a moral point of view. Such an attitude would be foolish since the parental disability is an outgrowth of the deepest early experiences that influenced the development of the parent's responsibility and is thus beyond direct control; it would also be completely out of keeping with the approach of the scientist whose aim is neither to blame nor exculpate but to establish causal-motivation chains that explain the empathically gathered, psychological data.[21]

3

The Problem of Scientific Objectivity and the Theory of the Psychoanalytic Cure

Returning now to a topic that I discussed in *The Restoration of the Self* (1977, especially pp. 63–69), I wish to consider the problem of scientific objectivity, in particular, the problem of scientific objectivity with regard to that new field of endeavor one might call the scientific humanities (Kohut 1980, pp. 504–5). It is within the borders of this new field that psychoanalysis, the science of complex mental states in general and psychoanalytic self psychology in particular, should be seen to lie. I will first approach my topic from a somewhat broader perspective before focusing directly on psychoanalysis (both clinical and applied) per se.

There are, broadly speaking, two attitudes that people may take when they contemplate the product of the mind of another. Some will say that they are interested not in the creator of a work, but only in the work itself. Others will maintain that some degree of knowledge about the creator, in particular about his intentions and purposes in creating the work, is helpful to them as they study the work, enriching their grasp of the meaning of the work and easing their access to it. The division of opinions is especially clear-cut with regard to works of art and literature. (An illustrative debate of this issue can be found in Kohut 1978*b*, 2:908 ff.) With regard to scientific works, however, one attitude is clearly and overwhelmingly dominant: virtually total unanimity exists that what is important is the content of the work itself, its truth value. The motivations and purposes of the scientist are, as far as our judgment of the value of his contribution is concerned, not only irrelevant but to be actively excluded from consideration. However challenging it may be to study the personality of a scientist, whether as the investigation of the personality of a specific individual or a contribution to our understanding of human creativity, his work must ultimately be judged on its intrinsic merits alone. Whatever the personal reasons for undertaking a scientific task might have been, as far as science is concerned, it is only the accuracy, truth, and relevance of the result that ultimately count.

Whereas workers in most branches of science have accepted the dissociation of the researcher's motivations from the results of his research as a matter of course, psychoanalysts, including Freud, have, understandably, never been as clear-cut with regard to this issue as their scientific colleagues. Just as analysts are accustomed to taking emotional factors into account whenever a patient begins to attack this or that tenet of psychoanalysis, so also in scientific arguments. When Adler, feeling that analysis during its first decade had underemphasized the importance of inferiority feelings, introduced ideas that deviated, at least in emphasis, from those of Freud and his loyal followers, Freud undermined the significance of Adler's contributions by stressing his personal motivations. In particular, he referred to Adler's statement that he (Adler) could not live forever in Freud's shadow. Although there is no dearth of similar events in the history of psychoanalysis, I believe that public statements about the personalities of colleagues whose ideas one opposes have now become rare. Admittedly, they have not disappeared altogether, but they are now, with a few notable exceptions, confined to more or less restrained rumor-mongering and gossip. Although such activities may at times constitute a very powerful force and may, as in the arena of politics, lead to the thoughtless rejection of valuable ideas (or at least to protracted delays) before fair and careful examination, they have no official status and are rarely affirmed in public.

The preceding statements appear to leave no doubt where I, personally, stand, with regard to the issue in question. Scientific work, including work in psychology in general and psychoanalysis in particular, must be judged on its intrinsic merits, that is, with regard to its explanatory power. The personality, the mental state, the specific motivations of the contributor should not influence our judgment about the value of the theories and findings presented to us. That Freud, to use a commonly adduced illustration, was ill and confronted death in a new and more tangible way when he formulated his crucially important ideas about a death instinct—a theory that in my opinion cannot be removed from the magnificent edifice of Freud's theoretical system without seriously damaging its cohesion and internal consistency—should have no bearing on our evaluation of the essential correctness and relevance of this theory. The theory should be accepted, partially accepted, emended, or rejected on the basis of its objective scientific features, independent of the moment in the personal life of its author when it was formulated.

All this appears to be true beyond the shadow of a doubt. But is the issue really as unambiguously settled as the foregoing reflections lead us to believe? The more one ponders the matter, the more difficult it is to arrive at a clear-cut verdict. Are there really truths of any significance and breadth that can be evaluated without regard to the observer who affirms them? Are there, in particular, psychological theories which, dealing with objectively ascertainable data, allow us to disregard the observing instrument, that is, the individuals who have formulated them and affirm their accuracy, relevance, and explanatory power? Modern physics tells us that in its realm the answer is quantitative. It has taught us that, in principle, the observing agency is always a part of what is being observed, that, again in principle, there is no objective reality. Still, it has also taught us that as far as the macrocosmos is concerned, the influence of the observer on the observed is so infinitesimally small that, in practice, it can be disregarded. Only when we turn to the world of microparticles does the observer's influence have to be taken into account; only then must the assessment of reality include the observer. It is only in this case, in other words, that, in a manner of speaking, objective reality is always subjective. The question we must therefore ask as we turn now from physics to our own field is this: in psychoanalysis, that is, in the psychology of complex mental states, and specifically in self psychologically informed psychoanalysis, that is, in psychoanalysis as it focuses not only on the gross disturbances of psychological functions but also and especially on the defects in the psychic structures from which the gross malfunctioning arises, are we dealing with conditions that correspond to the macrocosmos of Newtonian physics or to the Planckian realm of small particles that has become one of the principal foci of attention for physicists of our time?

I cannot give a simple answer to this question. In theory I believe that, as in the physics of small particles, objective truth does not exist in the psychology of complex mental states or, stated more accurately, that objective truths must always include an assessment of the observer. But the analogy to physics cannot be applied consistently, even if we disregard the fact that, in consequence of the vastly different nature of their subject matter, the methodologies of physics and psychoanalysis are also vastly different. The analogy can probably be most fruitfully applied in the clinical situation, leading to the reexamination of such crucial concepts as analytic neutrality, the notion of the analyst as a screen on which the patient projects the imagoes of his childhood, and the like—all formed at a time when, as I have pointed out (Kohut 1977, pp. 66–69), the leading theoretical ideal of analysis was total objectivity, that is, the removal of the influence of the observer on the observed.

It is by no means necessary for analysts to discard this nineteenth-century ideal to which Freud and his contemporaries subscribed. In a specific, circumscribed sense it is as valid a guide now as it was then: if we want to see clearly, we must keep the lenses of our magnifying glasses clean; we must, in particular, recognize our countertransferences and thus minimize the influence of factors that distort our perception of the analysand's communications and of his personality. But this purely cognitive approach to the problem of scientific objectivity in our field, however valid within certain limits, is inadequate. By restricting ourselves to it, we are preventing ourselves—unnecessarily, I will add, because enlarging our purview does not entail sacrificing one iota of our dedication to the ideal of scientific truth—from perceiving some of the most significant aspects of the analysand's responses in the psychoanalytic situation. The cognitive framework sees the analyst only as the observer and the analysand only as the field that the observer-analyst surveys. Since this orientation fails to do justice to one of the most significant dimensions of the psychoanalytic situation, we need an orientation that complements it and thus gives us a more complete picture of the analyst's significance in the analytic situation. Expressed affirmatively, we need an orientation that acknowledges and then examines the analyst's influence *in principle* as an intrinsically significant human presence, not his influence via distorting countertransferences. The former kind of influence characterizes the psychoanalytic situation in general, but is exemplified par excellence in the working-through process.

Let me restate my last point most unambiguously. If we are in a situation in which a human being listens to us in order to understand us and explain us to ourselves, and we know that such listening and explaining will go on for a long, at first seemingly unlimited, time, we are not in a situation that can be properly defined as being neutral. On the contrary, it is a situation that, in its psychological impact on us, is the very opposite of neutral—indeed it is a situation that may be said to provide us with the most crucial emotional experience for human psychological survival and growth: the attention of a selfobject milieu, that is, a human surrounding that, via empathy, attempts to understand and participate in our psychological life. And the quality of the understanding that is achieved, its relative accuracy, inaccuracy, insufficiency, or oppressiveness, is an immanent quality of the analytic situation, not an adventitious admixture to it. Indeed, the analyst focuses his attention on the inner life of his patient, and the successes and failures of his understanding activity are the essential motor of the psychoanalytic process. In view of the fact that the final part of the present work deals at length with this aspect of the psychoanalytic process, I will not pursue these reflections any further here.[1]

They were stimulated, it should be remembered, by the question of how far the analogy between psychoanalysis and the physics of small particles could be relevantly extended. Instead, I turn now to the field of applied analysis.

In applied analytic work, the analogy with small-particle physics vis-à-vis the immanent role of the observer in shaping the observed field would, with certain exceptions, be misleading. It would be misleading because the difficulties, the at-times well-nigh insurmountable difficulties that the observer faces, are not due to his influence on the field of observation but to his own shortcomings as an observing instrument. These great difficulties, in analogy to the reactions which in the clinical situation we view as countertransferences, are due to the distorting influence of emotional biases on our empathy-based perception. I refer to the fact that prejudicial tendencies deeply ingrained in us will often decisively influence what part of the potentially available data we perceive, which among the perceived items we consider important, and, ultimately, how we choose to explain the data that we selectively perceive.

The preceding considerations apply especially to the investigations of the events within that most portentous area of the applied field—the focus on the behavior of large groups via an approach that has become identified as "psychohistorical." Specifically, when we are dealing with current events (including the assessment of currently active political figures; see Kohut, Anderson, and Moore 1965, pp. 450–51), with events of the recent past that have affected our lives, or with events of the distant past that parallel important present events, we are often unable to free ourselves sufficiently from the distorting influence of our passions (e.g., our ambitions, cherished narcissistic commitments, or envy). And we cannot, therefore, claim with confidence that we have been able to assess the personalities of the actors in the historical drama—their motivations, intentions, narcissistic involvements, and conflicts—with that degree of objectivity that would place our findings and judgments within the borders of science, however vaguely these borders may be defined.[2] Still, while this is indeed a serious obstacle, the psychoanalytic psychohistorian must not give up hope. Significant new insights are never obtained easily, and any move into new territory requires the courage to set aside tradition-bound restrictions and to experiment with new methods and develop new skills. With reference to the distorting influence of our passions on our historical perceptions, for example, I believe that the ever deepening awareness of the tendency to make the history we write serve certain psychological ends (to give hope and support to the group with which we identify, for example, or to belittle the one that threatens us) should allow us to move toward greater objectivity, perhaps even to the kind of objectivity that includes the analysis of the subjective element, that is, of the way the historian's specific emotional involvement influences his perceptions.

Under average circumstances, then, our depth-psychological perceptions concerning the fields of literature, art, political science, jurisprudence, and, above all, history do not include the subjective element which, as I noted above, is as immanent in the clinical situation as it is in small-particle physics. Still, as I implied before, we must not disregard the fact that in certain rare but conspicuous instances the influence of the observer on the field that he observes is undeniable—even in the field of applied analysis. There are certain depth-psychological observers, in other words, who, via their observations, influence the field they observe in ways that, to a certain extent, parallel the observer's influence in the clinical situation and, par excellence, in the psychoanalytic situation. True, in the vast majority of instances, the depth-psychological observer within the applied field will exert no more influence on the field he observes than the physicist who observes the movements of the stars. This fact clearly differentiates applied analysis from clinical analysis where, by his very presence, the observer is an immanent constituent in the field. But there are instances when the depth psychologist, even in the field "beyond the bounds of the basic rule," not only will observe the world of man but, via the disclosure and discrimination of the results of his observations, will influence the views and motivations of his contemporaries and even of future generations. Here the adage *habent sua fata libelli*, "writings have their own destiny," at times applies with great force (see, in this context, my earlier examination of the influence of depth psychology on modern man, Kohut 1978*b*, 2:511–47, esp. p. 515). There are books—think of the writings of Rousseau, Hegel, or Marx, not to mention the oeuvre of Freud—that were destined to contribute to the shaping of social reality, despite their authors' protestations that they had simply meant to describe man's motivations and reactions with scientific objectivity.

The foregoing reflections can easily be extended in two directions. If the observed field is a limited one, then it may be especially difficult, if not impossible, to separate the aims of scientific observation and description from other objectives. To adduce an illustration that is close to home, I can point to the not inconsiderable number of references to the history of psychoanalysis in my own work (e.g., those in Kohut 1977, pp. 249–66, and 1978b, 2:511–46, 663–84, 793–843) and admit without hesitation that in the case of most if not of all of them it would be impossible to separate the aims of the objective historiographer from the aims of a man who wants to lay the groundwork for a reform. Furthermore, even when the observer is not of the caliber of a Rousseau, a Hegel, a Marx, or a Freud, the total impact of the contributions by the scientist-reformer himself and those who follow in his footsteps, the sum total, in other words, of the scientific observations adduced by a particular school of thought exploiting reality from a novel point of view, may well be said not only to depict the world, but also to make a contribution, however small, to shaping it.

Does the effect of the contributions of various schools of thought—and we are, of course, ultimately interested in the various theories and conceptions of man that underlie the treatment situation in psychoanalysis—invalidate these contributions? Does it, in other words, exclude them from the realm of science?

I do not think so. A particular psychohistorian, for example, may be more keenly in touch with the essence of his time than his contemporaries. He and his specific perceptive acuities are, to be sure, shaped by the time in which he lives. But then, as he employs perceptive equipment that is specifically attuned to the period of history in which he lives, he may, in turn, contribute to the unrolling of events by heightening the awareness of his contemporaries to what they feel themselves to be and what they themselves are striving for. (The best illustration in this context, I am sorry to say, is the now discredited historian von Treitschke, who, following in Hegel's footsteps, declared as an objectively ascertainable fact that wars are inevitable and that the ultimate end of cultural progress was the absolutistic German state that had to subdue all opposition in order to reach the goal of civilization. Clearly his "objective" assessment of historical reality helped prepare the soil for Hitler's Reich.)

Do these considerations imply that there *is* no objectivity, that what we want to call objective science is always some sort of moral pressure or propaganda veiled in the cloak of scientific respectability? Again, I do not think so. If we initially have the courage to acknowledge the fact that scientific objectivity in the sciences of man must always include the objective assessment of the observer—the influence of the observed on the observer and, especially, the influence of the observer on the field that he observes—then we can clarify our methodology. Through such clarification, we acquire the ability to separate the wheat from the chaff (e.g., we separate science from propaganda), not only by discarding one kind of contribution and upholding another but—and this is of the greatest importance to the field of depth psychology and, in particular, to our estimation of Freud's work—by separating the time-bound elements of certain contributions, however broadly they have ultimately been accepted and however strongly they have contributed to shaping man's concept of himself, from those elements that have a more enduring validity.

As I am now approaching the end of the present chapter, it behooves me to lay my cards on the table and point to the specific application of the preceding reflections in the present work, and to the forthcoming major part in which I will attempt to define the essence of the psychoanalytic cure. I have adduced the preceding reflections on objectivity in science—a relative objectivity since the field that is observed, of necessity, includes the observer in the various ways that I outlined—in order to lay the groundwork for the specific way in which self psychology explains the psychoanalytic process and evaluates its results. It was not an arbitrary move on my part—to restate in different words my belief in the relativity of scientific objectivity—that the first part of this book discussed the major theories of self psychology, specifically the aspects of these theories that deviate, if ever so subtly, from traditional maxims. My order of presentation follows from the assumptions about objectivity I have just spelled out: that the theories held by the observer influence not only what he sees—in our case, what he sees when he scrutinizes the psychoanalytic process and its results—but, and par excellence, how he evaluates what he sees, what he deems to be central and significant, and what he dismisses as peripheral, insignificant, or trite. To be specific: it is clear that a psychology—traditional psychoanalysis—that explains man in terms of a psychic apparatus that processes drives and, during therapy, focuses predominantly on the flaws of conflict solution of psychic macrostructures (id, ego, superego) will see the essence of the analytic process and the essence of cure in a different light from a psychology—the psychoanalytic psychology of the self—that explains man in terms of a self that is sustained by a milieu of selfobjects and, during therapy, ultimately focuses not on the flawed functional results of the faulty structures of the self (i.e., not on the mishandled drive as the *fons* and *origo* of psychopathology) but on the defects and distortions of the microstructures of the self. Thus, although self psychology does not disregard psychic conflict and analyzes it when it presents itself in the transference, it does so only as a preliminary step on the way to what it considers the essential task of therapeutic analysis: the exploration, in its dynamic and genetic dimensions, of the flaws in the structure of the self via the analysis of the selfobject transferences. The relationship between traditional analysis and analytic self psychology may thus be seen to parallel the relationship between the physics of Newton (who explored the macrocosm) and the physics of Planck (who explored the atomic and subatomic particles that form the micro-structures).

What Constitutes a Complete Analysis? What Is an Analytic Cure?

In focusing on the question of a "complete analysis" and an "analytic cure," I am both preparing the soil for the major section of this work and returning to the issue raised by a colleague with which I began this section, namely, the mistaken opinion that I advocate that some analyses of severe narcissistic personality disorders should, in principle, remain incomplete. It was this misunderstanding that initially induced me to undertake the writing of this book.

My entire presentation up to this point, however varied the topics covered and however divergent my reasons for taking them up, should nevertheless be considered as preparatory to the major task that lies ahead: the definition of the analytic cure and, interwoven with the definition of cure but still to be approached as a circumscribed topic, the elaboration of the method by which we strive to reach a cure. My discussion of analyzability, for example, in particular the summary of my therapeutic attitude vis-à-vis the three classes of psychopathology (the psychoses, the narcissistic personality and behavior disorders, and the transference neuroses),[3] was presented not only in order to compare the self psychological outlook on the nature of these classes of psychic disorder with the traditional point of view, but also with the aim of laying the groundwork for the ultimate task of this work.

These previously undertaken inquiries concerning the *differentiated* therapeutic outlook with regard to these three types of psychopathology should now allow us to make some *general* remarks about the self in health and disease. Specifically, I hope it will not be difficult to see, against the background of the previous discussion, that I differentiate sharply between, on the one hand, the description of the shape and content of the self—the distinctive individuality which distinguishes it from other selves with their respective shapes and contents—and, on the other hand, the assessment of its firmness and freedom to carry out its intrinsic program of action. It should be stressed, furthermore, that a healthy nuclear self, which, given minimally favorable circumstances, will be able to realize its nuclear program in the course of its life span, is in general not acquired only as a result of wholesome experiences. We know that early development can never be totally free of traumata. But we also know that the outcome of psychic development is determined not only by the relative frequency and severity of the traumata to which the self is exposed during its development, but also by the ability of the self—sometimes in the face of frequent and serious traumatizations—to establish the energic continuum from one pole to the other that I consider the dynamic-structural essence of mental health.

At this juncture, and in the context of the specific misunderstanding that I advocate that certain analyses be intentionally left incomplete, I will stress that the successful outcome of early development is often accounted for by the capacity of a self *in statu nascendi* to respond to certain traumatic frustrations of its developmental needs with a renewed and vigorous search for new solutions. This search continues until, in the narcissistic personality disturbances, in the structural neuroses, and in the conditions which, because the functional shortcomings of the self are not experienced as illness by the individual and his surroundings, we characterize psychological health or psychic normality, the outlines of an at least potentially cohesive self, that is, of a potentially efficient energic continuum, have indeed emerged. True, in the narcissistic personality disorders this process does not lead to secure consolidation, and the self, whose shape is already determined, must be strengthened with the help of the analytic process.[4] True, in the classical transference neuroses, a nuclear self which had been more or less able to maintain its firmness and cohesiveness during the early stages of development was unable to finish its development—because, as I explained before, of the faulty responses of the oedipal selfobjects—and remains enslaved by the fears and conflicts of the Oedipus complex. According to self psychology, therefore, not only the conflicts of the Oedipus complex, but also, ultimately, the specific self-selfobject relationships of the oedipal period on the basis of which the Oedipus complex arose, must be revived and worked through in the course of the psychoanalytic treatment. The result, in favorable instances, is that the early development of the self can now be completed. In this final developmental step, achieved with the aid of psychoanalysis, the establishment of oedipal self-structures is belatedly achieved: the fragments of the oedipal self (incestuous sexuality and destructive hostility) are replaced by an integrated oedipal self (an affectionate and assertive self) and the conditions are thus provided for the patient's living a meaningful life through the ability to realize the program of his nuclear self via the instrumentalities of work and love. But, to underscore the crucial issue, it is not possible to reactivate traumatic situations of infancy and childhood to which the self had on its own responded constructively during its early development. Even if the revival of these situations were feasible, moreover, no good purpose would be served if we could in fact bring it about.

In emphasizing this final point, I intend to clear up the misunderstanding of my friendly critic regarding certain passages in *The Restoration of the Self*. I argued in 1977, and I would reiterate now, that those traumatic aspects of its early selfobjects from which the nuclear self was able to withdraw successfully during its development are not revivable in the narcissistic transference. They cannot be revived because the developing self had turned away from them early in life and, since it was able to shift to different sources of structure formation—sources that culminated in the formulation of compensatory structures—it has no subsequent need for them. In such instances of self pathology, therefore, the essential task of treatment becomes the analysis of the manifestations emanating from the compensatory structures that had been incompletely established in early life. On becoming spontaneously reactivated in the form of a selfobject transference, these compensatory structures strive to complete their development via the projection of the favorable aspects of the infantile selfobject imago of the analyst.

At this point I will once more underline the fact that every self, not only in the narcissistic personality disorders but also in the structural neuroses and in health, consists to a greater or lesser extent of compensatory structures. There is not one kind of healthy self—there are many kinds. And there is no single analytic road toward cure—there are many, depending on the specific health potential of a specific analysand. But this much we can say: the healthy self will be predominantly composed of either primary or compensatory structures. Defensive structure, although never absent, will in most cases be at a minimum, though even this rule may, in some very exceptional cases, be invalid. While we are on firm ground in claiming that fully creative-productive selves are generally characterized by a relative paucity of defensive structures, we are less certain as to the most desirable ratio between primary and compensatory structure. On the basis of impressions gleaned from observing people who, I believe, are (or were) able to live especially meaningful and creative lives, I have come to assume that a self characterized by the predominance of compensatory structures constitutes the most frequent matrix of the capacity for high achievement. Stated in different terms, it is my impression that the most productive and creative lives are lived by those who, despite high degrees of traumatization in childhood, are able to acquire new structures by finding new routes toward inner completeness.

I will add to this brief discussion of the structural preconditions of a good life my conviction that traditional analysis cannot even approximate the meaningful message that self psychology can give us here. The theory of sublimation, in particular, which must not be taken as a counterpart to the foregoing statements, is tied to the concept of the primacy of drives and to the theory of drive-processing; it is in principle incapable of telling us anything about the meaningfulness and fulfillment or emptiness and sterility of a person's life. Conflicts, furthermore, are, again in principle, seen as having a deleterious impact on creative-productive activity as long as we remain within the confines of conceptualizations that explain man in terms of a mental apparatus fueled by the drives. Self psychology, on the other hand, while fully acknowledging the value of the traditional conceptualizations with regard to certain delimited experiences of man—temporarily paralyzing guilt feelings, for example, or even unconscious guilt that hampers performance throughout life—is able to show that, in the presence of a firm self, conflict per se is by no means deleterious, not even the largely unconscious conflict to which traditional analysis assigns the causative role in the psychogenesis of psychopathology. From the self psychological vantage point, even "the Unconscious"—in terms of the mental apparatus, the id, and the unconscious parts of the ego—if considered outside the procrustean bed of a cognitive approach that only asks whether a mental content is available to awareness or not, can provide a creative way of responding to the conflicts brought about by guilt. And a lifelong struggle to free oneself from such conflicts, ultimately leading to the functional rehabilitation and expansion of compensatory structures, will allow us to see even structural conflicts in a new light, that is, as potential challenges to our vitality and potential activating agents spurring "tragic man" to his successes and failures.

But even though I believe that self psychology has given us the means to understand the problems of psychic health more deeply and more broadly than the conceptual armamentarium of drive and ego psychology could, I realize that many of the questions touched on in this communication still require a good deal of further study—both in the direction of defining the life-contents that can be agreed upon as constituting health and in the direction of defining the structural composition of those selves that ultimately lead the most fulfilling lives. Even in the face of these uncertainties, however, I believe we can state with assurance that it is not a measure of pathology but a sign of resourcefulness and health when a self—nondefensively— demonstrates in the transference that it had, already during its early development, turned away from hopeless frustrations and found new paths or at least made partially successful moves in the new direction. The attempt to push such a self in therapy toward areas from which it had already disentangled itself in early life and with which it had severed connections not only is doomed to failure, but also betrays a gross misunderstanding of the patient. By insisting that his analysand's disease conform to the specific mold that he holds to be universal and by insisting, furthermore, that the analysand submit to the particular procrustean therapeutic process that the analyst considers the sine qua non of true analysis—be it the resolution of the Oedipus complex, the reliving of the emotions of the paranoid-depressive position, the abreaction of the trauma of birth, the reexperiencing of an early injury to the self, or any other theory-limited panacea—the analyst who undertakes such an attempt puts obstacles in the patient's path to recovery.

Part Two
The Nature of the Psychoanalytic Cure

Self psychology holds that self-selfobject relationships form the essence of psychological life from birth to death, that a move from dependence (symbiosis) to independence (autonomy) in the psychological sphere is no more possible, let alone desirable, than a corresponding move from a life dependent on oxygen to a life independent of it in the biological sphere. The developments that characterize normal psychological life must, in our view, be seen in the changing nature of the relationship between the self and its selfobjects, but not in the self's relinquishment of selfobjects. In particular, developmental advances cannot be understood in terms of the replacement of the selfobjects by love objects or as steps in the move from narcissism to object love.

4

Self-Selfobject Relationships
Reconsidered

Although I am eager to move forward and address the question that constitutes the title of this book, I think I should interrupt the flow of my argument at this point to discuss a problem that has arisen in the minds of several of my colleagues and friends. They ask the following question: How can I speak of self-selfobject relationships in general and claim, in particular, that self-selfobject relationships are present from birth to death, that the healthy self always needs the sustaining responses of selfobjects from the first to last breath?

Let me first dispose quickly of the second half of this question. This part of the question, as I should perhaps spell out, rests on an erroneous interpretation of the meaning of the term selfobject. Specifically, it rests on a confusion between the *general* meaning of the term selfobject as that dimension of our experience of another person that relates to this person's functions in shoring up our self and a *specific* meaning of the term selfobject—in this sense it should always be referred to as an *archaic* selfobject—that relates to the beginning stages of the development of selfobjects. During the earliest stage, cognitive indistinctiveness between self and selfobject may or may not exist. In view of the fact that I will discuss this issue from many sides later in this work, I will not pursue it further at this point. I will only say that, as with all genuine experiences in human life, the adult's experience of a selfobject is not segmental but sectorial. It is, in other words, an experience in depth: when the adult experiences the self-sustaining effects of a maturely chosen selfobject, the selfobject experiences of all the preceding stages of his life reverberate unconsciously. When we feel uplifted by our admiration for a great cultural ideal, for example, the old uplifting experience of being picked up by our strong and admired mother and having been allowed to merge with her greatness, calmness, and security may be said to form the unconscious undertones of the joy we are experiencing as adults.

But now to the first half of the question under scrutiny: is it not erroneous, is it not internally inconsistent, a kind of *contradictio in adjecto,* to speak of "self-selfobject relationships"? If, as is indeed the case, we claim that the concepts of a self and of a selfobject refer to inner experiences (see Kohut in prep.), that they are not part of physical reality but of psychological reality, observable only via intro-spection and empathy, how then can we speak of relationships between them as if we were dealing with actors on the stage of external reality?

There is no doubt about the fact that the objection implied in the foregoing rhetorical question is valid. But there is also no doubt, at least in my opinion—I know there are others, for example, Roy Schafer, who think differently about these matters—that the inconsistency in question is harmless and excusable, and greatly facilitates communi-cation. Why is it harmless and excusable? And why is it expedient to use it in the service of scientific communication? It is harmless because we can definitively clarify our usage of the term for the scientific community without feeling obliged to reiterate our basic explanation every time we use the term. In particular we need feel under no such obligation on those occasions—the vast majority of occasions, I will add—when the meaning of the concept of self-selfobject relations is not in the center of our attention but when our focus is elsewhere, for example, when we want to stress that the self needs selfobjects not only in infancy but throughout the whole span of life.

The problem is by no means restricted to the phrase self-selfobject relationships. We encounter the same dilemma whenever we are un-sure whether, insisting on conceptual consistency, we should be brief and evocative, trusting the mind of the reader to make whatever conceptual adjustments are necessary. Analysts are certainly used to living with conceptual ambiguities—perhaps too happily at times—that are much greater than the self psychological one under discus-sion. And I certainly am strongly in favor of pointing out these am-biguities, especially when, under the cover of terminology, the significance of a claim is actually falsified.

An excellent example of the harmless variety of terminological obfuscation within the framework of traditional analysis is the term and concept of "transference." An excellent example of the noxious variety is the term and concept of "drive." In view of the fact that I

have for many years (see Kohut 1978*b*, 1:205–32) discussed the deleterious consequences of a pseudoscientific usage of the term "drive"
and in view of the fact that I will do so again later in the present
work, I will not focus on them here. Instead, I will turn briefly to
"transference" to show that we are dealing with a conceptual inconsistency analogous to the one that typifies our use of the term "self-
selfobject relations."

"Transference" was originally a concept that was consistent with
the status of psychoanalysis as a psychology of complex mental states.
Since it was defined as a process going on between two areas of the
mental apparatus—the influence of the Unconscious on the Preconscious (Freud 1900, 1953, vol. 4)—it was clearly a psychological concept,
that is, an abstraction and generalization concerning data that had
been obtained, or that could now be obtained, via introspection and
empathy. I do not have to tell analysts, indeed I do not have to tell
anyone who is in any way involved with the mental health field, what
has become of this originally unambiguous concept. As everyone knows,
transference in its current usage is something that goes on between
people—in the analytic situation between analysand and analyst. As
a result, most people will be mystified when told that slips of the
tongue and hysterical-conversion symptoms are transference phenomena, and they will think of patients dreaming of analysts when
they learn that dreams are the result of transferences.

It would be easy enough to show that the shift from psychoanalytic
to social-psychological meaning that has occurred with regard to the
term "transference" is harmless enough, especially inasmuch as the
faulty but expedient usage has been clarified to the scientific community. But let me instead return to the ambiguity of the phrase "self-
selfobject relationship."

My justification for the usage of this term rests on the same reasoning that I alluded to in the foregoing remarks. In this instance,
however, an explanation, once given and understood, is even more
effective in preventing misunderstanding than was the case with regard to the concept of "transference." I put it this way in a letter to
a friend who questioned my use of the term "self-selfobject relationship" (Kohut, in prep.):

> I believe that, despite the gross terminological inaccuracies of
> this statement,[1] my meaning is clear. But think how clumsily,
> complicatedly, and, in the end, confusingly I would have to ex-
> press myself if I did not trust the reader to make the necessary
> allowances but tried to be conceptually accurate. I said that "self-
> selfobject relationships are present from birth to death." But
> what I should have said in order to be accurate would be some-

thing like this: "Throughout his life a person will experience himself as a cohesive harmonious firm unit in time and space, connected with his past and pointing meaningfully into a creative-productive future, [but] only as long as, at each stage in his life, he experiences certain representatives of his human surroundings as joyfully responding to him, as available to him as sources of idealized strength and calmness, as being silently present but in essence like him, and, at any rate, able to grasp his inner life more or less accurately so that their responses are attuned to his needs and allow him to grasp their inner life when his is in need of such sustenance."

And I stressed in my letter that

I wrote the foregoing sentence not in order to caricature the demand for exactness but only to show that there are no advantages—but many disadvantages—in being exact at all times. There *is* a place for sentences such as the foregoing one, namely, when the focus of the communication is on the definition of the sustaining effect of the self-selfobject unit. But when the point to be made lies elsewhere—e.g., in my example, on the fact that the need for this unit persists throughout life—then completeness and exactness become unnecessary burdens that do not need to be shouldered.

Having discharged as best I could the obligation to clarify a crucial self psychological term, I can now turn back to the more substantial, that is, experience-near, statement that prompted the foregoing excursion into concept formation and terminology. I am referring to the claim that a move from dependence (symbiosis) to independence (autonomy) is an impossibility and that the developmental moves of normal psychological life must be seen in the changing nature of the relationships between the self and its selfobjects—not as a replacement of selfobjects by love objects, not as a move from narcissism to object love.

As a sequel to the preceding tenet and in harmony with it, self psychology has also maintained from the beginning—an assertion that has retained its basic significance in our theories—that it is fruitful to look upon the "I's" experience of the "You" within two separate frames of reference: (1) with regard to the role the "You" plays in supporting the cohesion, strength, and harmony of the self, that is, to the experience of the "You" as "selfobject"; and (2) with regard to the "You" (a) as the target of our desire and love and (b) as the target of our anger and aggression when it blocks the way to the object we desire and love, i.e., to the experience of the "You" as "object." Whereas self psychology holds that the application of these two separate frames of reference makes a significant contribution to our ability to explain human experience in health and in disease, we also realize that there are occasions when the "I-You" experience is most fruitfully approached within a frame of reference that dispenses with this conceptual separation. We believe, furthermore, that the mutual influence of the two intertwining sets of experiences, one upon the other, deserves intensive study. Echoing Freud (1914, 1953, 13:241–44), I have emphasized (Kohut 1978b, 2:618–24) that object love strengthens the self, just as any other intense experience, even that provided by vigorous physical exercise, strengthens the self. Furthermore, it is well known that a strong self enables us to experience love and desire more intensely. Finally I would like to point out the conceptual clarity that results from differentiating narcissistic rage from the aggressions mobilized in the service of eliminating an obstacle to our goals: the first is characterized by unforgiving hatred and cruelty, the second by the absence of the need to hurt the opponent unnecessarily and the subsiding of aggression altogether when the goal in question is reached.

It should also be remarked at this point that, in view of the fact that traditional analysis has intensively investigated the vicissitudes of the self as it desires the "object" while neglecting and also misunderstanding the vicissitudes of the self as it needs the "selfobject"—low self-esteem expressed in the form of conscious self-preoccupations, for example, taken to constitute heightened instead of lowered narcissism within the framework of the libido theory—self psychology initially concentrated its efforts on the formerly neglected area. Only now is it beginning to investigate the relationship between self and self disturbance on the one hand and the experience of the object on the other. Self psychology is now attempting to demonstrate, for example, that all forms of psychopathology are based either on defects in the structure of the self, on distortions of the self, or on weakness of the self. It is trying to show, furthermore, that all these flaws in the self are due to disturbances of self-selfobject relationships in childhood. Stated in the obverse, by way of highlighting the contrast between self psychological and traditional theory,[2] self psychology holds that pathogenic conflicts in the object-instinctual realm—that is, pathogenic conflicts in the realm of object love and object hate and in particular the set of conflicts called the Oedipus complex—are not the *primary* cause of psychopathology but its result.

I have intentionally emphasized the word "primary" in the preceding statement about the position of the conflicts of the Oedipus complex in the classical transference neuroses. While we have come to appreciate the self-selfobject failures and self defects correlated with them as primary, the resulting distortions of the child's emotional life (its sexual instead of affectionate attitudes and its proclivity to respond

with hostile-destructive impulses instead of self-confident assertiveness) and the subsequent disturbance of its relationships should also
be considered pathogenic factors, that is, they should also be considered causal elements, at least in an intermediate sense, in the sequence
of events that ultimately lead to the formation of symptoms in the
classical transference neuroses.

I have repeatedly said that the difference between traditional analysis and psychoanalytic self psychology is one of emphasis—a shift in
emphasis which, while subtle, is still very significant. I can illuminate
the significance of this shift by pointing to Freud's view that his great
discovery, the discovery of the unconscious, was experienced by people
as a narcissistic injury of the first magnitude. This injury, which, by
implication, accounted to a considerable degree for the rejection that
Freud's own work suffered, was strongly influenced by a crucial confluence of the innovator's personal sensitivities and era-dominant psychological trends which is often the soil on which important
psychological insights grow. I have previously discussed both these
factors as they contributed to the establishment of psychoanalysis as
a fledgling science after its emergence in the pioneering step taken
by Anna O. and Breuer. (For an earlier consideration of Freud's personality in the foregoing context, see Kohut 1977, pp. 290–98; for a
related discussion of the era dominance of specific psychological vulnerabilities, see Kohut 1977, pp. 267–80.) Still, in view of the pivotal
significance of the issues that are at stake I will now restate and expand
on certain ideas I have introduced in earlier work.

Let us begin with the specific features of Freud's personality that
led him to see the psychological field in the specific way that culminated in classical or traditional psychoanalysis, that is, the science of
the unconscious, of the mental apparatus, and of structural conflict.
Turning first to Freud's moral stance, we can say that his morality was
above all a truth morality. And we can add in this context that his
self-esteem was intensely influenced by his sense of knowing something or not knowing it. To have knowledge withheld from him was
experienced as an intolerable narcissistic injury to which he responded
with rage. (See the discussion of this aspect of his personality in Kohut
1977, pp. 65–66.) He thus held, undoubtedly sensitive to this propensity in others on the basis of his own vulnerability in this area, that
confronting people with the fact that they did not know something
they thought they knew—that is, the full content of their own mind—
was the most serious injury to which psychoanalysis exposed them. It
was an injury, he added, that stood in proud succession to the injuries
inflicted on mankind by Copernicus and Darwin (cf. Freud 1917,
1953, 16:284–85, to a discussion of his views in Kohut 1978b, 2:515–
18).

I trust that I do not have to stress again that the personal element in the psychological truths that a psychologist affirms, like the quantum physicist's observing instrument, must not be separated from objective reality; objective reality always includes the subject (see chap. 3). Thus, (a) while I doubt Freud's claim that being confronted with the fact that one does not know what one thought one knew necessarily inflicts an unbearable narcissistic injury on people and (b) while I further doubt that such an injury would be equally severe in all periods of history, I do not derive these doubts about the appropriateness of Freud's emphasis from the evidence pointing to his own specific vulnerability in this area. And I will add that the same considerations obtain in the realm of the theories that Freud formed. I consider it very likely that it was a specific characteristic feature of Freud's personality—the same feature, in fact—that led Freud to subdivide mental life as he saw it into conscious and unconscious parts, to assign primacy to the contrast between knowing and not knowing when he first systematized his findings, and to employ the criterion of accessibility to knowledge as the ordering principle in the doctrine of man's dichotomized mind that he always considered the most crucial tenet in his entire system of thought. But, once more, my judgment concerning the relevance and explanatory power of Freud's theories should not, and will not, proceed from my conclusion that Freud was led to his particular explanatory framework by a highly personal—and, I will stress again, time-bound—outlook on man.

Surprising as it may seem at first sight, the same specific sensitivities that led Freud to his early formulations about the dichotomy between the unconscious and the (pre)conscious layers of the mind can also be invoked as having contributed to his later complementary formulations concerning the dichotomy between the id and the ego (Freud 1923, 1953, vol. 19). Not long before he introduced the new dichotomy—his addition of a third "agency," the superego, is irrelevant in the present context—Freud stated (1917, 1953, 16:284–85) that people found his tenet of the existence of the unconscious intolerable because it forced them to admit that they were not even *masters* (my italics) in their own psychological houschold (see, on Freud's views in this area, Kohut 1978*b*, 2:689–90). By thus juxtaposing knowledge with mastery—that is, knowledge with the ego, the functional seat of mastery—and, by implication, a lack of knowledge with a lack of mastery—that is, a lack of knowledge with passivity or paralysis of the ego—Freud achieved in one bold creative act a workable synthesis that was simultaneously the expression of a deep personal need and the formulation of a theoretical model of great explanatory power.

Here another vista opens, I believe, concerning the connection between the personality of the researcher and the theories he formulates.

Lack of mastery—passivity—was for Freud the ultimate not-further-analyzable biological bedrock of man's psychological life (Freud 1937, 1953, 23:252). By recognizing the two messages that converge in Freud's formulations, by recognizing the deeply significant correlations they imply between verbalizable knowledge and anxiety-dispelling mastery on the one hand and between lack of verbalizable knowledge and dreadful passivity on the other, we have not only made some headway in our subsidiary task of examining the influence of Freud's personality on his choice of theories, but by focusing on the origins of the traditionally accepted claims that the acquisition of verbalizable knowledge (often referred to as insight) constitutes the essence of the psychoanalytic cure—"the talking cure"—we have also moved closer to our principal task: the examination of the factors which psychoanalytic self psychology, in contrast to traditional analysis, believes to constitute the essential ingredients of the psychoanalytic cure. By having deepened our understanding of an important aspect of the traditional explanation of psychoanalytic cure, that is, we have prepared the way for our subsequent scrutiny of the process of cure in the light of self psychology. It is our aim, in other words, to identify those elements in the psychoanalytic process which in contrast to those emphasized by traditional formulations—or rather in complementation and emendation of these—can now be recognized as leading to the psychoanalytic cure.

It will be remembered that I began my present digression by focusing on a specific narrow issue, namely, Freud's belief that the rejection of psychoanalysis was motivated by the fact that his science confronted man with the painful recognition that he lacked full access to his own mind, that he was not master in his own psychological household. I must admit that in the past I always read Freud's lines expressing this view with pleasure and unquestioning belief. In particular, identifying with Freud as an analyst who could also look an unpleasant truth squarely in the eye, I felt uplifted in reading about the proud company in which he saw himself when he thus offended and angered man: Copernicus, who had taken from man the illusionary greatness of being in the center of the universe, and Darwin, who had taken from him the illusionary greatness of having been created separately as the crowning glory of God's work. I can still derive a great deal of pleasure from participating in Freud's pride in the magnitude of his achievement, but, as I have observed, I am no longer unquestioningly convinced of the universal validity of Freud's implied claim that the theory of the unconscious is by its very content intolerably offensive to man—in particular, that it is intolerably offensive to man as he is constituted at all times. And I must admit, furthermore, that I now have similar doubts with regard to the correctness of Freud's claim about the analogous effect on man (i.e., on man as he is constituted at all times) of the theories of Copernicus and Darwin.

Clearly we are dealing here with a very complex and difficult problem—the problem of where to draw the line between psychological tenets that are universally valid at all times and those that hold only with regard to certain individuals and/or during certain periods of history. I have discussed this issue before, specifically as it pertains to the analyst and psychoanalytically informed psychohistorians who examine the historical past; it is, however, an all-important issue not only in psychohistory but in all applications of analysis that examine man of past eras and his creations (see Kohut 1978b, 2:910–13, 916–19). In the present context, I will restrict myself to restating that while analysts must not let themselves be deterred from examining the historical past with the best tools at their disposal, they must not forget that they are always on dangerous ground while doing so. Even the most convincing conclusions, seemingly self-evident beyond question, may ultimately come into serious question. Freud's assertion—which, to repeat, I completely accepted until recently—that the three greatest discoveries of science were also, in harmony with his theory of resistance to insight, those discoveries most strenuously rejected by man may in fact be open to serious doubt. Specifically, the various negative reactions to revolutionary scientific discoveries may be less universally explainable than Freud thought; in fact, they may be time-bound (era-specific) and/or restricted to certain groups or individuals. I would be hoisting myself on my own petard if I went on to assert the definite conclusion that Freud's claims were in error. I cannot make this assertion since I have not undertaken, for example, the broad study that would be necessary to familiarize myself with the subtle biases, the threatened privileges, and the power positions undermined that one must understand in assessing the meaning of the rejection of the theory of a nongeocentric universe, of the evolution of species, or of the limits of the domain of consciousness in mental life. But consider the conception of the universe that was dominant before it was overthrown by the discoveries of the Renaissance. Pre-Copernican man saw his earthly existence, as the vernacular says, "at the bottom of the heap." The heavens above were populated by angels and, above them, by archangels; higher still, at the topmost peak, was God. Copernicus' theory, in other words, did not attack man's pride. On the contrary, his theory was promethean hubris, an insight that freed man from the conception of a universe in which he had to resign himself to a very lowly station indeed (see Lovejoy 1936 for a broad discussion of these issues).

Are there similar factors with regard to the rejection of Darwin's and Freud's teachings that would make us, here too, question the relevance of Freud's reference to the injury inflicted by his discoveries on that omnipresent residue of infantile omnipotence that his contemporary Ferenczi (1916) had described? I must admit once more that it is beyond my competence to evaluate fully and reliably the narcissistic injury inflicted on entrenched power groups in Copernicus's, Darwin's, or even Freud's time and to estimate whether the rejection of the theories under scrutiny was due to a defensive counterattack by these groups. I do think, however, that it would be a rewarding task for a psychohistorian to establish these causal connections, and I consider it likely that the task could be executed successfully. I am confident, in other words, that a causal chain could be identified by a competent historian that would enable us to dispense with explanations that see the motivation of a complex social action as issuing directly from a ubiquitous reaction at the deepest layers of our psychological organization. (An analogous objection can be raised to Freud's [1930, 1953, vol. 21, 1933, 1953, 22:203] psychological explanation of the cause of wars.)

Clearly—and this I want to stress in contrast to Freud's position still widely accepted by analysts—great new ideas, great discoveries should not be considered prima facie offensive to mankind. On the contrary, great new thought, great discoveries tend to be welcomed because, heightening the self-esteem of those who become acquainted with them, they enhance vitality through the merger with the idealized innovator—unless, of course, they threaten positions of personal privilege and power. In fact the self-esteem-enhancing effect of new ideas may prevent those who have enthusiastically embraced them from soberly identifying their inevitable shortcomings. In this way, the adoption of new ideas may embody almost as great a potential for error—in particular, for the perpetration of error via the changing of theory into dogma—as the rejection of these same ideas on the basis of wounded pride.

I said that Freud, for personal, undoubtedly psychogenetically determined reasons, was especially sensitive to having knowledge withheld from him and that he was, in general, inclined to give knowledge and truth values a disproportionately exalted position—alone at the pinnacle of his value hierarchy. To prevent all possible misunderstanding, let me say that I am not demeaning knowledge and truth values. I am emphasizing, however, that other important values exist—values that may at times occupy a rank as high or even higher than those concerning the facing of truth and the search for knowledge. I will not at this point expand on the hypothesis that the hierarchical position of truth values is lowered to the degree that truth-seeking and veracity have become ego function and ego attitude, respectively (see Kohut 1978b, 2:674–75). I will, however, underline once more that while some values may have absolute and abiding validity—at least within the foreseeable future[3]—their position within the hierarchy of values changes in response to changes in the internal (psychological) and external (e.g., sociocultural and political) milieu in which man lives at any given time.

Was Freud's time one that made truth and knowledge values especially important? Is Freud's genius partly accounted for by the fact that, because of the specific makeup of his personality, that confluence of personal sensitivities and era-dominated trends existed which I earlier characterized as a facilitator of significant psychological discovery? I believe that these questions can be answered affirmatively. Specifically, I think that Freud's personality unfolded during a transitional period of history—an era of change, of progress, of increasing political freedom, of increasing freedom of thought—the kind of period, I might add, that is often the most propitious for great achievement. It was unquestionably a time in which obscurantism in general was on the wane. But I would stress that this expression "on the wane" tells only half the story. Progress is never simple and unidirectional— the previously established order, the old morality, the prior system of values being overcome are not only waning, but simultaneously waxing, channeling their influence into covert but silently effective activities, and feeling threatened, pursuing their aims with intensified exertions. Thus, while in the laboratories and classrooms the sciences flourished and knowledge values held sway, sexual knowledge was still stringently withheld from children. Furthermore, scientific beliefs not only were rooted in the political life of the Vienna of Freud's time (as embodied, in particular, in the figures of von Schoenerer and Lueger) but often emerged in that strange admixture with pseudo-science (e.g., the work of J. A. de Gobineau 1884 and H. S. Chamberlain 1899) which many years later exploded into the great countermovement of racist fascism that nearly succeeded in destroying Western man and his values of freedom and reason.

The parallelism between the sociocultural layering to which I am referring here (for a sensitive evaluation of fin de siècle Vienna, see C. Schorske 1980) and Freud's conceptualizations is striking. Just as in the Europe of Freud's time, in general, and in the Austria in which he grew up, in particular, political liberalism held sway and the arts and sciences flourished while the forces of tyrannical mystical belief simultaneously made their presence known—at least in retrospect, though at the time their enormous potential was not appreciated and they tended to be disregarded and ridiculed—so also with Freud's dichotomized psyche. There was "the Conscious" (later the conscious parts of ego and superego) on one hand and "the Unconscious" (later the id and the unconscious parts of ego and superego) on the other. The very division that held true for the cultural and social life of Freud's time, in other words, pertained to the psyche of the individual as Freud conceptualized it. One realm—overt, easily recognized, its existence acknowledged—lived by logic and reason (in the language of Freudian metapsychology, it followed the laws of the secondary process); the other realm—hidden, hard to recognize, its existence denied—lived by archaic, prelogical rules (it followed the laws of the primary process).

Our own time, by way of contrast, seems to show the foregoing type of sociocultural dichotomization to a much lesser, indeed to a minimal extent. Archaic forces—from the John Birch Society to the Moonies to Jonestown—are active, just as they were during the fin de siècle— but their presence and potential for evil are now recognized, broadly discussed, and opposed. Yet, side by side, there is a flourishing of science, technology, and art—from penicillin and space exploration, on the one hand, to Picasso and Stravinsky, on the other—which, in its creative thrust has hardly been equaled in history. And, again in contrast to the personality structure of the fin de siècle patients whose investigation led Freud to his formulation of the dichotomized psyche and later of structural conflict, the prevalent personality organization of our time is not typified by the simple horizontal split brought about by repression. The psyche of modern man—the psyche described by Kafka and Proust and Joyce—is enfeebled, multifragmented (verti-cally split), and disharmonious. It follows that we cannot adequately understand our patients and explain them to themselves if we try to do so with the aid of a model of unconscious conflicts that cannot do the job.

To summarize my reasoning: Freud's scientific outlook—the choices he made in his observations, the nature of his theories—not only was strongly influenced by his personality, but also was an outgrowth of the fact that he was a child of his time. I would stress two points once more: (1) My distinction between specific features of Freud's person-ality and the character of his time serves heuristic and expository purposes; the distinction is actually an artifact since the mores, pre-dilections, and social conditions of the time will also decisively influ-ence the behavior of adults toward their children and thereby produce the milieu in which the personality of the child is formed. (2) My statements concerning the era-specificity of Freud's views do not per se constitute a criticism; they were offered as a contribution to our understanding of how his great achievements came about.

But let me now expand on these two points. Concerning the first point we can say that the formative era-specific imprints made on

Freud via the personalities and behavior of the adults who surrounded him during his childhood were ambiguous. Stated differently, the children of his time, in general, and those of the Central European middle class to which Freud's family belonged, in particular, were simultaneously exposed to two separate antithetical influences. There was, on the one hand, the influence of that strong era-specific cultural current that expressed itself as an overt self-enhancing admiration for freedom of action and thought. There was, on the other hand, the influence of self-stifling conservative religious beliefs threatened and thus defensively intensified by the overt expansion of self-enhancing scientific thought and the stirrings of self-enhancing nationalism. These conservative beliefs entailed the withholding, especially from children, of knowledge beyond the area permitted by the religious authorities; this withholding is usually correlated with intensified religious (and political) authoritarianism. Concerning the second point—that is, concerning Freud's propensity to make those specific choices in his observations and theories that gave the science of analysis its specific content and shape—I will only reiterate my belief that it was the very fact that his personality had been formed by his time that provided him with a specific sensitivity toward certain psychological trends which, as he moved toward personal and scientific maturity, were dominant in the society whose members he investigated.

But having affirmed once more the era-specificity of the fit between observer and the observed with regard to Freud, I will now unhesitatingly claim the same privilege for the psychological observer in our time, in particular for the self psychologically oriented observer. People in our time—especially people of the Western democracies—are not, as I have stressed many times before, predominantly exposed to the traumatic effect of being deprived of knowledge (by governmental censorship as adults, by "Victorian" parents as children). And being confronted with a scientific theory such as classical analysis that demonstrates to them that aspects of their own minds are beyond their awareness will not lead them to reject the theory angrily or, turning the tables, to assume an attitude of contempt and ridicule toward it. Man of our time is the man of the precariously cohesive self, the man who craves the presence, the interest, the availability of the self-cohesion-maintaining selfobject. It is the very intensity of this need that via a wall of secondary prideful disavowal accounts for the fact that he may experience our theory that the self's autonomy is only relative, that, in principle, a self can never exist outside a matrix of selfobjects, as a serious narcissistic blow. Could it be that some of the intense antagonism that self psychology has aroused, that some of the distorting ridicule to which it is exposed, can in part be explained by this factor? And could it be that the warmth with which self psychology is accepted by others—by those, that is, who are more directly in touch with modern man's primary need—is also explained in this way?

Yes, I do indeed believe this may be the case. But I can do no more than give voice to this opinion and affirm it as a likely possibility. I must immediately add, moreover, that I do not consider it likely that this factor is the decisive one in bringing about the often intense rejection of self psychology by a number of psychoanalysts—their refusal to accept it as a developmental step in analysis and their attempt to demean it as a "deviant school" or, even worse, as a "cult." I have not forgotten, in other words, my earlier conclusion that new ideas affect people on many levels and that we should not take immediate recourse in depth-psychological explanations but rather investigate carefully the variety of motivations that render people unwilling to give new ideas a fair hearing. And I have not forgotten in this context my own call for courage in commending the analysis of group attitudes by someone who, as a member of the group, is himself involved in the group dynamics to be explained (see Kohut 1978b, 2:831–43).

Why then do I not undertake such an investigation? An objective assessment of the complex attitudes encountered in our profession with reference to the rejection and acceptance of my own ideas would be an enterprise that—without a clear promise of success—would require all my energies for a considerable time, energies that I feel should be devoted to insufficiently explored areas of clinical self psychology and self psychological theory. I cannot deny that I abstain from the self psychological investigation of the reactions—pro and con—to my work with considerable regret. I feel regret because, despite the potential pitfalls of my personal emotional involvement with the processes that need to be investigated, I believe that, on the whole, this task can be done and done with sufficient objectivity to be worthwhile. I have told myself, moreover, that I should not shrink from this undertaking out of faintheartedness, anticipating ridicule and the summary dismissal of my findings. Still, having considered all these factors and faced my own conflicts, I have decided to remain faithful to more important scientific commitments and to spend the time left to me not attempting an objective assessment of my colleagues' positive and negative reactions to my work, but pursuing primary research in the area of my primary professional and scientific competence.

Certainly, even apart from any consideration of the potential pitfalls due to my personal involvement, the task of analyzing the attitudes of my professional colleagues vis-à-vis the teachings of self psychology would be a difficult one. My earlier comment, furthermore, concerning the limited explanatory power of Freud's assessment of the role of narcissistic wounds in accounting for the rejection of his own theories as well as those of Copernicus and Darwin applies as well to an analogous assessment of the emotional aspects of the resistances evoked by self psychology. The rejection of classical analysis by the neuropsychiatric establishment of Freud's time was not only due to the fact that Freud's professional opponents (and others who ridiculed him) felt narcissistically injured by a theory that claimed man did not have full access to his own mind. Many other motivating factors were involved—essentially "narcissistic" factors to be sure, such as those arising on the basis of threatened professional and religious prestige and power—which in my opinion were the decisive ones. The same considerations now hold with regard to the teachings of self psychology. To be confronted with man's lifelong need for selfobjects, to be told that autonomy is impossible, may well be experienced as a narcissistic injury by many, particularly in an era in which the survival of the selves of many individuals depends on the sustenance of selfobjects at archaic levels. But there are also issues of professional prestige and power at stake. Just as classical analysis was rejected by members of the neuropsychiatric establishment during the early phases of its development—it was generally supported by those who perceived themselves as "outsiders"—so now with the rejection of self psychology from the side of established analysis.

It is clear and hardly needs mentioning that the preceding reflections concerned only the irrational elements that fuel the antagonism toward new ideas. There is no doubt whatever that Freud's system was from the beginning also exposed to serious criticism, to rational doubt—and the same is true, I am happy to say, with regard to self psychology. In addition, even among the nonrational motivations underlying extreme reactions toward new ideas, there are those that cannot be explained by referring to the self, whether sustained or threatened. But, clearly, I cannot pursue any longer the secondary topic into which I have strayed—the fascinating field of the role of narcissistic injury, narcissistic rage, and subsequent antagonistic-inimical reactions to new ideas in the realm of scientific thought. I must move forward to the major task I have set myself: the investigation of the process of cure in psychoanalysis. In view of the fact, however, that I do not think we should deprive ourselves of the results of the preceding reflections insofar as they are relevant to this major task, I will make my return in a specific way, namely, by asking whether the preceding considerations contribute to our ability to assess the process of cure in psychoanalysis. Predictably, my answer to this question will be in the affirmative.

5

The Curative Effect of Analysis:

A Preliminary Statement Based on the Findings of Self Psychology

Self psychology does not find the essence of the curative process in the cognitive sphere per se. In the terms of Freud's earlier topographic model, it does not believe that we have defined the essence of the curative process when we say that the unconscious has become conscious. Although the step toward cure that self psychology considers to be decisive is usually preceded by, accompanied by, or followed by a broadening of the area that is accessible to introspection, this increase in the scope of consciousness does not always occur, and it is not essential.

But let us now consider Freud's later structural or tripartite formulation of the mind. What is the self psychological evaluation of Freud's conceptualization of cure in the terms of this second step in his theory formation? It is no different from the self psychological assessment of the earlier topographic conceptualization of therapeutic success. *Expressis verbis,* self psychology believes that the essence of the curative process is defined neither by reference to the expansion of the realm of awareness nor, at least not per se, by reference to the increased ability of the psychic apparatus to modify the drives. In comparison with the conception of the effect of psychoanalytic therapy that derives its explanatory power from Freud's later structural model of the mental apparatus, self psychology does not see the essence of the curative process as lying primarily in the expansion of the domain of the ego. True, the movement in the psychoanalytic process of therapy that the self psychologist does consider essentially curative will frequently be followed by an increase in the scope of the ego—an increase in the sphere of its influence which, it should be stressed, may manifest itself in particular in the patient's increased ability to express himself verbally with regard to the formerly pathogenic sector of his personality. But I must immediately add that ego expansion (in particular as manifested by an increase in verbal mastery)[1] does not eventuate in every instance of cure. More significantly, even when this desirable development has indeed transpired, it is a secondary result of the basic curative alteration and must not be regarded as constituting the essence of the cure.

I am familiar with the objections that will be raised to the preceding contrast between the formulations of ego psychology and those of self psychology—objections, I will add, which will arise among the very best of analysts who, without taking the decisive step from mental apparatus psychology to self psychology, attempt to make the old system relevant to what they actually perceive in their patients by straining it beyond its capabilities. (For some remarks concerning my own struggles "to adjust the classical tenets to the data that I accumulated as I added year after year of clinical experience," see Kohut 1978b, 2:931–38, esp. p. 933.) I know that a sensitive and intelligent analyst will up to a point be able to employ the concepts of the tripartite model of the psyche in a reasonably satisfactory way, by emphasizing the synthetic function of the ego and construing it as roughly parallel to the conceptualizations of self psychology (parallel, that is, to such introspectively accessible features of self experience as the self's cohesion, firmness, vigor, vitality, and harmoniousness). But, to repeat, he will be able to do so only up to a point.

I have never claimed that the formulations of ego psychology are wrong or useless. I have only claimed that they do not allow us to formulate in a satisfactory way those crucial attributes of the psyche as it moves toward health: the capacity for self-soothing, the sense of continuity of the self in time, and the crucial role of the selfobject in providing the opportunity for the acquisition of these attributes. An unforced theoretical conceptualization of these psychic states and processes is, to my mind, not possible with the armamentarium of even the most sophisticated ego psychology; it requires the complementary framework of the psychology of the self.

But now, having expressed the view that the traditional explanations of cure have only limited validity, we must turn to the decisive question: how does self psychology perceive the process of cure? The answer is: as a three-step movement, the first two steps of which may be described as defense analysis and the unfolding of the transferences, while the third step—the essential one because it defines the aim and the result of the cure—is the opening of a path of empathy between self and selfobject, specifically, the establishment of empathic in-tuneness between self and selfobject on mature adult levels. This new channel of empathy permanently takes the place of the formerly repressed or split-off archaic narcissistic relationship; it supplants the bondage that had formerly tied the archaic self to the archaic selfobject.[2]

To demonstrate the essential correctness of the preceding formulation concerning the essence of the cure achieved by psychoanalysis, to demonstrate, in other words, the encompassing explanatory power of the simple formulation that the gradual acquisition of empathic contact with mature selfobjects is the essence of the psychoanalytic cure, is an enterprise of monographic proportions. But it is an enterprise that I know could be carried out successfully, and I hope very much that some of my colleagues will undertake this task. At present, I myself can do no more than sketch the outline of such an undertaking.

The work that must be done relates to both the clinical and the theoretical fields. Concerning the first of these two areas, the researcher who wishes to demonstrate the correctness of the hypothesis under scrutiny must show, with the aid of numerous detailed clinical illustrations, how analysands who had originally been restricted to archaic modes of self-selfobject relationships because the development toward maturity in this sector of their personality had been thwarted in childhood became, in the course of successful analyses, increasingly able to evoke the empathic resonance of mature selfobjects and to be sustained by them. Using existing clinical reports or adducing unpublished clinical material,[3] the researcher must in particular demonstrate how, after the original resistances motivated by the fear of retraumatization by the current selfobject's empathic failures—in the selfobject transference: the analyst's failures as manifested by his erroneous, inaccurate, ill-timed, or unfeelingly blunt interpretations[4]— had been overcome, the ultimate opening of a channel of reliable empathy between self and selfobject was reached via a characteristic undulating path. He must show, in brief, that the quietly sustaining matrix provided by the spontaneously established selfobject transference to the analyst that establishes itself in the early phases of analysis is disrupted time and again by the analyst's unavoidable, yet only temporary and thus nontraumatic, empathy failures—that is, his "optimal failures." In response to the analyst's errors in understanding or in response to the analyst's erroneous or inaccurate or otherwise improper interpretations, the analysand turns back temporarily from his reliance on empathy to the archaic selfobject relationships (e.g., to remobilization of the need for merger with archaic idealized omnipotent selfobjects or remobilization of the need for immediate and perfect mirroring) that he had already tentatively abandoned in the primary selfobject transference of the analysis. In a properly conducted analysis, the analyst takes note of the analysand's retreat, searches for any mistakes he might have made, nondefensively acknowledges them after he has recognized them (often with the help of the analysand), and then gives the analysand a noncensorious interpretation of the dynamics of his retreat. In this way the flow of empathy between analyst and analysand that had been opened through the originally established selfobject transference is remobilized. The patient's self is then sustained once more by a selfobject matrix that is empathically in tune with him.

In describing these undulations, the researcher must show how each small-scale, temporary empathic failure leads to the acquisition of self-esteem-regulating psychological structure in the analysand—assuming, once more, that the analyst's failures have been nontraumatic ones. Having noticed the patient's retreat, the analyst must watch the analysand's behavior and listen open-mindedly to his associations. By listening open-mindedly, I mean that he must resist the temptation to squeeze his understanding of the patient into the rigid mold of whatever theoretical preconceptions he may hold, be they Kleinian, Rankian, Jungian, Alderian, classical-analytic, or, yes, self psychological, until he has more accurately grasped the essence of the patient's need and can convey his understanding to the patient via a more correct interpretation.

This is, I think, the place to refer again to a fact which I and others have discussed on several occasions before (e.g., Kohut 1978b, 2:749–50) and which I will discuss again more extensively later in this work (see chap. 9). I am referring to the fact that an observer needs theories in order to observe. The specific issue that I want to underline at this particular point is that these theories must be the helpmates of the observer, not his masters. If an analyst is convinced that a particular set of theories has ubiquitous applicability and relevance at all times, he will often misinterpret his patients' reactions and, in compliance with his unshakable convictions, will look upon their protestations as resistances. It must be stressed, in particular, that the appropriateness or inappropriateness of the analyst's interpretations has to be evaluated with regard to the particular moment in the analysis at which they are given. For long times during the analysis of an oedipal transference, for example—that is, for long times during the analysis of an Oedipus complex that has been remobilized in the transference—the analyst will properly function as the analysand's selfobject only if he focuses his interpretations on the latter's incestuous desires and death-wishes and on the well-known conflicts of ambivalence that accompany these drive-fed impulses. Should the analyst attempt to bypass the Oedipus complex and push the patient prematurely toward the failures of the oedipal selfobjects of childhood which led to the Oedipus complex, the analysand will feel misunderstood and retreat, whether via open resistance and protest or—one of the strongest resistances encountered—via external compliance.

It follows that the self psychologically informed analyst will stay with the here and now of the transference and will shift the focus of his interpretations only when, after the working through of repressive oedipal material, the beginnings of a joyfully entered oedipal stage can be discerned and the revival of the faultily responsive oedipal selfobjects of childhood becomes evident via the patient's transference experiences. During the transitional period in the transference, the characteristic oscillations between the patient's return to the Oedipus complex and his tentative forward moves toward the experiences of the normal oedipal stage place especially great demands on the analyst's empathic perceptiveness. At this period in the analysis, it is incumbent on the analyst to be able to respond in three different ways, each specifically appropriate at different moments: (1) he must acknowledge the presence of the beginnings of the oedipal stage with appropriately phrased and appropriately felt interpretations; (2) he must acknowledge the analysand's retreats—especially frequent in the early part of this transitional period—to the experience of the Oedipus complex; and (3) he must explain with increasing emphasis the dynamics of the oscillations between the two aforementioned sets of experiences, via both the dynamic interpretation of the here and now of the transference and the genetic reconstruction of the original situation in childhood.

Does all this mean, we will ultimately ask ourselves, that the theory held by the self psychologist concerning the genesis of the Oedipus complex—that is, his recognition that it came about as the result of the pathological and pathogenic responses of the oedipal selfobjects—plays no role whatever during the protracted period when the experiences of the Oedipus complex are confronted in analysis? My answer to this question is clearly and emphatically in the negative. There can be no doubt that, as decisively influential background knowledge, the analyst's understanding of the pathogenic role of the selfobjects in oedipal neuroses will not only enable him to recognize the beginning of the shift toward the normal oedipal stage as soon as it occurs, but also subtly influence the tone of his interpretations, even during the earlier phase of the working-through process. It is clear that the oedipal interpretations of the analyst who, in harmony with Freud's major emphasis—his reference to a complementary series in which traumata have a role notwithstanding—puts the drives into the center of the child's experience will sound different (even though the content of the interpretations may be the same) from the interpretations of an analyst who looks upon the Oedipus complex as a disintegration product that follows the destruction of the normal oedipal self.

It bears repeating, in this context, that however correct an analyst's theories are, and however open-minded he is in applying them, he cannot avoid erring many times in his understanding of the analysand and in the explanations he offers to him. This obtains whether the analyst is dealing with a narcissistic personality or behavior disorder or with those self disorders to which we have traditionally referred as oedipal neuroses. In all such instances, as I have stressed repeatedly, no harm ensues if the analyst recognizes the patient's retreats and responds to them with appropriate interpretations. Such errors constitute optimal failures; they can, I am sure, be demonstrated easily by any clinically experienced researcher since they occur literally hundreds of times in every good analysis. Each optimal failure will be followed by an increase in the patient's resilience vis-à-vis empathy failures both inside and outside the analytic situation; that is, after each, optimal new self structures will be acquired and existing ones will be firmed. These developments, in turn, lead to a rise in the patient's basic level of self-esteem, however minimal and by itself imperceptible to analysand and analyst each such accretion of structure may be. As I said, I will dispense with the task of giving specific clinical examples, trusting that the reader's clinical experience, the previous clinical contributions of my colleagues and me, and work still to be presented by others will fill the gap. But while I am foregoing clinical illustrations at this point, I will attempt to support my hypothesis by examining it against the background of a number of theoretical issues.

In thus restricting my focus to the theoretical field, I must at once undertake to restrict it still further. To wit, I cannot undertake here the broad, systematic comparison that will eventually have to be done between the theory of psychoanalytic cure offered by self psychology and the theories of cure that have been proffered by analysts, beginning with Breuer and Freud, who, like self psychologists, wanted to understand the nature of their successes and the reasons for their failures in theoretical terms. This ambitious task, too, I will leave to others and restrict myself to clarifying the meaning of the self psychological definition of cure and to supporting it in the theoretical area via a less systematic approach.

I will begin with an argument in favor of the self psychological hypothesis concerning the factors that bring about a psychoanalytic cure which, however important to the self psychologically oriented analyst, will carry little weight with those who are skeptical of the self psychological outlook in all its aspects. We can claim, I believe, that the theory of the psychoanalytic cure advanced by self psychology is in harmony not only with the general theories of self psychology, in particular with those of its formulations concerning the nature of the various kinds of psychopathology, but also with the developmental tenets that are correlated with its explanations of adult psychopathology. Let me summarize both of these theories—the self psychological theory of the nature of psychopathology and the self psychological theory of psychological development—with two brief statements. (1) Self psychology holds that, with regard to a large number of patients who now enter psychoanalytic treatment,[5] the essence of psychopathology is the defective self (i.e., the self prone to states of fragmentation, weakness, or disharmony). (2) Self psychology holds that the pathological condition of the self is due to disturbances of the self-selfobject processes in early life; these processes normally lead to the building up of a healthy self. A healthy self, it should be added, is a structure that—except perhaps as an outcome of the most severe forms of traumatization such as prolonged confinement in concentration camps and other protracted dehumanizing experiences—is not prone to become fragmented, weakened, or disharmonious during maturity, at least not severely and/or for long periods.

What are the wholesome self-selfobject processes that build up the healthy self? We see them as occurring in two steps. First, a basic intuneness must exist between the self and its selfobjects. Second, selfobject failures (e.g., responses based on faulty empathy) of a nontraumatic degree must occur. We refer to the results of such failures on the part of the selfobjects of childhood as "optimal frustrations." This two-step sequence of psychological events in early life, occurring in countless repetitions, has two important consequences: (1) it brings about structure formation (cf. Kohut 1978*b*, 1:137–38, and Kohut 1978*b*, 1:248–49) via a process to which I have given the name "transmuting internalization" (Kohut 1971, pp. 49–50), and (2) it prepares the soil for a shift in self-selfobject relations that is of great significance, namely, a gradual shift from the self relying for its nutriment on archaic modes of contact in the narcissistic sphere (in particular on mergers with the mirroring selfobject, mergers with the idealized selfobject, and twinship mergers [i.e., mergers with a selfobject that is experienced as an alter-ego replica of the self]) to its ability to be sustained most of the time[6] by the empathic resonance that emanates from the selfobjects of adult life.

In order to be capable of cure by psychoanalysis, the analysand must be able to engage the analyst as selfobject by mobilizing the sets of inner experience that we call selfobject transferences. Analyzability—as differentiated from accessibility to other forms of psychotherapy—thus rests on the patient's not being psychotic—neither manifestly nor in the covered-over form that we designate "border-line."[7] To approach the problem of analyzability from still another direction, we may say that the analyzable patient who suffers from a conflict neurosis or a narcissistic personality or behavior disorder is an individual whose self—or, to be more exact, a remnant of whose self—is still, potentially at least, in search of appropriately responsive selfobjects. The remnant in question may be either repressed or split off, and it may be searching primarily for appropriately responsive selfobjects from the first years of childhood or from a later period (e.g., the oedipal phase). Concerning this latter possibility, I will add that the positively toned, joyfully engaged oedipal phase which emerges, seemingly de novo, in the terminal phase of some successful analyses of narcissistic personality disorders bears witness to the fact that the search for empathically responsive oedipal selfobjects had not been totally given up by these patients in childhood. This search was then reactivated during the analysis and ultimately brought to its devel-opmentally appropriate conclusion.[8]

In order to be capable of cure by psychoanalysis therefore, the analysand must be able to mobilize in the psychoanalytic situation the maturation-directed needs for structure building via transmuting in-ternalization of the revived selfobjects of childhood. As precursors of the child's psychological structure (Kohut 1971, p. 19n.), these self-objects perform the functions (e.g., in the area of self-esteem regu-lation) which the psyche of the adult will later be able to perform with the aid of a selfobject milieu composed of his family, his friends, his work situation, and, last but not least, the cultural resources of the group to which he belongs. It should be stressed, however, that the curative processes of transmuting internalization that are mobilized in the course of analysis, while analogous to the processes that bring about maturation in the child under normal circumstances, are not identical with them.

By way of comparing the structure-building processes of childhood with the analogous ones in analysis, let me return to the example of structure building in a wholesome childhood that I invoked in an early contribution (Kohut 1978b, 1:248–49) when I wanted to dem-onstrate the relationship between optimal frustration and the firming of that psychic area I then equated with the superego but which I subsequently conceptualized as the idealized pole of the self. I wrote: "A child's lie remains undetected and thus one aspect of the omniscient idealized object is lost. But omniscience is introjected as a minute aspect of . . . the all-seeing eye, the omniscience of the superego" (1977, pp. 248–49). Now it is obvious that, while undetected lies may well provide an important structure-building experience—an "optimal frustration"—for the child who, via the undetected lie, discovers that the parents are not omniscient, in particular, are not able to penetrate into his mind, the undetected lie does not have a similar function and is not of equal importance in the analysis of adults with analyzable disturbances of the self. The place of the undetected lie is rather taken by the analysand's discovery that his own understanding of his mental states and attitudes is at times better than that of the analyst, that the analyst is not omniscient, that his empathy is fallible, and that the patient's empathy with himself,[9] including, par excellence, his empathy with his childhood experiences, is often superior.

Although the undetected lie, as pointed out above, does not significantly contribute to the building up of self structure during analysis, lying does at times play a specific role in the analysis of certain patients with narcissistic personality disorders. Within the context of an adult analysand's overall endeavor to strengthen his self—and to indicate this by announcing via his lie the rights of an individual self— the significance of the lie may well be regarded as analogous to the significance of the undetected childhood lie understood within the context of the child's overall endeavor to establish a firm self in the first place. Focusing on the self psychologically informed analyst's response to such traditionally construed "acting out" behavior on the part of the patient will allow us simultaneously to demonstrate how the self psychologist's subtle shift in theoretic orientation may at times lead to a change in technique, in this case to replacing a confrontational posture with an attitude that aims (at least potentially) at the employment of an interpretation.

Early in analysis, not infrequently during the first session, a patient may confront the analyst with an easily discoverable lie or some thinly disguised or even quite open delinquent move, such as the attempt to cheat with regard to the analyst's fee or the payment of taxes. I have come to realize that such acts may have important maturational implications and that they must not be responded to out-of-hand with moral indignation and rejection. The perceptive analyst, especially if he is self psychologically informed, will, in certain instances at least, be able to recognize a patient's lie as a first, testing assertion of the rights of an independent self and, while not condoning the lie in a moral context, will therefore accept it with equanimity. His attitude, in this respect, differs from the attitude usually assumed by analysts. I know that there are some analysts, perhaps the majority, who, on the basis of their conviction that the goal of analysis is expanded cognition—translated into moral terms: truthfulness despite shame, fear, or guilt—not only will confront the patient with the fact that he has lied with openly expressed indignation (and the expressed or unexpressed conviction that it indicates the patient's resistance to telling the truth about himself) but also will, as I have not infrequently witnessed, relate these confrontations to colleagues and students with pride, as an example of the incorruptible firmness with which they deal with a resistance against analysis that had to be nipped in the bud. (Compare, by contrast, my remarks about the favorable implications of certain resistances to analysis [1977, pp. 146–51].)

One of my analysands, a forty-year-old university professor, began his analysis with me—a previous analysis, ten years earlier, had relieved him of some circumscribed inhibitions but had left him dissatisfied about a persisting restrictedness of his personality and life-style—by saying that he would like to postpone the payment of my fees for several months because he wanted to make a down payment on some property in a Colorado resort, a favorable opportunity, to which he had to commit himself at that point. Would I be willing to wait for the payments? My reply—not without misgivings at that time—was that, yes, as far as my finances were concerned, I could wait. But I added that, although I appreciated the realistic issue that had prompted him to make the request, I did not know what else might be involved for him. It might well be, I said, that we would later discover that his request and my compliance with it had a significance for him that went beyond what we could know at this point.

I cannot in the present context give the evidence for my ultimate conclusions about the significance of this event for the patient and the fact that it provided a favorable start for his successful analysis with me. Here I will mention only that I ultimately became convinced that the patient, a very moral, straitlaced person, had neither embroiled me in a delinquent maneuver by inducing me to accede to his request nor "acted out" a specific drive-wish from childhood. He had simply begun his analysis with an act that expressed the hope that this analysis, perhaps in contrast to his previous analysis, would be for him and not for the analyst, that is, not for me. As we recognized years later, the buying of the property did in fact reinstate a specific situation from his early life: a situation away from home in which, for brief periods, he could give himself over to expansive, imaginative, creative play with an alter-ego friend. For short periods he could be temporarily unencumbered by the stifling restrictions to which his creative potentialities had been exposed at home. There, his joyless, guilt-producing mother had remained unresponsive to his attempts to demonstrate his intellectual gifts and physical prowess, whereas his self-absorbed, attention-demanding father had actively belittled and ridiculed him. That he had started the analysis by asking me to support a joyful move in his present life had been tantamount to saying that, in order to be successful, this analysis had to begin with a reinstatement of the one situation of his childhood in which his personality had been able to unfold its potentialities without the restrictions of his home.

In the foregoing I presented an example which demonstrates how the self psychological viewpoint may enable the psychoanalyst to extend the scope of the interpretive approach—the *ultima ratio* of the analyst—and thus to substitute appropriate and correct understanding for inappropriate and incorrect confrontation. I will now, for the sake of completeness, adduce an illustration of the opposite move; I will give an example of a self psychologist's employment of the analytic variant of the *ultima ratio regum,* namely, the employment of force in the form of confrontation. I will specify immediately that confrontation within the analytic setting can only be justified in terms of analytic appropriateness: the confrontation must not be an end in itself but must safeguard the road that leads to understanding and interpretation. My illustration is taken from a recent analysis.

The analysand, who was in his third year of treatment with me, was a psychiatric resident at a university hospital where I occasionally give seminars on the theory and practice of psychotherapy. He arrived about twenty-five minutes late to his analytic session. Entering the office, the door of which was open, he tossed his leather jacket on the chair and, hardly saying hello, tossed himself on the couch with a crash. He began at once to talk rapidly and related, with what seemed to me a trace of challenging arrogance, that he had once again been stopped for speeding on the expressway, that he had responded belligerently to an officer who had originally been inclined to let him off with a warning because he was a physician but who, undoubtedly amazed at my patient's provocative manner, ended up giving him an expensive ticket for driving well beyond the speed limit. The patient reported these events to me in an unrepentant, angry tone of voice, recalling similar incidents that had occurred over the years, before and during the analysis, including occasions when, while driving "like a bat out of hell," he had become involved in accidents—none of them of a very serious nature thus far. I listened to his outpouring in complete silence, but when, after about five minutes, he stopped, I said to him in seemingly utter seriousness that I was going to give him the deepest interpretation he had so far received in his analysis. I could see his utter surprise at this announcement; it was totally different from anything I had ever said to him before. Then, after several seconds of silence, I said very firmly and with total seriousness: "You are a complete idiot." There was another second or so of silence, and then the patient burst into a warm and friendly laughter and relaxed visibly on the couch. I then spoke to him for a couple of minutes, expressing my concern about certain aspects of his behavior, especially his potentially destructive and self-destructive outbursts of reckless driving, but also about other forms of tantrumlike behavior, including aggressive behavior at his place of work, when dealing with unresponsive salespeople, and the like. I ended by saying that we of course needed to understand what in his past, and, in particular, what in his childhood, had made him so vulnerable in certain situations and led him to respond as he did, but that first things came first: if he killed or injured himself in an accident, we certainly could not analyze his motivations.

Since I am adducing the present case vignette to illustrate an instance in which the self psychologically informed analyst (like the traditionally informed analyst under similar circumstances) employed a technique that one might call confrontative, I will not dwell at length on what followed the incident recounted. I will only report that what was left of the session in question plus the subsequent one the next day were very successfully devoted to the analysis of the events that had triggered his outburst of narcissistic rage. In a nutshell: at the level of the dynamic transference, it was a reaction to the fact that I had not responded to a contribution he had made during a seminar for residents, but had instead responded to the discussion remark of another resident. At the genetic level, his associations led him to intensely emotional memories concerning his father's responsiveness to his brother (e.g., in working in the basement with tools) while the patient was, as it were, left in the care of his mother. The patient had in effect been the young genius, all brains, from whom the father felt estranged, and who was deeply disappointed at being excluded from the company of men, specifically, the team formed by his father and elder brother.

After the foregoing digression—meant to demonstrate that there are (a) instances in which the expanded scope of self psychological theory will allow the analyst to continue to employ the primary analytic tool of therapy (interpretation) whereas without the self psychological orientation he might turn to the use of a secondary tool (confrontation), as well as (b) instances in which the self psychological orientation will not prevent the analyst from confronting the patient with the necessity of curbing his dangerous behavior, to control his "acting out"—we now return to our examination of the psychoanalytic cure. In this context, I want to reiterate that whereas self psychology relies on the same tools as traditional analysis (interpretation followed by working through in an atmosphere of abstinence) to bring about the analytic cure, self psychology sees in a different light not only the results that are achieved, but also the very role that interpretation and working through play in the analytic process. We believe, in brief, that the old theories of the analytic cure, although correct within their respective frames of reference, were incomplete. To repeat, the wholesome movement from archaic mergers with archaic selfobjects to the establishment of a bond of empathic resonance between self and selfobject is, indeed, often accompanied by an expansion of consciousness (by a "becoming conscious" in accordance with the topographic theory) and by the expansion of the domain of the ego (Freud's mental apparatus theory)—the ascendancy of secondary processes, particularly of verbal thought and verbalizations,[10] over primary processes, that is, preconscious and conscious verbal imagery and fantasies on various levels of formal regression (Freud 1900, 1953, 5:548). But while expansion of consciousness and of verbalizable insight are often encountered in the late stages of successful analyses, some unqualified analytic successes include in the main neither of these gains. An analysand's increased capacity to be reassured by a friend's wordlessly putting his arm around his shoulder, his newly obtained or rekindled ability to feel strengthened and uplifted when listening to music, his broadened sense of being in tune with the preoccupations of a group to which he belongs, his liberated ability to exhibit joyfully the products of his creativity in order to obtain the approval of a responsive selfobject audience—all these wholesome results of the successful analysis of a patient who has suffered from a narcissistic personality or behavior disorder connote that the patient's former reliance on the security provided by ancient merger states has been superseded by his reliance on the security provided by the resonance he elicits from his human surroundings and other humanness-sustaining aspects of present-day reality.

Even a person's greater freedom to create substitute selfobjects via visual imagery when external reality is devoid of tangible selfobjects must be counted among newly acquired assets when the successes and failures of an analysis are being evaluated. This is an assumption—a self psychological refinement of the regression-in-the-service-of-the-ego principle of ego psychology—whose application transcends the analytic situation. On the one hand, it leads to a positive evaluation of certain hallucinatory creations. These include (1) the hallucinatory conjuring of a company of mirroring selfobjects created by some people in solitary confinement which protects their personalities from suffering permanent damage (see Miller 1962; Modell 1958) and (2) the hallucinatory conjuring of the presence of the idealized Godhead which enables certain individuals to carry out acts of supreme courage not only without the aid of a supportive group, but even in the face of near-total social disapproval (e.g., martyred solitary resisters to the Nazis, like Franz Jägerstätter; see Zahn 1964 in this context). It leads, in addition, (3) to a nonapologetically positive assessment of the role and significance of art and religion (see Kohut 1978a) which differs from the assessment of classical analysis (cf., for example, Freud 1908,

1953, vol. 9, 1927, 1953, vol. 21, and as quoted in Binswanger 1956, p. 115).

To repeat and summarize, then, a successful analysis is one in which the analysand's formerly archaic needs for the responses of archaic selfobjects are superseded by the experience of the availability of empathic resonance, the major constituent of the sense of security in adult life. Increased ability to verbalize, broadened insight, greater autonomy of ego functions, and increased control over impulsiveness may accompany these gains, but they are not the essence of cure. A treatment will be successful because, allowing himself to be carried by the momentum of the analytic process, an analysand was able to reactivate, in a selfobject transference, the needs of a self that had been thwarted in childhood. In the analytic situation, these reactivated needs were kept alive and exposed, time and again, to the vicissitudes of optimal frustrations until the patient ultimately acquired the reliable ability to sustain his self with the aid of the selfobject resources available in his adult surroundings. According to self psychology, then, the essence of the psychoanalytic cure resides in a patient's newly acquired ability to identify and seek out appropriate selfobjects—both mirroring and idealizable—as they present themselves in his realistic surroundings and to be sustained by them.[11]

But how about structure formation? Is it not rather the replacement of selfobjects with self structure that is the essence of psychological health and thus of the process of psychoanalytic cure? My answer to this question, if I must answer with an unambiguous yes or no, is in the negative. A yes—the yes that is compatible with the traditional attitude of psychoanalysis—would indicate, to my mind, that the attitude of the empirical scientist had been replaced by that of the moralist. True, psychological structure is acquired through psychoanalysis and the self becomes more firm. But this increased firmness does not make the self independent of selfobjects. Instead, it increases the self's ability to use selfobjects for its own sustenance, including an increased freedom in choosing selfobjects. True, the person who grows up in a good selfobject milieu in childhood will in later life be blessed with the possession of a core of self-confidence along with nuclear ambitions, values, and goals. But by themselves these internal resources are never enough. We must have a healthy biological apparatus in order to utilize the oxygen that surrounds us, but we cannot live without oxygen. Similarly, we must be in possession of available nuclear self-esteem and ambitions, on the one hand, and of core ideals and goals, on the other, in order to seek out mirroring selfobjects and be nourished by their response to us and in order to seek out idealizable selfobjects and be enlivened by the enthusiasm we feel for them. The analyst's protracted and consistent endeavor to understand his patient leads to two results that are analogous to the outcome of normal childhood development: (1) his occasional failures, constituting optimal frustrations, lead to the building up of self structure, while (2) his on the whole adequately maintained understanding leads to the patient's increasing realization that, contrary to his experiences in childhood, the sustaining echo of empathic resonance is indeed available in this world.

If an ill-disposed critic now gleefully told me that I have finally shown my true colors and, with this last statement, demonstrated that I both believe in the curative effect of the "corrective emotional experience" and equate such an experience with analysis, I could only reply: so be it. To my mind, the concept of a "corrective emotional experience" is valuable so long as, in referring to it, we point to but a single aspect of the multifaceted body of the psychoanalytic cure. This, in itself, legitimate concept has been relegated to a position of disrepute because Franz Alexander, who coined the expression, used it in the context of what he considered to be "brief analysis," that is, the replacement of the working through of the transference with the patient's exposure to the analyst's playacting the opposite of the patient's transference expectations—the opposite, that is, of the traumatic behavior of the patient's parents in childhood. Regretfully, then, a perfectly serviceable term became tainted by a seemingly irrevocable guilt by association because it conjured up the clinical theories and technical maneuvers of Alexander's brief-analysis days. Still, by whatever name it may ultimately come to be known, the concept involved— independent of the adulterated meaning evoked by the term because of the circumstances of its origination—is a valuable one, and we should not shy away from its legitimate use.

At any rate, whether or not we wish to refer to the patient's increasing realization that "the sustaining echo of empathic resonance is indeed available in this world" as "corrective emotional experience," this recognition does not prompt him to cling forever to the analyst. The interrupted maturational push, the maturational push that was thwarted in childhood, will begin to reassert itself spontaneously as it is reactivated in the analysis in the form of a selfobject transference. The analyst will maintain this basic momentum toward the establishment, firming, and maintenance of a vigorous self by appropriate responses, namely by noncensorious dynamic (transference) interpretations and genetic reconstructions. And the patient, finding either appropriate understanding or optimally limited and infrequent misunderstanding, will build up internal structures that allow him to turn toward an ever broadening spectrum of selfobjects for support, confirmation, and sustenance. Thus, without being pushed away by the analyst—whether by being urged to consider termination or being confronted with an unalterable termination date—the patient will spontaneously move toward new modes of sustenance by an increasing variety of selfobjects outside the analytic situation.

6

The Curative Effect of Analysis:

The Self Psychological Reassessment of the Therapeutic Process

The Analyst's Attitude, the Analytic Ambience, and the Theory of Cure

Having to this point presented the self psychological explanation of the process of cure in the analysis of the narcissistic personality and behavior disorders, that is, of the analyzable self disturbances in the narrow sense of the word, we must now compare our theory of the psychoanalytic cure and the therapeutic procedure correlated to it with the analogous theories and procedures of traditional analysis (including those of psychoanalytic ego psychology). As we undertake this task, we will be striving toward three goals: (1) We want to clarify whether the therapeutic approach of self psychology toward the narcissistic personality and behavior disorders differs in essence from the approach of traditional analysis (including that of psychoanalytic ego psychology). (2) In view of the fact that we have begun to consider even the psychoneuroses—Freud's "transference neuroses"—as specific variants of self disturbances, that is, as analyzable self disturbances in the wider sense, we want to ascertain whether the specific approach of self psychology must also be applied to the analysis of these conditions. (3) We want to provide an explanation for the fact that psychoanalysts of varying theoretical orientations have treated many of their patients with good results, even when these patients suffered from analyzable self disturbances in the narrow sense of the term, that is, when they suffered from narcissistic personality or behavior disorders. How, if our theory of the therapeutic process is correct, could they have achieved their successes without subscribing to self psychology? And how could they have been successful without the benefit of the formulations that evolved from the investigations of psychoanalytic self psychology during the last fifteen years?

In view of the fact that the territories covered by these three inquiries overlap widely, I will for the most part not pursue them separately in the following discussion. I hope, however, that my reflections, while not systematically focusing on them, will ultimately succeed in providing adequate answers to each of the three questions.

Does the therapeutic approach of self psychology toward the narcissistic personality and behavior disorders differ from that taken by analysts toward their patients up to now? It is not easy to give an unambiguous reply to this question since the techniques employed by analysts and the emotional climate in which analysts conduct their analyses vary widely. Still, in principle, the approach of self psychology toward patients with analyzable self disturbances is the same as the approach of traditional analysis toward patients regarded as analyzable. To this general statement, however, we must add two amplifying remarks.

The first remark, however crucially important with regard to specific analysands who were severely traumatized by the emotional unavailability of selfobjects in childhood, is to my mind of lesser differentiating significance. It concerns my belief that, on the whole, self psychologists tend to work in a more relaxed fashion, are more easygoing with their patients, have fewer misgivings about making themselves emotionally available to their patients if the need arises, and generally behave in a (comparatively speaking) less reserved manner than the majority of analysts. I base this opinion on observations over the last decade that accompanied the supervision of colleagues who turned to me for guidance in the analyses of their patients. As I implied before—whether this difference indeed exists, as I believe, or whether, as some may maintain, the sample on which I base my opinion is too slanted to support my conclusion—the gross behavior of the analyst and his overt attitude toward his patients are not, in my view, significantly relevant to the frequently debated issues that determine the analyst's adherence to the more or less codified set of procedures and responses that are called psychoanalytic technique. By way of underlining this point, I will admit without hesitation my conviction that the difference in attitude under scrutiny, if it does in fact exist, is by no means universal: there is certainly a respectable number of analysts among those uninfluenced by the discoveries of self psychology whose behavior toward their patients is as relaxed and easygoing as the behavior of the majority of self psychological analysts. Furthermore, there is a by no means negligible number of self psychological analysts who, whether because of their personality makeup, their general convictions concerning the doctor-patient relationship, or their particular convictions about the proper behavior of an analyst toward his analysand, are conforming to the straitlaced reserve that is still espoused by many traditional analysts.[1]

But—and I am now turning to the more important of the two amplifying remarks I announced—if the self psychologist's basic approach to the psychoanalytic situation and to analytic technique does not in principle deviate from the classical model, how can we explain the fact that, disregarding the exceptions mentioned above, the analyst's attitude vis-à-vis his patients is less strained, the analytic atmosphere more relaxed, and the analyst more emotionally available to the analysand, if the analyst's perception is not restricted by an exclusive reliance on a drive-defense-conflict orientation but has been expanded by his access to self psychological conceptualizations, especially vis-à-vis the analysand suffering from a narcissistic personality disorder? My answer is that the greater relaxation of the self psychologist, his greater freedom to respond with deeply reverberating understanding and resonant emotionality, and the generally calmer and friendlier atmosphere of self psychological treatment—these developments do not rest on the self psychologist's increased use of empathy, on the fact that he is "more empathic" than his non–self psychological colleagues. They rest instead on the expanded *scope* of empathy that is the product of the self psychologist's expanded theoretical understanding.

The best definition of empathy—the analogue to my terse scientific definition of empathy as "vicarious introspection" (1978*b*, 1:205–32)— is that it is the capacity to think and feel oneself into the inner life of another person. It is our lifelong ability to experience what another person experiences, though usually, and appropriately, to an attenuated degree. Under normal circumstances, this ability will change in specific ways along an individually variable but, on the whole, predictable developmental road. At the beginning of life, the baby's empathic perception of his surroundings seems to be tantamount to total suffusion with the emotional state of the other. There is empathic flooding, in other words, as opposed to that attenuated taste of the other's experiences that characterizes the adult in general and the depth psychologist who employs empathy scientifically in particular. From the beginning of life, therefore—and the analytic situation is no exception—the desideratum is exposure to attenuated empathy, not exposure to total and all-encompassing empathy. The baby is anxious and the mother experiences a taste of the baby's anxiety; she picks up the baby and holds it close. As a result of this sequence, the baby feels simultaneously understood and calmed because the mother has experienced as an empathic signal not the baby's total anxiety but only a diminished version of it. If the mother's empathic ability has remained infantile, that is, if she tends to respond with panic to the baby's anxiety, then a deleterious chain of events will be set in motion. She may chronically wall herself off from the baby, thus depriving him of the beneficial effect of merging with her as she returns from experiencing mild anxiety to calmness. Alternatively, she may continue to respond with panic, in which case two negative consequences may ensue: the mother may lay the groundwork in her child for a lifelong propensity toward the uncurbed spreading of anxiety or other emotions, or by forcing the child to wall himself off from such an overly intense and thus traumatizing empathic echo, her uncurbed empathic resonance may foster in the child an impoverished psychic organization, the psychic organization of a person who will later be unable to be empathic himself, to experience human experiences, in essence, to be fully human.

It follows from the foregoing considerations that the capacity to employ empathy in a way that facilitates the collection of undistorted data, particularly in the area of scientific depth psychology, will vary greatly depending on many factors. These factors, which include both biological equipment and, especially, childhood experience, deserve much careful investigation. Still, *within an average range*, variations in empathic ability are not of decisive importance with regard to a person's ultimate proficiency as a depth psychologist just as, within an average range, the fact that one person has sharper eyes than another will not in itself make him more proficient in a branch of science whose methodology entails visual skills (such as histology and histopathology, which depend on the use of microscopy). Put in different terms—and I am here only emphasizing what I have pointed out in the past (see Kohut 1980, pp. 485–86)—we must beware of mythologizing empathy, this irreplaceable but by no means infallible depth-psychological tool. Empathy is not God's gift bestowed only on an elect few. For the average individual, training and learning make the difference, rather than the fact of endowment. Admittedly, these considerations, as I indicated earlier, do not pertain to people whose empathic capacities lie outside the average range. For a variety of reasons, certain individuals are indeed severely restricted in their ability to feel and think themselves into the inner lives of others (see Kohut 1971, pp. 301–7) while, at the opposite end of the spectrum, certain individuals exist whose empathic capacities may be unusually great.

These remarks suggest that the self psychologically informed psychoanalyst's increased ability to understand the self pathological aspects of his analysands is not due to some special gift, to some new kind of empathy.[2] It rests on the fact, which cannot be affirmed too emphatically, that his broadened theoretical grasp, while not altering his basic capacity for empathy, has expanded the potential range of application of this instrument of observation. Via the theories of self psychology, in other words, the self psychologist can empathically perceive configurations that would otherwise have escaped his notice. Specifically, the new theoretical formulations allow him to acknowledge that he may become the target not only of his analysand's drive-wishes, but of his analysand's selfobject needs as well. And since the theories of self psychology enable the self psychologically informed analyst to focus his analytic empathy on the formerly thwarted but now reactivated selfobject needs of his patients—assuming the data supplied by the analysand warrant the conclusion that selfobject needs and not instinctual wishes are being mobilized in the transference—he is able to explain these needs (and their frustration) in a noncensorious way, that is, he can explain them as primary needs that had not been responded to in childhood, that had gone into hiding, and whose transference reactivation is to be welcomed. The self psychologically informed analyst realizes, in other words, that the remobilization of these needs constitutes a positive analytic development, that it is a positive achievement. He realizes, accordingly, that it would be an error to reject them by interpreting them either as unwelcome defensive maneuvers, as attempts to escape the painful confrontation of anxiety- and guilt-provoking aggressive and sexual drive-wishes, or as a clinging to outdated drive-pleasures that must be opposed by the reality principle and the strictures of adult morality.

As an illustration of the change in attitude and ambience that appears to be correlated with the broadened compass of self psychological theory, I can point to "The Two Analyses of Mr. Z.," on which I reported not long ago (1979). The change in the atmosphere that prevailed in the two analyses emerges clearly when one compares the different ways in which I communicated to the patient my understanding of his inner life. So far as I myself can judge—it is not easy to be fully objective here—I did not consciously attempt in the paper to show that in the first analysis my communications incorporated a greater degree of reality-principle morality and that a modicum of educational pressure was therefore occasionally amalgamated with my interpretations. But there can be no doubt that this was indeed the case, and a number of colleagues have focused their attention on this particular aspect of my report. As far as I was concerned—and my view on this matter has remained unchanged—I presented "The Two

Analyses of Mr. Z." in order to demonstrate how a shift in theory, namely, the shift from a focus on faulty psychic functions to a focus on the faulty psychic structures to which the faulty psychic functioning is due,[3] enabled me in the second analysis to help the patient move on in his life with more profound zest and joy than had resulted from the first analysis. I did not attempt to exaggerate or even to highlight issues of attitude and ambience that differentiated my approach during the first analysis from my approach during the second.

The professional colleagues who have remarked on my attitude toward Mr. Z. fall into two groups: (1) an inimical group who claim that the first analysis was conducted poorly or even that I was the victim of a countertransference and (2) a friendly group who chide me for making myself appear more moralistic than, in their opinion, I could have been. This friendly group, I will add, supports its criticism by pointing to a clinical case I reported in 1957 (1978b, 1:233–53), long before my first analysis of Mr. Z. Here, these critics point out, my attitude toward my patient reveals none of the educational admixtures that subsequently perverted my analytic approach (the poor technique theory; the countertransference theory) or, at the very least, led to a slanted description of my therapeutic attitude (the theory that in "The Two Analyses of Mr. Z." I was intent on making some kind of propaganda about the self psychologist's greater humanness).

It is my opinion that none of these criticisms are valid—at least not to the extent that they would invalidate the essential message that my case report was meant to communicate. In the following remarks, I will respond to the three major lines of criticism—the "poor technique" criticism, the "countertransference" criticism, and the "propaganda" criticism—one by one.

Is it accurate to say that my behavior during the first analysis of Mr. Z. would have been condemned by traditional analysts as an example of poor technique? Although I do not believe this question can be answered in a single, simple way, I would, from the vantage point of my overall assessment of the prevailing practices and opinions of the time, be inclined to answer it in the negative. First of all, I believe there are many analysts who would even now find my technique entirely appropriate and who, give or take a few details, would claim that they always have conducted, and still continue to conduct, their analyses in approximately the same way in which I conducted the first analysis of Mr. Z. I would also point out that the pressure I brought to bear on Mr. Z. when I "consistently, and with increasing firmness, rejected the reactivation of his narcissistic attitudes, expectations, and demands" and told him "that they were resistances against the confrontation of deeper and more intense fears connected with masculine assertiveness and competition with men" characterized my interpretations not in the early part of this four-year analysis but "during the last years," that is, after we had worked on his (as I then saw it, defensive) narcissism and on his (as I then saw it, defensive) mother-attachment and infantilism for a long time. Finally, it must be borne in mind that my efforts in this regard seemed clearly rewarded by (what then seemed to me) a frank oedipal dream that (as I believed then) ultimately led us to the resolution of his essentially oedipal neurosis.

But are there not also analysts who are truthful in their assertion that they would have conducted the analysis of Mr. Z. from the beginning in a way that more closely approximates my approach to the patient in my second encounter with him? Again, it is difficult to give an unambiguous answer, but I am on the whole inclined to respond in the affirmative. We are dealing here with an issue that I have already discussed at several points in this presentation: that many analysts have over the years held half-formulated opinions about a variety of topics, including analytic technique, that were not in tune with traditional dogmas. I thus have no doubt that some of my colleagues conducted their analyses in ways that, intuitively, moved on paths that contemporary self psychology is tracing more firmly and decisively with the aid of new, explicitly articulated theories.

Still, when all these relevant facts have been taken into account, I must append to them a decisive question pertaining to the dream of the return of the father from Mr. Z.'s first analysis. Would those of my critics who now claim that they would have conducted the first analysis of Mr. Z. in the way I conducted the second one really have recognized that this dream was a self state dream dealing with the child's need for paternal substance in order to build psychic structure? Would they have recognized, in other words, that the patient's attempt to slam the door which his father tried to open was not motivated by castration anxiety, but was a desperate attempt to forestall a traumatic state that threatened the patient's self cohesion in the face of the overwhelming prospect of a need fulfillment that should have taken place gradually over the years (in this context see Kohut 1978*b*, 1:229–38)? I think not. I believe that the shift required to interpret the dream in this way—a shift in technique based on a shift in theory—would not have been made, even by those who now claim that the ambience of their analyses has always been relaxed and emotionally open. Indeed, I believe that the crucial significance of the necessary shift from a focus on faulty psychic functioning to a focus on the faulty structures responsible for the faulty functioning even now remains unclear to my critics: witness the fact that all of them fail even to mention this all-important point.

But what of the assertion that I was the victim of a countertransference, in particular, that my attitude toward Mr. Z. toward the end
of the first analysis was one of harshness and that this harshness, in
turn, was due to my being angry at him for reasons of which I was
unaware? I have thought a great deal about this possibility and have
searched within myself for any set of motivations that could be considered countertransferential, even in a broadly defined sense of the
term. And I must admit, in retrospect, that there was something in
my attitude toward Mr. Z., especially toward the end of the first analysis, that might be classified under this heading. I would not reveal
what I have come to recognize were it not for the fact that I will be
owning up to an attitude that, I have no doubt, characterizes the
analytic stance of great numbers of analysts—a chronically present
attitude that has become well rationalized. But let me first talk about
myself before I apply the lesson I have learned from my early work
with Mr. Z. to this chronically established attitude of my colleagues.

As I have revealed before (e.g., 1978b, 2:663–84, 931–38), I had
throughout a professional lifetime been deeply committed to the
teachings of classical psychoanalysis and to the technical prescriptions
correlated with the established theoretical tenets. It was, therefore,
not easy for me to admit to myself that I was seeing the psychological
world in a way that differed from the traditional view. Throughout
the decades of my clinical practice, I mostly did what those colleagues
did, and still do, who claim they do not need self psychology to tell
them how to analyze: I put theory on one side and practice on the
other and, in my teaching, strained to talk about ego psychology as
if it were in harmony with what I did in my practice. This apparently
worked most of the time—I will again mention my case report of 1957
in this context—though clearly not always without some tensions and
misgivings on my part. But when I analyzed Mr. Z. for the first time,
the situation was different. Without knowing it, I stood at the thresh-
old of finally telling myself openly that psychoanalysis needed a decisive shift in emphasis, in both theory and practice, if it was to be in
harmony with the psychic problems of man as I saw him, both inside
and outside my consulting room. I had tried to escape my dilemma
by devoting years to administrative work—to tasks, in other words,
that are not naturally congenial to me. But while I discharged the
time-consuming organizational duties that left me so little time to think
and write, I dimly realized that at some point these external delays
would cease to exert their restricting force and I would be free to
express what I thought. It was during this final period of not yet
confronting what deep down I knew I would ultimately have to confront that the first analysis of Mr. Z. came to its end. To be exact, the
last period of this analysis coincided with my first attempts to escape

from the inner conflicts I have described by making diversionary moves toward organizational and administrative tasks.

Having said this much, I believe no perceptive analyst will have any difficulty understanding why I was so "consistent" in my demand that Mr. Z. face his Oedipus complex; why "with increasing firmness [I] rejected the reactivation of his narcissistic attitudes, expectations, and demands." This patient, as I saw clearly in the second analysis, must have confronted me, as many other analysands throughout my professional life undoubtedly had, with the recognition that his needs were primary and real and not defensive. But whereas formerly (see the 1957 report) I had silently made my compromises with established theory and technique, I was this time in greater need of keeping those forces in check which demanded that I acknowledge what I saw and how I saw it. These forces whispered to me that I should not only stand up for my new insights in the clinical situation but also, overcoming the third barrier of resistances (see Kohut 1978*b*, 2:589–614), raise "the findings of individual psychology to more general levels, by expressing them in a carefully chosen, well-defined terminology, and by communicating them to the broad scientific community" (minutes of the Ad Hoc Committee on Scientific Activities of the American Psychoanalytic Association, quoted in Kohut 1980, pp. 592–93).

Still, having admitted my emotionally grounded contribution to the essential failure of the first round of Mr. Z.'s analysis, I believe that I would not be reporting facts as I truly see them if I left the impression that I now believe that my especially strong emotional reluctance to face the new insights that I only began to communicate "to the broad scientific community" in 1966 was a decisive factor in the failure of the first analysis to lead to a permanent cure. Two further circumstances must be kept in mind: (1) that many other analysts—including some of my most highly respected colleagues—would have reacted with the same firmness that characterized my stance toward Mr. Z. in the later phases of his analysis; and (2) that the clinical picture that unrolled in Mr. Z.'s first analysis was, or at least convincingly appeared to be, different from (for example) the case described in my 1957 clinical report and seemed to justify the interpretive stance I adopted. The clinical picture of Mr. Z.'s first analysis, in other words, was totally consistent with what the traditional orientation would lead an analyst to expect with a neurosis in which the Oedipus complex forms the center of the psychopathological structures. I believe, pointing once more to Mr. Z.'s dream of the intruding father—including both the manifest content of the dream and the patient's associations to it— that the analysis clearly focused more and more on oedipal themes, in particular on drive-conflicts between active competition with the father and passive submission to him. Can I really blame myself for

not knowing then what I came to know later: that the need for structure from the selfobject becomes sexualized (see, for example, Kohut
1978*b*, 1:71–73) and that the resistances evoked, while appearing to
be directed against primary drive-wishes, are in reality only directed
against the traumatic intensity of the sexualized version of the analysand's developmental need? Can I really blame myself for not having
overcome a countertransference to Mr. Z.? Or should I not rather
affirm that the "countertransference" involved was directed at having
to make a scientific step that, as I dimly realized, would arouse strong
controversy among my colleagues and require the mobilization of all
my intellectual and emotional resources for the rest of my life? Clearly,
it is this latter affirmation that I unhesitatingly make.

Finally, I must respond to the criticism that the contrasting ambience
of the first and second of the two analyses of Mr. Z.—a contrast which
apparently emerges from my description of these two analyses—did
not really exist but is a piece of propaganda. Critics who adopt this
viewpoint contend that the contrasting ambience of Mr. Z.'s two analyses aims at demonstrating the greater kindness, humanness, and
compassion of the analyst who has benefited from the theories of self
psychology by comparison with the analyst who has not. In the case
of Mr. Z.'s two analyses, this point is of course made with reference
to the same analyst at two different stages of his career. With regard
to this reproach, I will give two responses that are contradictory up
to a point. As far as the specific case report is concerned, my focus
was on the theory change: the shift from conflict to structure via the
shift from the vicissitudes of the drives to the vicissitudes of the self.
The ambience that characterized the analytic situation was, to the best
of my memory, never the focus of my attention when I wrote the
essay in question. But while I am thus certain that the reproach that
I was exaggerating my "firmness" in the first analysis in order to drive
home a point is unjustified, I will add that I would not feel particularly
blameworthy even if I *had* consciously emphasized the differences in
question in order to make my point.

Psychoanalytic case histories, however conscientiously presented and
skillfully disguised in order to protect the patient while preserving
the essential clinical content, can never prove a theory. Case histories—
not to speak of the brief case vignettes that I often use in my writings—
can never be more than illustrative; they are a special means of communication within the professional community intended to clarify
scientific information from a clinical researcher to his colleagues. Even
if the professional colleagues can grasp the meaning of the message,
it is still up to them to make use of it in their own work. As I have
explained before (Kohut 1978*b*, 1:140–70), clinical-empirical support
for a new hypothesis in the field of analysis can only be obtained via

the application of the new theory by the clinician who, shedding pre-
conceived notions to the best of his ability and voluntarily suspending
disbelief, applies the new theory for protracted periods and with a
variety of patients until he can form his own conclusions. Thus, returning to the question of whether "propaganda" distorted my pre-
sentations of the two analyses of Mr. Z., I can only reply—in an
acceptable variant of the parable of the broken pitcher that had been
returned whole yet had also already been broken when the borrower
first got it—that while I did not, to my knowledge, exaggerate or
otherwise distort my description of the analytic ambience in "The
Two Analyses of Mr. Z.," even if I had emphasized certain features
of my behavior, played them up, as it were, in order to make a point
with special clarity, I would see nothing in such a move that would be
out of keeping with our scientific communications.

But while I did not intentionally focus on the important subject
matter of the analyst's attitude and of the analytic ambience in my
paper on Mr. Z., I do indeed believe that the self psychologist's broadened understanding does tend to lead to a change both in the analyst's
attitude and in the analytic atmosphere (see Wolf 1976). Specifically,
self psychology results in an attitude and an atmosphere that differ
from those that tend to prevail as long as the analyst sees narcissistic
demands as defenses and drive manifestations (especially the patient's
rage) as primary rather than reactive phenomena. And his broadened
understanding does indeed tend to lend to the self psychologically
informed analyst's interpretations a certain accepting coloration,
whereas interpretations given by the analyst who, on the basis of his
theoretical convictions, holds the opinion that the analysand's narcissistic demands should be rejected as either escapist moves or a clinging
to infantile gratifications do tend to contain at least a trace of rejection
and censure. Put in different words: the friendlier, more relaxed
atmosphere that tends to prevail when a patient suffering from a
narcissistic personality or behavior disorder is analyzed within the
framework of self psychology is due to the fact that his narcissistic
demands, in general, and his narcissistic transference demands, in
particular, are welcomed as tentative moves toward maturity.

The same point can be made with reference to the sexual and
aggressive drive manifestations encountered in the narcissistic personality and behavior disorders. If the analyst sees the infantile erotism
and aggression that emerge in the analysand's transference as in essence fueled by primary infantile drives that are being reactivated,
he will respond to them in a different way from the analyst who
considers them secondary, symptomatic manifestations and looks at
the undernourished self as the locus of the primary disturbance. However softened by the compassion and tact of the analyst, interpreta-

tions of infantile seductive and aggressive behavior toward him that fall back on a theory of the narcissistic transferences as defensive will be experienced by patients as subtly censorious and disapproving. Conversely, interpretations of the self psychologically informed analyst who sees the same behavior as a manifestation of the disruption of a selfobject transference (i.e., as a rupture of the empathic bond between the patient and himself) and who often, after establishing the role that he himself played in the disruption, can explain the appearance of the infantile drives to the patient as an outgrowth of the disrupted self-selfobject bond, will be felt as accepting and development-enhancing. Thus do we grasp the lesson of the two analyses of Mr. Z. The case not only highlights the way theoretical changes enable the analyst to see new clinical configurations, but further demonstrates how the analyst's apprehension of the selfobject transference affects his handling of clinical material via the expanded empathy that results from the new theoretical framework.

Understanding, Explaining, and the Therapeutic Impact of Erroneous Interpretations

But let us now change the direction of our inquiry and return to a question that I raised earlier. If the oedipal neuroses are to be conceptualized as specific disturbances of the self, that is, as arising in consequence of flaws in the selfobject functions of the surroundings of the child during the oedipal stage of development, would it not follow that the specific therapeutic approach of self psychology should also be employed in the analysis of these disorders?

It is by no means easy to provide a definite answer to this question. Still, even if we are unable to respond in a way that is satisfactory in all respects, the mere attempt to do so will move us toward greater clarity with regard to some of the fundamental issues involved. Let me begin by expressing my belief—and this should come as no surprise to those who have firsthand familiarity with the therapeutic approaches of both traditional analysis and self psychologically informed analysis—that much of what many analysts have long been doing, including the successes they have achieved with the traditional technique, can in fact be explained, and explained well, within the conceptual framework of self psychology. It is my claim, in other words, that given the analytic situation and the analyst's reliable responsiveness to his analysands, good—if not optimal—therapeutic results can be achieved even though the theories that guide the analyst in his assessment of the patient's psychopathology and in his understanding of the therapeutic process may be in error.

Let me illustrate my meaning with an example. Many years ago, during an informal workshop at an international congress, an analyst from Latin America reported, in the course of a presentation on a then ongoing analysis, that she had told her patient at the end of a session that she would have to cancel an appointment in the near future. When the patient came to the next session, she was silent and withdrawn and did not respond to the analyst's promptings to tell her what she was experiencing. The analyst finally said to the patient, obviously in a warmly understanding tone of voice, that she felt her announcement about being away had decisively shifted the patient's basic perception of her. Formerly, the analyst said, she had been the good, warm, feeding breast, but now she had become the bad, cold, nonfeeding one. And she added that the patient had come to feel intense sadistic rage against her qua bad breast: that the patient wanted to tear the analyst apart and, furthermore, that she defended herself against these impulses to bite and tear by inhibiting her activity, in general, and by her oral activity (i.e., talking via "biting" words), in particular. To my surprise this, to me, farfetched interpretation of the patient's mental state elicited a very favorable response from the patient. She began to talk more freely, reported that she was now aware of the fact that her jaw muscles had been very tight since the last session, was able to verbalize a number of "biting" fantasies and verbal reproaches toward the analyst, and ended the session again on good terms with the analyst. Analyst and patient thereupon agreed—with easygoing, unforced conviction—that the analyst had been reinstated as the good breast that she had been before the brief interruption had been announced.

Although I happen to have chosen an illustration pertaining to the theories of a specific, recognizable school of thought in analysis—the Kleinian school, in general, and the Latin American subgroup of Kleinianism, in particular—I did not intend it to serve as a vehicle of criticism directed against this specific school. Had the analyst, in other words, responded to the patient by saying that she had withdrawn because she had experienced the analyst's cancellation in terms of being abandoned by the mother who was locking the bedroom door in order to engage in sexual intercourse with the father, the point at issue would be just as valid. And the same, I will add for the sake of completeness, would hold true if the analyst's response had been framed in self psychological terms vis-à-vis a patient suffering from a narcissistic personality disorder, for example, if the analyst had said that the analysand's self-esteem had been lowered just as it had been in childhood when the friendly cook who had allowed her to assist in the kitchen and praised her for her help was abruptly dismissed by the cold distant mother, and the child, in consequence of the loss of a self sustaining selfobject, had experienced herself as empty, drained, and not fully alive. The point I wish to make rests not only on the claim that in all these instances the patient might feel genuinely understood, but on the stronger claim that in all these instances the patient's feeling of being understood would, in essence, have been in harmony with the facts.

No reader who is familiar with my outlook will now, on the basis of my preceding statement, suspect me of utter nihilism vis-à-vis the tenets of psychoanalytic theory, experience-distant or experience-near. And indeed I am not a nihilist. Specifically, I am convinced that only one of the three proffered interpretations is closest to the mark, even though from what I know about the patient in question I cannot decide which one it would be. But this is not the issue under discussion. Whether, in the case at hand, a reconstruction in terms of oedipal drive-conflict psychology, a genetic-dynamic formulation concerning archaic experiences vis-à-vis archaically perceived, instinctually cathected objects, or a self psychological formulation concerning the self-selfobject unit and its vicissitudes would be the most accurate is not the question we are confronting. The fact is that all of these proposed interpretations are irrelevant. Indeed, they exemplify "wild analysis" because they are not based on the analyst's prolonged empathic immersion in the patient's associations and do not proceed in accordance with the valid precept that—in traditional terms—interpretations must first focus on the psychological surface before they can move into the psychic depths and into the past, or that—in self psychological terms— a phase of accurate understanding must precede the phase of accurate explaining via interpretation and reconstruction. But, to repeat, I am not attempting to explain what is wrong with the interpretation given by the analyst in the example I have selected but, paradoxically, what is right about it. Glover, in his well-known contribution to the therapeutic effect of what he termed "inexact" interpretation (1931), concluded that it is the nonspecific suggestibility of the analysand that leads to pseudosuccesses in such instances. Regretfully, I must admit that here I am in almost total disagreement with the opinion of one of the great heroes of my psychoanalytic education, a contributor from whose writings I have probably benefited more than from those of any other psychoanalyst with the exception of Freud. I believe, in other words, that to dismiss the analysand's positive response to the interpretation given by the analyst as a result of the analysand's suggestibility would be a mistake.[4]

If there is one lesson that I have learned during my life as an analyst, it is the lesson that what my patients tell me is likely to be true—that many times when I believed that I was right and my patients were wrong, it turned out, though often only after a prolonged search, that *my* rightness was superficial whereas *their* rightness was profound.

How do these considerations apply to the episode under discussion? If the patient responded positively to the analyst's communication that she had been transformed for the patient from a good breast to a bad breast, could it be that, even though the content of the interpretation was wrong, the interpretation itself was still right? I think so. To my mind the interpretation was right in its essential message to the patient. Its specific content was actually of negligible importance and should be understood as being the nonspecific carrier of the essential meaning that was transmitted.

And what was this meaning? The message that was transmitted to the patient was easy to understand. Independent of the mode in which the message was expressed, as far as the patient was concerned the analyst had said no more than this: you are deeply upset about the fact that one of your appointments was canceled. It is this simple but, I believe, profoundly human message, expressed with human warmth, that the patient heard—never mind the transference revival of the archaic experience of the bad breast, the transference repetition of a catastrophic damming-up of libidinal impulses resulting from exclusion from the parental bedroom, or the recurrence in the transference of the profound loss of self-esteem that followed the abrupt loss of the mirroring selfobject that had sustained her self. And I am convinced, furthermore—to make my point from the opposite direction—that the analyst could have spoken the same words without the patient's wholesome response to the interpretation if she had failed to transmit her correct empathic perception of the patient's devastated state via her choice of words, the tone of her voice, and probably many other still poorly understood means of communication including bodily movements, subtle body odors, and the like.

What is the nature of the therapeutic effect of psychoanalytic therapy on the analysand? Does the foregoing vignette bring us closer to an answer to this crucial question? I believe that it does if we keep in mind the self psychological principle (see Kohut 1977, pp. 84–88) that therapeutic interventions consist of two separate, identifiable, but interdependent steps, just as the two steps of reassuring and feeding in the childhood prototype of the selfobject-object interventions that promote psychic health are comparably separate but interdependent (pp. 86–88). These two steps, which, together, constitute the substance of the basic therapeutic act, are (1) understanding and (2) explaining. In terms of the clinical vignette under discussion, we need only refine this simple formula by stating explicitly that, during certain stages of their analyses, certain analysands will respond exclusively to their analysts' accurate empathy even when, as I demonstrated with the foregoing vignette, the (correct) understanding may have been transmitted through the vehicle of an (incorrect) interpretation, that is, an incorrect explanation. Clearly, it is not enough for the analyst to be "nice" to his patients, to be "understanding," warmhearted, endowed with the human touch. While I acknowledge that if empirical research should ever demonstrate that the therapist's consistent protracted friendliness and kindness could by itself lead to the patient's cure, we would have to bow to this evidence,[5] all the evidence now available indicates that being nice, friendly, understanding, warmhearted, and in possession of the human touch cures neither the classical neuroses nor the analyzable disturbances of the self—at least not in the sense in which psychoanalysis, in general, and psychoanalytic self psychology, in particular, define the therapeutic goals of treatment.

Seen from the point of view of the topographic model of the mind, the essence of the cure lies in the cognitive field: it lies in the expansion of consciousness. Seen from the point of view of the tripartite model of the mind, the essence of the cure lies in an increase in the territory of the ego. The traditional conception of cure, then, is defined not only in terms of expanded knowledge but also in terms of the expanded terrain over which the ego operates. This, in turn, is equated with the dominance of the reality principle over the pleasure principle, of the secondary process over the primary process. Ego psychology formulated these therapeutic goals of psychoanalysis by two implicit expectations: (a) that a "conflict-free" sphere of the ego should be acquired (or that it should expand to the extent that its influence will prevail) and that "ego autonomy" (Hartmann 1964, pp. 113–41) should be achieved (or should increase); and (b) that the "area of progressive neutralization" (Kohut 1978b, 1:337–75, 137–38) should become broadened and that not only ego autonomy but also, and par excellence, "ego dominance" (Kohut 1978b, 2:620–21, 1:415–22) should be established (or should increase, again to the extent that its influence will be the prevailing one).

And what has self psychology up to now contributed to our understanding of the psychoanalytic cure? Let me, before addressing myself again to this question, point out that, with reference to the issue of cure, the continuity between ego psychology and self psychology is most palpable. This continuity lends weight to our assertion that self psychology, although at the present time still unassimilated by the majority of analysts, is placed squarely in the center of the analytic tradition, that it is in the mainstream of the development of psychoanalytic thought. What psychoanalytic self psychology has contributed in this area is the following: (1) it has emphasized the importance of the sequence of (a) experience-near understanding (i.e., the gathering of relevant data about the inner life of the analysand)

and (b) explaining these data in more or less experience-distant dynamic and genetic terms (see Kohut 1978b, 2:511–46); (2) it has pointed out the central role of the process of transmuting internalization, that is, of structure-building in consequence of optimal frustration (Kohut 1978b, 1:337–75, 1971); and (3) it has formulated the essence of psychological health and thus the goal of psychoanalytic therapy in self psychological terms—that is, (a) in dynamic structural terms and (b) as related to a meaningfully unrolling life process (see Kohut 1977). Expressed in structural terms, self psychology points out that psychological health requires the presence of a sectorial functional continuum from one pole of the self to the other, whether the structures that form the continuum are acquired during a wholesome childhood or, belatedly, during a successful analysis later in life.

I believe that we can profitably address the crucial questions concerning the nature of the psychoanalytic cure that I enumerated earlier if we examine the curative process in the light of these three major contributions of self psychology.

Let us initially focus on what I consider "the basic therapeutic unit" of the psychoanalytic cure. The basic step that constitutes the essence of the psychoanalytic cure—or, to express myself more exactly, I should say the basic step, the countless repetitions of which during the course of an analysis collectively constitute the essence of the psychoanalytic cure—begins with the apperception by the analyst of something that the analysand experiences. Since we are dealing with the analyst's grasp of a state or event in the *inner* life of his patient, we say that the analyst comes to a closure via empathy, that is, via vicarious introspection. It has to be stated, furthermore, that while we understand that there is a "decisive difference between (a) the tentative and ad hoc use of preformed, vaguely outlined configurations during the act of observation which makes possible the collection of data and (b) the development of sharply defined mental configurations, that is, of theories to which the researcher has a long-term, conscious commitment" (Kohut 1978b, 2:750n), we must admit that, strictly speaking, there can be no observation without theory. The number of different explanatory configurations available to an analyst, in other words, will influence the scope of his observations vis-à-vis a given patient. And if he is able to compare the explanatory power of a number of different configurations by postponing a definitive commitment either to a specific one of them or to a specific combination of them, he will ultimately be best able to explain to the analysand those experiential configurations mobilized in the therapeutic situation that are most relevant to his psychopathology. (I am speaking here mainly of the reconstruction—from the assessment of its revival in the transference—of the genetic context in which the analysand's psychopathology arose in childhood.)

The preceding remarks will, I suppose, not arouse much opposition. But there is a certain conclusion which I draw from them—a conclusion which, in its further elaboration, is of considerable significance in understanding some otherwise puzzling successes in psychoanalytic therapy—that some may well view with a degree of skepticism. This is the conclusion, already mentioned in the context of the report of my Latin American colleague, that the therapeutic effectiveness of certain interpretations that are based on erroneous theorizing is basically due not, as Glover (1931) believed, to the fact that the patient submitted to the analyst's suggestive pressure, but to the fact that the interpretation, though conveying an erroneous message via its verbal content, was, paradoxically, in its essence more right than wrong. It is in this sense that many analysts (and their patients) are right in accepting the theories (and the therapeutic interpretations based on these theories) of a variety of mutually contradictory schools of thought that share only one thing in common: an opposition to the classical emphasis on the Oedipus complex. They are right because the theories of these schools, however incorrect or inaccurate their content, at least attempt to respond to the crucial experiences that lie at the center of the forms of psychopathology prevalent in our day. The classical theory, on the other hand, does not.[6]

Let us assume, for the sake of argument—as I said before, I do not know what the dynamic-genetic facts of the case were—that the patient of the Latin American analyst was suffering from an analyzable disturbance of the self, a narcissistic personality disorder. It follows that she reacted to the analyst's announced absence with depression and rage, just as she had reacted to the loss of the cohesion-maintaining mirroring selfobject or harmony-providing idealized selfobject in childhood. And let us surmise, furthermore, that, at the time when her treatment took place, her analyst had no knowledge of the formulations of self psychology, which indeed existed in only a rudimentary state at the time and were certainly unknown in the geographical area in which this analyst worked. Under these circumstances the analyst had two choices: she could have seen the patient's reaction to her announced absence in the context of experiences with the instinctually cathected objects of the oedipal phase, or, as in fact she did, in the context of experiences with the maternal breast qua instinctually cathected object of early infancy. Although neither conceptual framework could explain the patient's experience if she indeed suffered from a disorder of the cohesion and vitality of the self, I submit that, in most instances, though not in all, the Freudian misinterpretation would have been perceived by the analysand as more erroneous than the Kleinian misinterpretation to which she was in fact exposed. Why?

If the analysand was suffering from a narcissistic personality disorder and not from a structural neurosis, if, in other words, her basic psychopathology lay in the area of the self and not in the area of unresolved conflicts over incestuous desires, then, ceteris paribus, the Freudian interpretation would have been felt as farther off the mark, that is, as less understanding, than the Kleinian. By this I mean that the patient would have felt that the Freudian analyst's empathic grasp was less accurate than that of the Kleinian analyst, that, in particular, the Freudian analyst was less in tune with the state of her self than the Kleinian. The Freudian and the Kleinian interventions would have been equally erroneous in their explanatory dimensions (i.e., the interpretive aspect), but the Freudian intervention would have been wider of the mark in terms of the first step of the "basic therapeutic unit," that is, as far as the understanding phase of this two-step process is concerned. It would have been farther off the mark because in essence it would have been concerned with the conflicts and emotions of a firmly cohesive self and not with the devastating experience of a crumbling or seriously weakened self. The Kleinian interpretation, on the other hand, while failing to focus squarely on the self state of the analysand and, on the basis of an erroneous theoretical bias, mistakenly conjuring up a concretized picture of primary drives and archaic drive objects, dealt, at least tangentially and by implication, with the experience of an encompassing disturbance of the psyche. Thus, as far as the nonverbal message conveyed by this analyst's tone of voice and her overall attitude toward a patient with such a disturbance go, the analysand experienced this Kleinian empathic understanding, if not her dynamic-genetic explanation, as being reasonably in tune with what she experienced.

Optimal Frustration and Structure Formation in the Curative Process

From this consideration of the basic therapeutic unit of the psychoanalytic cure and the way this unit helps us conceptualize the therapeutic impact of theoretically erroneous interpretations, we can return to the question of just *how* psychoanalysis cures with a broadened perspective. The most general answer that self psychology gives to this question is a simple one: psychoanalysis cures by the laying down of psychological structure. And how does this accretion of psychological structure take place? The most general self psychological answer to this second question is also simple: psychological structure is laid down

(a) via optimal frustration and (b) in consequence of optimal frustration, via transmuting internalization.

But now I must add a number of specific points to these general statements. When the self psychologist speaks of "psychic structure," he is referring neither to the structures of a mental apparatus nor to the structures of any of the constituents of a mental apparatus but to the structure of the self. The structure of the self, in other words, is the theoretical correlate of those attributes of the self which, in their sum total, define this central concept of self psychology. While the notion of psychic structure is, like all theoretical constructions, no more than a tautology, it is still an invaluable aid to our thought and an indispensable tool when we communicate with one another. It allows us to speak of the attributes of the self in general terms, without specifying whether we have in mind its cohesion, its strength, or its harmony—that is, without specifying whether we refer to a person's experience of being whole and continuous, of being fully alive and vigorous, or of being balanced and organized (see Kohut and Wolf 1978, especially p. 414). And it allows us to evoke, again without being specific, such diverse yet defining attributes of the self as those given by our abiding experience of being a center of initiative, of being a recipient of impressions, of having cohesion in space and continuity in time, and the like. (On the definition of "the self" see Kohut, in prep.)

There is yet another point that needs to be made with regard to the simple statement that analysis cures via the laying down of psychological structure. Are these structures new, we will ask, or are we, with the aid of the analytic process, simply strengthening and rehabilitating structures that are already present, that have in fact been present since childhood? This is a significant question which is best answered, I believe, if we divide it into two parts.

1. As far as the overall program of the self is concerned, that "action-poised programme arched in the energic field that established itself between [the patient's] nuclear ambitions and ideals" (Kohut and Wolf 1978, p. 424) and that gives the self a dimension directed toward the future (see Kohut in prep., 1979), we will say that psychoanalysis does not lay down new structure. This is tantamount to saying that the analytic process, so far as we know, cannot establish a nuclear self de novo.

2. Still, since the structure of the nuclear self and the layers of the self that are acquired in later childhood may in certain cases of severe yet analyzable self disorder be composed of structures that are riddled with defects and lacunae, and/or seriously enfeebled, and/or disharmonious, new structures will indeed be laid down during the process of working through to fill the defects of the self, to strengthen the

existing fabric of the self, or to provide those connecting links that allow the patient to experience himself as a harmonious, balanced unit that is continuous in time and cohesive in space. Nevertheless, however extensive these aforementioned structural accretions may be, they do not, so far as we know, create the basic program of the personality that was outlined in early life and do not create a nuclear self de novo.

But I will not pursue any further the examination of the intricate problems that arise as soon as one begins to contemplate the question of how to define the concept of a "psychic structure"—problems that are by no means specific to self psychology. Instead, I will briefly touch on certain tasks that lie ahead in the continuing elucidation of the process of transmuting internalization. It will come as a surprise to no one, I am sure, if I point out that what is required is the testing, with the aid of detailed clinical observations, of the various claims that I have made. Which claims in particular need to be tested and, if need be, modified or contradicted? I will not give an exhaustive list but merely a few representative examples: (1) We need to examine the accuracy of my "foreign-protein" analogy (see Kohut 1971, p. 49, and Kohut and Wolf 1978, p. 416). The question that needs to be investigated here, putting the foreign-protein claim in the obverse, is whether psychic functions can be established reliably and abidingly that constitute a direct takeover of selfobject functions, that is, psychic functions that are not being altered in the process of being taken over from the selfobject. (2) Can enduring psychic functions be acquired with the aid of selfobjects (their listening presence, their silent mirroring, their silently present calmness and strength) that are ab initio neither identical with any features displayed by the selfobject nor even derived from such features? Can the presence of the selfobject, in other words, activate innate functions without the detour of an intermediate gross borrowing of the selfobject's functions? (3) Even if the term "frustration" is used in the specific sense that I have employed it in defining the relationship between optimum frustration and the laying down of psychic structures (Kohut 1978b, 1:433–34, and 1971, p. 50), including, for example, disappointments in the formerly assumed perfection of the selfobject, can abiding psychic functions be acquired by the self without a preceding frustration, however tiny and/or fractionated, from the side of the selfobject? (4) We need a careful and detailed study of those not infrequently occurring instances (see Kohut 1971, pp. 166–68) in which, often after prolonged and severe resistances against the establishment of a selfobject transference, a loss of the selfobject analyst (e.g., during a vacation) is responded to by a gross, concretely enacted identification with him. We particularly need to know how—if the analyst does not reject the

identification as a resistance but interprets it as a first acknowledgment
of the presence of a reactivated developmental need—such moves
toward gross incorporation become gradually and increasingly replaced by processes that conform more and more to that mode that
we characterize as *transmuting* internalizations. Such a study would be
especially valuable because, with its aid, we might see with greater
clarity than we do now how the shift from a traumatically experienced
frustration to a gradually less traumatically experienced series of disappointments is accompanied by a shift from gross (and we assume
ephemeral) identifications to the laying down of enduring structures
that are increasingly in harmony with the preformed outline of the
patient's preanalytic self. (5) Finally, by way of rounding out this list
of specific investigative tasks that need to be undertaken in the area
under scrutiny, I will ask two questions that are interrelated with the
preceding ones in a number of ways: (a) Is there a decisive difference
(a difference in principle) between the acquisition of psychic structure
in adult life, for example, in the course of psychoanalytic treatment,
and the acquisition of psychic structure in childhood, and (b) if such
a decisive difference indeed exists, of what does it consist?

Having thus pointed to certain aspects of the process of transmuting
internalization that await further clarification, I will now put this widely
discussed concept to one side and turn to the concept that, in the
context of our investigation of the psychoanalytic cure, is unquestionably the crucial one. I refer to the concept of "optimal frustration"
on which the self psychological theory of the psychoanalytic cure may
be fairly said to hinge. How, I will ask, is the analysand—specifically,
the analysand with a self disturbance who is analyzed from the vantage
point of psychoanalytic self psychology—exposed to those optimal
frustrations which, in innumerable repetitions throughout the years
of treatment, ultimately bring about the cure?

Let me, to begin, return once more to my experience with the Latin
American analyst whose announcement of an impending absence provoked a crisis in her patient. Again, for the sake of my argument, I
will assume that her patient had been suffering neither from an oedipal neurosis nor from the revival of the instinctual ambivalence of
earliest life, but from an analyzable disturbance of the self. Was the
erroneous interpretation of the analyst curative in the self psychological sense of cure? Or, to put it more cautiously, could the erroneous
interpretation have contributed an increment of health to the analysand, however tiny and insignificant? The answer, in principle, is
affirmative: I believe that the events I have described could have been
experienced by the analysand as an optimal frustration and could
thus have brought about a tiny accretion of structure via transmuting
internalization. But how, it will be asked, could this possibly have

occurred? How could an erroneous interpretation have brought about a result that was not merely psychotherapeutic (i.e., the patient's pleasure at feeling that she had, in essence, been understood and supported by the experience) but genuinely analytic? Let us, again for the sake of argument, disregard Glover's (1931) hypothesis that the erroneous genetic reconstruction could have been nonanalytically therapeutic via suggestion and instead look squarely at the pivotal hypothesis that the analyst's correct empathic understanding of the intensity of the patient's unsettled psychological condition—an understanding that was communicated to the analysand more via nonverbal cues including the analyst's tone of voice than by the verbal interpretation—was curative in the psychoanalytic sense.

In view of the fact that I have defined the basic therapeutic unit of psychoanalysis as consisting of the two steps of understanding and explaining, it is clear from the outset that the result of an intervention such as that of the Latin American analyst cannot be optimal since only the first of the two steps has been successfully taken. Still, provided that an analyst has correctly grasped the essence of his patient's inner state via vicarious introspection (empathy) and, in one form or another, communicated this understanding to the patient, it is my claim that even this first step of the basic therapeutic unit alone exposes the patient to a modicum of optimal frustration and thus, secondarily, to the laying down of new, that is, defect-filling or cohesion-firming, psychic structures. But how, it will be asked, can "understanding" alone constitute optimal frustration? Am I not merely describing "cure through love," "cure through being kind," and the like? The answer to these questions is no, and it is no whether we are considering the first step (understanding) of the two-step (understanding, explaining) sequence in a case of self pathology or in a case of conflict neurosis; whether, that is, we consider a moment in an analysis when the analyst communicates a reasonably accurate understanding of a transference experience that is due to a revived developmental need in the analysand or a reasonably accurate understanding of a transference experience that is due to a revived incestuous drive-wish. My hypothesis remains the same, in other words, whether the patient's self disintegrates temporarily because the withdrawal of the mirroring selfobject repeats the traumatic unavailability of self confirming responses in early life or whether, in a case of structural neurosis, the analyst's absence is experienced as a repetition of the primal scene, with an intensification of incestuous desires on the one hand and hostility and reactive guilt-depression on the other.

The analyst's communication to the patient of his more or less correct understanding of the patient's inner life is optimally frustrating in either event. It is *frustrating* because, despite the analyst's *understanding* of what the patient feels and his *acknowledgment* that the patient's upset is legitimate (e.g., both as the revival of an old unfulfilled need and as the manifestation of a universal need for selfobjects that persists throughout life), the analyst still does not *act* in accordance with the patient's need. Thus, in the case of the Latin American analyst, the regularity and continuity of the sessions will still be interrupted by the analyst's forthcoming absence. It is *optimally* frustrating because the communication is still in compliance with the patient's need—though to a lesser degree. It is optimal *frustration* rather than optimal *gratification* because, through the analyst's more or less accurate understanding, an empathic bond is established (reestablished) between analyst and patient that substitutes for the de facto fulfillment of the patient's need. All these components, it should be noted, still remain part of the understanding phase of the basic therapeutic unit.

The foregoing considerations concerning the process of the psychoanalytic cure may seem rather undramatic in comparison with such traditional formulations as "to make the unconscious conscious" or "where id was, there ego shall be" (Freud 1933, 1953, 22:80). But I think the significance of the sequence I have just described—(1) reactivation of need (in conflict-neuroses: of instinctual wish); (2) nonresponse by the selfobject (in conflict-neuroses: by the object); (3) reestablishment of a bond of empathy between self and selfobject (in conflict-neuroses: between self and object)—cannot be overestimated with reference to both normal development in childhood and the movement toward cure in psychoanalysis.

Before we can move forward and, leaving the examination of the understanding phase of the basic therapeutic unit behind us, turn our attention to the explaining phase, two clarifications concerning the preceding inquiry must be made. The first one concerns my reason for spelling out the aforementioned three-step sequence of the therapeutic miniprocesses that lead to the laying down of psychic structure and thereby prepare the soil for the analytic cure. The second one concerns a definitional question that arises from my consideration of the three-step sequence that constitutes "understanding." Specifically, should we characterize the acquisition of the minute amounts of new psychic structures that are provided via the understanding phase alone—even when the analyst is unable to supplement his accurate understanding with a correct interpretation (e.g., because he is informed by a nonfitting theory or because he has explained too soon)— a psychoanalytic success or should we subsume it under the heading of "psychotherapy"?

My main reason for detailing the three-step sequence of (1) need-activation and optimal frustration via (2) nonfulfillment of the need ("abstinence") and (3) substitution of direct need fulfillment with the establishment of a bond of empathy between self and selfobject was not to demonstrate that self psychologically oriented psychoanalytic therapy is, in fact, different from traditional psychoanalytic therapy. On the contrary, my intention was to demonstrate that it is in principle exactly the same. To put the matter differently, self psychology does not differ from traditional psychoanalysis in its characterization of what is going on between analyst and patient that eventuates in a cure. But self psychology *does* differ from traditional psychoanalysis in: (a) the explanation it provides for the process of cure and (b) the theories that, at least in some instances, inform the analyst's interpretations during the explanatory phase. To present my meaning *in nuce,* I believe that psychoanalysis—traditional psychoanalysis—has *always* achieved its successes via the three-step process that I have laid out and that the only real forward move provided by self psychology is its expansion of psychoanalytic theory, specifically, its theoretical elucidation of the whole area of the reactivation of thwarted developmental needs in the transference via the discovery of the selfobject transferences.[7]

I turn now to my second clarification which, as I said above, concerns the question of whether or not we should call the limited structure accretions that are acquired on the basis of correct understanding alone an analytic result. In approaching this issue, I cannot help but smile at the complexities into which I feel forced by entirely nonscientific considerations. Clearly, what should be at stake is not a name— "analytic" or "nonanalytic"—but the deepest and broadest grasp of the processes with which we are dealing. Having to this point attempted to elucidate these processes to the best of my ability, I will now leave science behind and, submitting to internal and external pressures—I admit that they are related to what I once (Kohut 1978*b,* 2:663–67) characterized as tool-and-method pride or tool-and-method snobbishness—affirm that it would be quite justifiable to reserve the name "analytic" only for those emotive results that come about via the complete understanding-explaining sequence, that is, via accurate understanding followed by dynamic-genetic interpretation. It follows that the structure accretions that came about as a result of the Kleinian (one could substitute "traditional" or "self psychological") "wild analytic" intervention that I described earlier should be called "psychotherapeutic" rather than "analytic." But this classificatory issue is not my major concern, at least not within the context of the present work. My inquiry at this point is not directed at an issue of nomenclature— whether, as I believe, the ascription "analytic cure" should be reserved for treatment results in which the laying down of structures is achieved via a working-through process that includes the dynamic-genetic interpretation of the transference—but on the elucidation of the specific effect brought about by interpretation, the second step of the two-step basic therapeutic unit.

I will be as direct in my approach as I can and ask whether it might not be concluded on the basis of the preceding discussion that the second step might just as well be omitted. If structure-building optimal frustrations are already provided by the first phase of the basic therapeutic unit, it might be argued, why do we need the second one at all? Or do dynamic-genetic explanations make a contribution to the curative process that understanding makes incompletely or fails to make? The answer to these questions is unambiguous: the explanatory phase indeed provides a great deal that the understanding phase does not. Although, as I have observed elsewhere (1977), some patients will require "long periods of 'only'understanding before the second step—interpretation . . . can be usefully and acceptably undertaken" (p. 88), the interventions of the analyst must ultimately include both phases of the basic therapeutic unit in order to bring about a result that we may call a psychoanalytic one.

It is my claim, in other words, not only that the second phase of the basic therapeutic unit increases the impact of the first phase quantitatively, but that, through its influence, the therapeutic effect of the basic therapeutic unit itself becomes qualitatively different from the effect that resulted from the understanding phase alone. I know that an accurate depiction of the maximizing effect of the second phase and of the interaction between the effects of the two phases cannot be given in black and white; it would require the use of many shades of gray. Nevertheless, in order to keep my presentation concise, I will dispense with nuances—I know they can be easily supplied by the experienced clinician once the basic principles have been clearly set forth.

The reason why the phase of dynamic-genetic explanations is an indispensable constituent of the basic therapeutic unit in psychoanalysis is twofold. (1) Without it the understanding phase remains of necessity incomplete. The analyst's communication to the analysand of his dynamic-genetic formulation of the patient's reactions, in other words, not only broadens and deepens the patient's own empathic-accepting grasp of himself, but strengthens the patient's trust in the reality and reliability of the empathic bond that is being established between himself and his analyst by putting him in touch with the full depth and breadth of the analyst's understanding of him. (2) Whereas the analyst's more or less accurate empathic understanding of the current condition of the analysand's self (phase one of the basic therapeutic unit) promotes the movement toward health and leads to the laying down of new psychological structure, the result of this experience tends to be ephemeral. Well-designed verbal interpretations, on the other hand—which explain the patient's psychological reactions (in particular and par excellence his transference experiences) in dynamic terms (substep one of this explanatory phase of the basic therapeutic unit) and which, furthermore, refer to the genetic precursors of his vulnerabilities and conflicts (substep two of the explanatory phase of the basic therapeutic unit)—will implant the wholesome but, heretofore, ephemeral experience of having been understood into a broader area of the upper layers of the analysand's mind—expressed in the terms of Freud's bi- and tripartite models of the mind, into a broader area of the system preconscious or of the ego, respectively—and will thus allow him to recall this experience during the subsequent all-important period of working through. Thus, experiences similar to those that had previously led to the interpretation of a transference disruption—such as the analysand's reaction to the analyst's canceling a session—can now, and ab initio, be actively faced by the analysand himself. Or, to state this matter differently, during that stage of treatment in which a particular sector of psychopathology is being worked through, the analyst's active interventions (interpretations) are needed less and less. The patient takes over the analyst's functions—though, as I will discuss shortly, only temporarily and transitionally.

I will now make a claim whose full meaning may not be apparent on first sight but which I consider very significant: I believe that the mode by which, in innumerable repetitions throughout the course of an analysis, the two-phase basic therapeutic unit brings about the psychoanalytic cure is the same in properly conducted analyses of analyzable self disorders in the narrow sense (narcissistic personality and behavior disorders) and in properly conducted analyses of conflict neuroses (the classical transference neuroses).

It will be immediately and erroneously concluded that the preceding statement about the identity of the curative process in the narcissistic personality disorders and in the oedipal neuroses is simply an expression of the fact that oedipal neuroses are now also conceptualized by me as self disturbances in the broad sense of the term (see Kohut 1977, pp. 246–48, and the extensive discussion of this issue in chap. 2). I hasten to explain, therefore, by way of preventing this misunderstanding from taking root, that the self psychologists' conviction about the essential identity of the curative process in these two forms of psychological disturbance does not rest on our having indeed come to the view that conflict neuroses are in every case embedded in the genetic matrix of a self disturbance. Even if we had not come to this latter view, our claim of the essential identity of the curative process in analyzable self disturbances and conflict neuroses could be maintained. To put this as concretely as possible: our claim would still apply to an analysis conducted by an analyst who did not share our view that conflict neuroses are always rooted in the soil of a damaged self and who believed that he had dealt with the deepest layers of the patient's disturbance when the structural conflicts had been worked through. The claim would apply, in other words, even if the analysis did not penetrate to the transference reactivation and recall of those traumatic selfobject failures of childhood which, according to self psychology, are laid down in the deepest layers of the patient's unconscious and are regarded as the ultimate genetic factor of psychological disturbance, not only in the narcissistic disorders but in the classical oedipal conflict neuroses as well.

The preceding reflections are significant because they make clear that the expansion of analytic theory that self psychology considers the unavoidable consequence of its clinical discoveries does not per se imply a change in the way self psychologically informed analyses are being conducted. This is tantamount to saying—and I use the time-honored term with some inner reluctance—that it does not lead to a change in basic psychoanalytic technique. Rather, the foregoing discussion emphasizes that our reinterpretation of the curative process applies to all properly conducted analyses—that is, to all analyses in which the unfolding of the transference is not interfered with and in which the transference, having unfolded, is systematically interpreted and worked through—and not only to analyses conducted by self psychologically informed analysts. The theory of structure building via optimal frustration advanced by psychoanalytic self psychology, that is, applies not only to the analysis of the analyzable narcissistic disorders but also to the classical conflict neuroses. And, what is even more important in this context, it is meant to apply not only to analyses conducted at present by my colleagues and me, but to all analyses conducted *lege artis* ever since this form of psychotherapy was perfected by Freud, Strachey, Anna Freud, Fenichel, Eissler, Greenacre, Glover, Loewald, Stone, and many others.

At the risk of overextending the discussion of the issue at hand, I will demonstrate my meaning once more with the aid of an extreme example. Psychoanalytic gossip has it—whether accurately or not is unimportant here—that an especially cautious colleague, worried that he might provide corrective emotional experiences to his patients, removed the Kleenex boxes from his office so as not to provide a source of psychoanalytically deleterious gratification for patients when they cried. Now, while I, presumably in harmony with the opinion of most of my colleagues, consider such a move the outgrowth of a ridiculous misunderstanding of what constitutes a psychologically defined "neutrality" (see Kohut 1977, pp. 249–64), I believe that it would not per se preclude the development of a psychoanalytic process that could lead to a psychoanalytic cure. If this analyst, however mistakenly, believed that what he was doing was really for the long-term benefit of his patient, that is, if his action was not motivated by unconscious sadism, then the patient would simply, after a while, adapt to this particular analyst's conception of neutrality. When this occurred, the analyst's conception of neutrality would become the baseline for determining, throughout the treatment, what constituted optimum (structure-building) frustration and what did not.

I would not be candid, however, if I failed to admit that I actually believe the foregoing statement holds only within certain limits. Returning for a moment to the perhaps factitious illustration I have invoked, even if the removal of the Kleenex was a well-meant action, an analyst's employment of this measure would demonstrate, in my opinion, not only that he failed to grasp the true meaning of psychoanalytic "neutrality," but also that he failed to realize that, should a particular patient indeed use Kleenex for gratification—should he "act out," in other words, instead of "remembering"—the ensuing absence of meaningful free associations would be dealt with not by an *action* from the side of the analyst, but by appropriate interpretations that enlist the patient's cooperation in the analytic task.

But we must not lose ourselves any longer in side issues. Returning to our discussion of the curative factors in analysis, we will derive a more general lesson from the specific reflections we have undertaken thus far and say that it is not what the self psychologically informed analyst does, that is, his "technique," that has changed, but how he views what he does. In contrast to those—including James Strachey (1934)—who believe, in harmony with the spirit of the Age of Enlightenment of which Freud was a true child, that it is the power of reason which cures, the self psychologically informed analyst holds that with regard to all forms of analyzable psychopathology the basic therapeutic unit of the psychoanalytic cure does not rest on the expansion of cognition. (It does not rest, for example, on the analysand's becoming aware of the difference between his fantasy and reality, especially with reference to transference distortions involving projected drives.) Rather, it is the accretion of psychic structure via an optimal frustration of the analysand's needs or wishes that is provided for the analysand in the form of correct interpretations that constitutes the essence of the cure.

I have held these views, it must be emphasized, for many years. And it is of particular significance that I held them before I became interested in narcissistic personality disorders. Specifically, I held them before I began to formulate my conceptions concerning the mode of cure in the narcissistic disturbances and began to describe (Kohut 1978b, 1:427–60, 477–509, 1971) the interrelated processes of optimal frustrations and transmuting internalization as they applied to both the theory of self development and the theory of the therapeutic action in the analysis of patients with developmental disturbances of the self. These theories concerning optimal frustration and structure formation, in other words, were advanced before I turned to the investigation of the self. This significant fact, demonstrating once more that my changed conception of the analytic cure is not meant to apply only to the treatment process in narcissistic personality disorders, becomes evident if we consider certain passages from my essay of 1963, "Concepts and Theories of Psychoanalysis" (1978b, 1:337–75). Because of the significance of the theory of structure building within the framework of my thoughts, I will quote the following representative excerpts from this pre–self psychological contribution:

> The neutralizing psychological structure which constitutes the nondichotomized portion of the psyche . . . was formed by the internalization of innumerable experiences of optimal frustration. [P. 369.]

> Replicas of the experiences of . . . optimal frustration (identifications) are established in the mind via the mechanism of introjection. . . . The child's drives are opposed originally by the prohibitions of the parents. If these prohibitions are of nontraumatic intensity, the child incorporates the parents' drive-restraining attitudes in the form of innumerable benign memory traces. . . . As a result of having introjected many experiences of optimal frustration in which his infantile drives were handled by a calming, soothing, loving attitude rather than by counter-aggression on the part of his parents, the child himself later acts in the same way toward the drive demands that arise in him. [P. 370.]

> The most important source of a well-functioning psychological structure . . . is the personality of the parents, specifically their ability to respond to the child's drive demands with nonhostile firmness and nonseductive affection. . . . If a child is exposed chronically to immature, hostile, or seductive parental reactions . . . then the resulting intense anxiety or overstimulation leads to an impoverishment of the growing psyche. [P. 371.]

Here is convincing evidence that my opinion regarding the role of optimal frustration in structure formation preceded (1) my investigation of the narcissistic disorders and (2) my subsequent contention that, within the framework of a psychology of complex mental states, the experience of isolated drives should be conceptualized as a secondary rather than a primary phenomenon.

Why am I stressing the fact that my basic outlook on those analogous psychic processes that bring about psychic maturity during normal development and lead to successful psychoanalytic treatment in adult life was formed before my interest began to focus on the disturbances of the self, and before I began to differentiate between those healthy drive experiences in which an active lively self participated and those potentially pathogenic drive experiences which are isolated and which appear secondarily after the functional disruption of the self? I believe that the answer to this question is by now clear. I wanted, once more, to underline the fact that—at least up to this point—the theory of therapeutic cure that I am presenting (1) does not apply only to the analysis of analyzable self disorders (in the narrow sense) but to the analysis of *all* analyzable disorders and (2) does not apply only to analyses that are conducted by self psychologically informed psychoanalysts but to all analyses, past and present, in which transferences were interpreted and worked through.

7

The Self Psychological Approach to Defense and Resistance

The foregoing overview of the self psychological conception of the psychoanalytic cure prepares us to explore a more delimited topic that is centrally implicated in our understanding of the therapeutic process. I am referring to the place of "defense" in contemporary psychoanalytic theory and, more especially, to the question of whether the analysis of defenses, that is, "resistance analysis," is still as indispensable an element in clinical analysis as Freud considered it to be. Specifically, we want to ask how self psychology evaluates the traditional conceptualization of the treatment process as an overcoming of resistances in order to make the unconscious conscious.

To a significant extent, the self psychological reevaluation of the concepts of defense and resistance represents a continuation of the discussion of scientific objectivity that I undertook earlier (chap. 3). In a nutshell, the contrast between traditional psychoanalysis and psychoanalytic self psychology vis-à-vis defenses and resistances resides in the contrast between the former's commitment to a scientific objectivity that typifies the nineteenth century and the latter's commitment to a scientific objectivity that incorporates the breakthroughs of our own century. Whereas the traditional analyst is on the lookout for discrete "mechanisms" tied to the functioning of a mental "apparatus," the psychoanalytic self psychologist acknowledges his own impact on the field he observes and, through such acknowledgment, broadens his perception of the patient through empathic contact with the data of the patient's inner experiences. In the following historical observations, I shall try to demonstrate how the traditional estimation of the defenses and resistances has become intertwined with the perspective on the analyst's objectivity handed down by Freud.

I begin by recalling that the theoretical model that shaped Freud's earliest (i.e., preanalytic) therapeutic efforts was, and for a time remained, hypnosis. It is important to note, in this connection, that the decisive step toward analysis was not the replacement of hypnosis with a different therapeutic technique, but a pivotal change in the understanding of the psychopathology that was to be cured via hypnosis. As long as hypnosis did not conceptualize a psyche in depth (and, correspondingly, a psychopathology in depth), it remained nonanalytic hypnosis. As soon as it conceived of a psyche in depth, however (and, correspondingly, of a psychopathology in depth), it became, so to speak, "psychoanalytic" hypnosis. The preanalytic hypnotist ordered the hypnotized patient to get rid of his symptoms; the analytic hypnotist ordered the patient to produce an account of the dynamic (and, later, genetic) background, that is, to produce the data that illuminated the endopsychic causes of his symptoms. The significance of this step—a decisive step forward, despite the fact that the hypnotic technique was retained—cannot be overestimated.

I offer this historical caveat because it is of the utmost importance in understanding the contemporary analyst's attitude toward defenses and resistances. Specifically, Freud's early attempt to graft an analytic theory of therapy onto preanalytic assumptions about the therapeutic mechanism of hypnosis introduced a mode of thinking into the psychological field that would prove congenial to the medically trained mind of the researcher, but was ill adapted to the requirements of a science of complex mental states. In brief, the imagery evoked by this mode of thinking, and the type of metaphor it encouraged, were basically foreign to a field observed via introspection and empathy. The unconscious was the abscess that had to be drained (cf. Freud 1895, 1953, 2:305)—the intervening tissue had to be pierced, by whatever means were necessary, and the healing would take care of itself once the noxious substance had been removed. Freud's well-known reference to the *ferrum* and *ignis* of psychoanalysis (1915, 1953, 12:171) and his famous injunction that analysts should "model themselves during psycho-analytic treatment on the surgeon, who puts aside all his feelings, even his human sympathy" (12:115), are clear evidence that the theory of an unconscious that must be penetrated exerted a strong influence on the therapeutic attitude of the analyst toward his patients.

Ego psychological analysis might have led to a decisive shift in emphasis but, in fact, did not do so consistently. Ego psychology contributed vastly more to the refinement of psychoanalytic theory and to the increased articulation of its borders with the surrounding theories of science than it did to the theory of technique and the conduct of clinical analyses. Admittedly, there are a few noteworthy exceptions to this claim. Certain analysts (e.g., Loewald 1960; Stone 1962) did indeed oppose the attitude of "the surgeon, who puts aside all his feelings, even his human sympathy," as he proceeds to drain the pathogenic abscess in the unconscious. They began to espouse the attitude of the psychologist who seeks to understand and explain so that stunted psychological development can be resumed. In general, however, the hold of the old conceptualizations on the analytic profession persisted despite the contributions of ego psychology and remains strong, even today.[1] For purposes of reexamining the concepts of defense and resistance, moreover, even the theoretical modifications introduced by ego psychology are of little consequence. Specifically, the introduction of the ordering concept of a mental apparatus, of the ego as the seat of anxiety, and of the adaptive motivations underlying defenses and resistances adds little of decisive importance to our topic.

What does the penetration-to-the-unconscious-via-the-overcoming-of-resistances model explain? And what does it fail to explain? I have no difficulty answering these questions, at least in an approximate way. The explanatory power of the old model is best—fully satisfactory, I would say—when it is applied to isolated processes and isolated, circumscribed sectors of psychic life. It is worse—indeed, quite often unsatisfactory—when it is applied to the complexities of man and his personality and, in particular, to man's personality viewed along the time axis of his unrolling life. To be specific: the traditional model explains slips of the tongue and other forms of the psychopathology of everyday life to perfection; it also does well with regard to the interpretation of the majority of dreams—self-state dreams being the exception[2]—as long as they are viewed as delimited units of psychic function; and it is also satisfactory with regard to understanding the symptoms of the transference neuroses as long as they, too, are viewed as delimited units of psychic function or, more accurately, as delimited units of psychic dysfunction. The model is unsatisfactory, however, in explaining personality in general and the psychopathology of personality disturbances in particular—especially disturbances in which the essential psychopathology results from the thwarted development of the self.

In accord with the type of explanation to which the traditional model proves congenial, it has tended over the years to legitimize the analyst's preoccupation with mechanisms, encouraging him to focus on his analysand's unconscious drive-wishes, on the defenses instituted against them, and, ultimately, on the concretization of these defenses in the set of actions, enactments, and psychological attitudes vis-à-vis the psychoanalytic process that we call "resistances." What has been the offshoot of this tendency? In the final analysis, defenses and resistances are themselves mechanisms. They are psychic configurations that emerge when we examine the activities of a "mental apparatus" from the "dynamic point of view." Because they are "mechanisms" or "dynamisms" that are intrinsic to a drive-psychological/ego-psychological orientation, they are necessarily restricted in their explanatory power by the confining influence of the moralistic framework provided by the "pleasure principle" (i.e., the clinging to childish pleasures and the avoidance of anxiety) and the "reality principle" of which Hartmann's (1964, pp. 1–18) "adaptive point of view" is merely a sophisticated extension. Despite these built-in limitations of the traditional model, the analysis of drive-wishes, defenses, and resistances has long constituted a therapeutic end station. Analysts, that is, have not traditionally focused on this constellation as a transitional issue pointing to more significant, underlying problems of the patient. Instead, they have concentrated on it at length in the belief that once drive-wishes, defenses, and resistances were thoroughly analyzed and worked through, everything else would follow. Needless to say, self psychology, in both its conception of scientific objectivity and its governing theoretical commitments, takes issue with this traditional belief. Does it follow, then, that self psychology advocates the elimination of the concepts of defense and resistance from our clinical theory? I would reply to this question in the negative when it is put in such an oversimplified form. Specifically, certain experiences of our patients, and certain aspects of their behavior in analysis that are correlated with these experiences, are indeed appropriately referred to as resistances. These resistances may be directed against the analytic process in general (see Kohut 1978b, 2:547–54) or they may arise at certain specific junctures of analysis in reaction to the analysand's apprehensiveness that the analysis threatens the psychic status quo, in particular as it pertains to the maintenance of a residual self, however precariously established and stifled in its functions it may have been. My personal preference is to speak of the "defensiveness" of patients— and to think of their defensive attitudes as adaptive and psychologically valuable—and not of their "resistances." Still, I believe we should not be pedantic about the complete accuracy of the established nomenclature. To that end, I am willing, at least temporarily, to pour new wine into old bottles and simply redefine the meaning of "defense" and "resistance" in a way that accommodates the insights of self psychology. (The steps by which I tend to proceed are not difficult to demonstrate. In 1971, after all, I was still willing to pour new wine into old bottles. In 1977, however, I came to the decision that I would have to reformulate the old theories decisively and that I required a terminology that was in harmony with the new interpretations of the clinical data that I had presented.)

The elimination of terms, then, is crucial only when they contribute to the perpetuation of substantive conceptual errors. This danger can often be obviated by the careful redefinition of meanings and, especially, by pointing out exactly where old meanings may apply and where they do not. Thus, with regard to the issue at hand, I will say that we speak appropriately of an analysis of defenses during an interim phase of the analytic process, before it has begun to deal with the crucial issues that explain the analysand's psychic disturbance.

It follows, then, that neither the theoretical concept of defense-resistance nor the clinical concept of defense-resistance analysis is wrong or at present superseded by newer concepts. They are, however, less important today than they once were and should no longer be construed as centrally important to theory and practice. They are, to be sure, still important for the beginning student who undertakes his first analyses under supervision, and they deserve, once more, to be addressed at appropriate junctures in the therapy. And they *were* of great importance during the years when analysis itself was still in its infancy and *all* analysts, including Freud, may be said to have been beginners. But the focus of our attention has now shifted both with respect to our science as a whole and with respect to the therapeutic orientation of the experienced practitioner. The result is that the preoccupation with psychic mechanisms is diminishing while the attempt to grasp the condition of the self and its position in time—its future as well as its past—is in the ascendancy.

Thus, the analyst—and especially the self psychologically informed analyst—who has achieved a degree of therapeutic mastery will only very rarely look at his patient in terms of his drive-wishes and defenses; if he does, moreover, he will do so within the framework of his overall understanding of the needs of the patient's self. Defense motivation in analysis will be understood in terms of activities undertaken in the service of psychological survival, that is, as the patient's attempt to save at least that sector of his nuclear self, however small and precariously established it may be, that he has been able to construct and maintain despite serious insufficiencies in the development-enhancing matrix of the selfobjects of childhood.

Case Illustration: The Traditional Approach to Defense and Resistance

Having thus sketched the self psychological perspective on the role of the defenses and of resistance analysis in contemporary psychoanalytic theory, I will elaborate my viewpoint via a clinical illustration.

My case vignette concerns a middle-aged lawyer who had come to me for analysis because of marital difficulties and dissatisfaction with his work. As the basis of my discussion of the significance of the resistances in this patient's analysis, I will consider material from a specific interval of the treatment—a period of approximately three and a half months from the beginning of the fourth year of analysis. In particular I will focus on three dreams that occurred at the beginning, middle, and end of this period, respectively. The manifest content of these dreams, in the chronological sequence according to which they occurred, is as follows:

Dream 1. A summer resort, a hotel or motel or bungalow. The patient, however, was sleeping not inside the building but on the front lawn. He was ill at ease, uncomfortable, thrashing about restlessly with the result that he became uncovered. People began to walk by. He was dismayed by the thought that they would see him partially uncovered.

Dream 2. The patient had reported at the beginning of the session that during a recent disagreement with his wife he had behaved more maturely than in the past. Specifically, instead of getting enraged with her, as would formerly have been the case, he had canceled an engagement of his own in order to allow her to attend a concert with a girl friend to which she had unexpectedly been invited. He then reported a dream from the night preceding the session. He was honored by the lawyer's association and was to get a prize. Although he himself had not heard the announcement that he was to be honored, the man sitting next to him told him about it and also explained to the patient that, as a compromise, he was sharing the prize with someone else. The patient then went to the podium and was given the award; it was a camera. To the surprise of everyone he lifted the camera and took a picture of the audience. The audience was stunned.

Dream 3. His friend John W. was with the patient during the analytic session. John was lying next to the patient on the couch. There were other people in the room too, quite a few of them. Somebody seemed to have a heart attack. The patient sprang into action to help that man—an older person—doing mouth-to-mouth resuscitation as he had learned in a Red Cross course.

Having thus presented the manifest content of the three dreams that constitute the empirical basis of my discussion, I must temporarily put the dreams aside and provide some additional data concerning this patient whose resistances we are examining. The material I shall adduce constitutes neither the history of the case nor an account of the analytic process. For the purposes of this chapter, I am presenting only those aspects of the analysis that will be relevant to my subsequent consideration of the phenomena that are traditionally referred to as defenses or, as activated in treatment, as resistances. I will first enumerate the various resistances of this patient that I was able to identify and then discuss them separately. In proceeding in this way, I am adopting for expository purposes a schematism that would naturally be out of place in the clinical situation. The experienced analyst, of course, will have little difficulty arriving at an estimation of the general significance of defenses for this patient—his need to employ them and their constructive development-potential safeguarding functions—on the basis of my remarks. Finally, I should note that while I am, on the whole, focusing on the patient's resistances in connection with the analysis of the three dreams that are the clinical foci of my discussion, I will of necessity broaden my focus at times and adduce data concerning his personality in toto, present and past, in order to explain the meaning and significance of the specific resistance that opposed the work of analysis in general and the analysis of dreams in particular.

The four kinds of resistances that I could identify in the course of this man's treatment, manifested during the analysis in general but specifically operative during the analysis of the three dreams in question, were (1) resistances emanating from complex childhood experiences which, according to traditional analysis, are correlated to sibling rivalry; (2) resistances emanating from complex childhood experiences which, according to traditional analysis, are correlated to exhibitionism and voyeurism; (3) resistances emanating from complex childhood experiences which, according to traditional analysis, are correlated to anal-retentive erotism; and (4) resistances emanating from complex childhood experiences which, according to traditional analysis, are correlated to the incomplete resolution of the Oedipus complex.

I will now take up these four types of resistance in sequence, separating them—with somewhat artificial neatness, as I mentioned before—in order to distinguish between the various single aspects of their ultimately interconnected, overall significance. As I discuss them one by one, I will attempt to demonstrate that the models of traditional analysis, although adequate up to a point, fail to provide a conceptual framework that enables us to appreciate the most important functions of these so-called resistances, whereas self psychology, by contrast, does provide such a framework.

Certain resistances against dream analysis were clearly related to a theme with which the patient was familiar from a previous analysis with a senior analyst whose stance was consistently in line with the traditional psychoanalytic view that unsolved conflicts concerning object-instinctual attachments in childhood are the fons et origo of adult psychopathology. Specifically, these resistances related to sibling rivalry with regard to a brother who was two years younger than the patient. But while the topic of sibling rivalry had already played a significant role in the previous analysis—the unveiling of unexpressed hostility to the brother seemed to have been the aim of the analyst— the resistance aspects of this rivalry, so far as I could ascertain, had not been illuminated. Both the analytic work on dream 2 (the dream of sharing the prize) and on dream 3 (the dream of sharing the analytic couch with his friend John W., in reality a man several years younger than he) allowed us to grasp the meaning of these resistances. I will first explain this specific set of resistances from the dynamic-genetic point of view and then describe the form they took, particularly within the framework of the clinical transference.

From the beginning of the patient's analysis with me the topic of rivalry with younger brother figures had been an important theme— one of the three principal themes that I could identify. As I noted above, this theme had also been addressed in the patient's preceding treatment, a classical analysis that had been interrupted after about three years because the analyst, a man in his sixties, perhaps in anticipation of his retirement, had moved to another part of the country. The patient's sibling rivalry, I learned, took as its development nexus the fact that his only sibling, a brother two years his junior, had been the mother's favorite and that—at least as the patient experienced the relationship—the brother had attained this position by being compliant, by conforming to the mother's wishes, and by behaving in just the way that the mother expected children to behave. The patient, feeling first displaced by the new baby and later outclassed by the younger brother's physical attractiveness and adeptness (the patient, by contrast, felt that he was physically unattractive and clumsy), withdrew from competition and angry jealousy into an attitude of superiority, isolation, and nonconformity, particularly in the intellectual field, in which he was indeed superior not only because he was older, but also because of innate talents in this area.

And what were the resistances to the analysis of dreams that were correlated to these interpersonal tensions? The answer is simple. Analysts are much interested in dreams; dreams, as the previous analyst had admonished the patient more than once, are the "royal road to the unconscious." Thus, to supply dreams and to be willing to submit to their analysis represented "conformity," obedience, a playing up to authority in competition with the younger sibling (e.g., my other patients), who would sweetly comply and, in the end, be preferred. Specifically, this attitude would often manifest itself in the analysis via the patient's telling me a dream fragment and then veering off into intellectual side issues about the general meaning of dreams, introducing information he had gathered both from popular psychology magazines and from more scientific publications directed at the educated layman.

In the clinical situation he insisted that I was—covertly if not overtly—putting pressure on him to proceed in accordance with the rules of analysis. In particular, I was pressuring him to have dreams, to remember them, and to analyze them during the sessions—just as the previous analyst was recalled as having done and, perhaps to some extent, really had done. And I will only add, by way of stressing the fact that this specific resistance to dream analysis was specifically related to the brother rivalry of his early life, that it increased and decreased in response to events in the course of the analysis that the patient interpreted as my own turning to a younger brother—who conformingly played up to me—and away from him. In addition to the specific intensification of this set of resistances in response to such specific events—this dynamic connection was at first not recognized and I believe that I only began to see it during the second year of analysis—I have no doubt that this originally specific response had spread out in the course of his life and become nonspecific and diffusely embedded in his personality. The patient had, in other words, become a nonconformist and rebel in many areas and tended to take a negative stance toward what he understood as the cliché attitudes of the majority. (He was opposed, for example, to the liberal views— pro–public aid, pro–environmental protection, anti–death penalty, and so on—that were, according to him, held by most of the colleagues in his law firm and, as he further took for granted, held by most psychoanalysts including me.)

Let me now, at this point, return to dreams 2 and 3 and see whether, against the background of these remarks, we can broaden and deepen our understanding of the sibling rivalry theme and the resistances correlated to it by scrutinizing these two dreams. Dispensing in the context of this presentation with an account of the many associative links that illuminated the latent content of the two dreams, but also, and par excellence, with the whole analytic material emerging during the three-month period on which we are focusing, I can say that both dreams contained clear inferences to the brother theme: in dream 3 the patient was pushed off the analytic couch by a brother figure, whereas in dream 2 he and a brother figure shared a prize. In both dreams, however, the patient established a special bond with the analyst that, in a sense, made him victorious in the end: in dream 2 he lived up to the analyst's expectation that he should be a mature older brother who could share "the prize" with the younger one; in dream 3 it was he—not the brother—who saved the analyst's life. I believe it is clear from the foregoing, even without spelling out those associative

links that led to the specific precipitation of the current clinical transference or those links that led to the past, that the patient had made
progress in the analysis, that features of his personality that had formerly tended to isolate him (rebelliousness, nonconformity, resistance)
were being replaced by attitudes which, while still making him feel
special and superior (pride in displaying an older brother's mature
ability to share the parental offerings with the younger one; pride in
being able to help the parent effectively), did so in a nonisolating,
friendly, and socially acceptable way.

We now leave the sibling-rivalry theme and, continuing to assess
the clinical material from the viewpoint of traditional analysis, turn
to those resistances which emanate from complex childhood experiences that are traditionally correlated to exhibitionism and voyeurism.
I will again artificially restrict myself to this particular resistance without elaborating the obvious interconnections between this resistance
and the preceding one, for example, without commenting on the
competitive aspects of the wish to exhibit (the body, the feces, the
penis) to the mother.

To begin with, I will point out that the themes of exhibitionism and
voyeurism—or rather the inhibition of those component instincts, to
refer to this sector of his personality in drive-psychological terms—
had apparently played only a minor role in the previous analysis as
compared to the theme of sibling rivalry and, especially, as compared
to the theme of anality to be discussed below. And yet, in the analysis
with me, the patient's intense preoccupation with his body—in particular, his negative preoccupation with his body as flawed—was
inescapable.

Rather than gather the data pertaining to the patient's inhibited
exhibitionism and shame along with his inhibited urge to look (as
these impulses became available during the analysis via transference
experiences and via memories especially from adolescence when he
had felt outclassed by his peers in physical appearance and athletic
ability), I will turn directly to the dreams on which I am focusing. In
particular, I wish to examine the exhibitionistic and voyeuristic elements in dreams 1 and 2.

Dream 1, we recall, dealt with the patient's shame at being seen
naked, at exhibiting himself publicly. The relevant drive-psychological
associations should, again, be taken as evidence of the increasing loosening up of his personality, that is, as evidence of analytic progress.
These associations referred to his wish to have some light in the bedroom while having intercourse with his wife, enabling him to see her
and—clearly the more intense craving—enabling her to see him. (His
voyeuristic wish was in the main that of watching the woman looking
at him.) The dream occurred in the aftermath of the frustration of

this wish during the preceding evening. During sexual relations, his wife had insisted on total darkness in the bedroom and had, as he had experienced it, gone through the sexual act mechanically and without the accompanying visual gratification that he craved. Thus, to formulate it in traditional terms, the frustrated exhibitionistic urge had intensified and was therefore defensively inhibited, censoring the wish and underlining the patient's shame in the manifest content of the dream. During the analysis of the dream, the inhibition of this wish resulted in resistances to the emergence of the associative links that dealt with the underlying drive-wishes.

The exhibitionistic desire was also clearly expressed in dream 2. The analyst—the neighbor in the dream—told the patient that his performance was being honored; the honor involved an exhibitionistic display (on the podium). The patient, at the height of his exposure, turned the experience around: it was he who looked at the onlookers (he stunned them by suddenly taking their picture). The camera is, of course, a symbol of the eye—of being looked at, of looking.

Dispensing again with any attempt to provide an account of the associative material that followed the dream and of the relevant content of the ongoing analytic process in which the dream was embedded, I will focus directly on the most striking defensive maneuver depicted in the imagery of the manifest content of the dream: the patient's suddenly turning the situation around, as it were, by taking a picture of the applauding and admiring audience. He surprised and shocked them by his action; by employing the well-known mechanism traditionally characterized as "turning passive into active," he was able to convert the uncomfortable situation of being looked at into a situation in which it was he who did the looking and thus made those who looked at him feel uncomfortable. He (visually) counterattacked when he began to feel (visually) attacked; he embarrassed (shamed) others when he experienced the discomfort of being embarrassed (shamed). Dream 1, I will add, may be said to depict the passive aspect of the problem, whereas dream 2 demonstrates the conversion into activity.

Rather than speculate at this point on possible drive-psychological precursors of the patient's shame (none of his associations led to phallic or anal exhibitionism in early life or to his feeling of inferiority in overall physical equipment vis-à-vis his younger brother in childhood and his peer group during adolescence), I will give a short account of some relevant transference interactions that took place during two sessions about midway between the occurrences of dreams 1 and 2. Toward the end of the first of these two hours the patient told me with great warmth—with an emotionality that would have been almost unimaginable during earlier phases of the analysis—that he had recently, on several occasions, been able to converse freely and openly with his colleagues in the law office and that he had similarly been able to talk warmly with his wife and children instead of acting morose and withdrawn from them as he had generally done in the past. He gratefully added that he believed his newfound ability related to me—that it had been brought about not only by what he had learned from me about himself, but also by what he had learned from the way in which I would speak to him, that is, from the way I would make reconstructions of his past and review situations at home and at work before giving him explanations of his behavior. Indeed, he added that at certain times when he performed more humanly, more securely, more assertively than ever before, it fleetingly crossed his mind that I would be pleased with him and, barely noticed by him but acknowledged in passing, that he spoke with a little bit of my voice, with my choice of words, with my general human attitude. Since this communication came at the end of the session, I said nothing about it beyond remarking that I too had noticed that he was now freer, that things were better, and that I was glad about it.

The next session began, almost with the patient's first words, with an attack on psychoanalysis. Analysts were dogmatic, he said, forcing their opinions on their patients. Some analysts were sicker than their patients—for example, an analyst about whom he had read in a newspaper article had been psychotic, involved with the law, and was ultimately put into prison, where he died. After listening quietly to this tirade for a while, I remarked that this broadside against analysis was in striking contrast to the spirit in which the previous session had ended and I wondered whether there was not some meaningful connection between these two antithetical attitudes. Specifically, I commented that his attack on me must in some way be connected with his gratefully telling me that, via an identification with me and in anticipation of the pleasure that I would experience when learning about his progress, he had been acting in an increasingly relaxed and mature way.

He then proceeded to recount without any logical bridge a memory that had never emerged before in his analysis. The memory dealt with an event that had taken place in law school when he was in his early twenties in the context of a specific educational experience occurring rather late in the curriculum that was called "mock court." Although I am not able to supply details about this pedagogical exercise, I do know that it involved for him (and probably for all the students) a considerable emotional hardship since the performances of the participating students (as attorney for the defense, as prosecutor, as judge, etc.) not only were observed by the faculty and, in particular, by all the students not participating in the trial, but were afterward subjected to frequently scathing criticism, not only concerning the knowledge of the law displayed by the students, but also concerning what one might term their coolness under fire. The patient recalled that he had been very scared of the assignment—he had to act the role of the lawyer for the defense—but that he had handled it in a specific and, as we came to understand more and more profoundly, very characteristic way. He had turned the tables on the audience by pursuing a seemingly erroneous route in his defense of the accused, only to reveal, suddenly and to everyone's stunned surprise, that he had consciously misled them and that what had seemed to have been an error was actually a clever trap destined not only for the participants in the trial but also, and par excellence, for the audience.[3] As matters turned out, the discussion of the participants' performance that followed the trial almost totally bypassed the patient. Through his cunning strategem, in other words, he had fully achieved his purpose, at least at this particular juncture in his career as a law student.

I believe the foregoing memory from law school establishes the fact that the patient's tendency to employ the mechanism of turning passive into active—of shaming, embarrassing, stunning others when he felt that he himself was at the point of being shamed, embarrassed, and stunned—was an old one, ingrained in his personality, and had not occurred de novo in the analytic transference. Having demonstrated this much, I will leave the topic of exhibitionism and of the defense-resistances connected with this patient's exhibitionistic urges and turn to the drive-psychological examination of the next defense-resistance characteristic of this patient. I refer to his resistances emanating from childhood experiences that traditional analysis correlates to anal-retentive erotism.

It is, no doubt, of considerable significance that the theme of anality played hardly any role during the analysis with me, while, according to the patient, it had figured prominently in his previous analysis. As a matter of fact, the patient reminisced, not infrequently, and especially during the first year of the analysis, about this topic as it had been discussed by the previous analyst. In this connection, he tended to repeat with what seemed to me genuine fondness certain phrases that the analyst had used in his (transference) interpretations, such as "first you are shutting yourself off tight and then, suddenly, you are making a big production." It seemed that what little mourning about the loss of the previous analyst this patient could experience was expressed via these memories of the former analyst's interpretations—an important point to which I will later return in a different context.

Thus, even though the theme of anality per se played no important role in this patient's analysis with me—as far as I could ascertain, for example, the patient's associations to the three dreams I am examining did not lead to anal preoccupations and did not, at least as far as I was able to perceive, even allude to "anal" fantasies and/or memories— I will nevertheless provide those data concerning his early life that may be taken as most relevant to anality as a source of resistance in treatment. I do so in the context of my attempt to provide as complete a picture as possible of the traditional outlook on defense-resistances, and especially in view of the fact that the patient's previous analyst had clearly put great stock in this dynamic-genetic connection.

I was alerted from the outset to the possible presence, even to the prominence, of the anal theme via the indirect evidence provided by the fact that an experienced and skillful colleague had seen—and interpreted—the presence of a tendency toward anal holding back, followed by an overwhelming discharge of fecal material. This tendency was purportedly manifested in the interrupted and then overly abundant flow of associative material that the patient "produced" in the analysis. But, to repeat, I was not able to confirm these observations via the careful scrutiny of the transference as it unfolded toward me and became the target of consistent analysis and working through. I did, however, gather a set of specific data from the patient's childhood that can easily be made to accommodate the former analyst's point of view. What I have in mind, specifically, is the fact that the patient's mother gave the patient enemas throughout his childhood—indeed that she continued this regimen until the patient was ten or eleven years old. She did so because she was of the opinion that cleaning out the bowels in this way was a remedy for the patient's "irritability." And she did so, furthermore, because she thought that the patient should have his bowel movements in the morning and not, as seemed to have been his spontaneous tendency, in the later part of the day. This information about the patient's early life would seem to be in tune with the outlook of the former analyst, namely, that the patient resisted the analytic process (i.e., that he resisted the relinquishment of dream material and free associations) just as he had resisted parting with his cherished feces. Furthermore, it ostensibly fits the former analyst's interpretation that only pressure could force the patient to comply with the basic rule—and that such pressure resulted in a sudden outpouring of material after a protracted dearth of it, just as his childhood constipation had given way to the sudden "big production" when he could no longer fight the effect of the enema. As I said earlier, the patient recounted these interpretations of his former analyst with warm approval—at least he did so at those times, especially

during the first year of treatment with me, when he wanted to emphasize that he still preferred the previous analyst to me.

Finally, having discussed the resistances that appear to be correlated
to drive-psychological constellations bearing on the patient's competitiveness with his brother, his fear of passivity and need to turn passive
into active, and his stubborn insistence on the retention of his anal
possessions, we turn now to those resistances emanating from complex
childhood experiences that traditional analysis correlates to an incomplete resolution of the Oedipus complex.

As we begin to scrutinize the analytic material for evidence of an
incompletely resolved Oedipus complex, we should first acknowledge
that all the preceding defense-resistances could be said to be the secondary result of an overall defensive retreat from the conflicts of the
oedipal situation to the conflicts of the preoedipal years. And we could
speculate, furthermore, that the patient's competitiveness with the
younger brother constituted a regressive version of a nuclear competitiveness with his father, that his voyeuristic-exhibitionistic features
and fear of passivity derived from frightening primal-scene observations, and that the anal theme was in toto a defense against castration
anxiety. In arguing this latter point, we might further conjecture that
the patient combated castration anxiety by emphasizing the phallic
aspects of the mother (the active mother with the enema syringe) and
by considering himself the woman, seemingly accepting a castrated
state while secretly preserving the penis.

I believe that I used to be quite skillful at such speculations, and I
am still able, given the almost infinite variety of data obtainable in the
course of every analysis, to demonstrate a drive- and ego-psychological
etiology that can explain the symptoms and character traits of any
patient I see. But, as every analyst knows, our conclusions are not the
result of our intellectual ability to create coherent and meaningful
configurations via the skillful manipulation of the innumerable single
data that we collect; rather, they are the result of our capacity to
postpone closures, to apply closures tentatively, to observe the analysand's reactions to our (tentative) interpretations, and to consider
as great a variety of explanations as possible. When these strictures
are followed, the trend of the total living analytic process as informed
by our cohesive understanding of the patient's total personality and
our in-tuneness with the decisive experiences of his life ultimately
begins to tell us an understandable story. Clearly every explanation,
however valid within the framework of our current knowledge, must
not only be considered a gain, but also a barrier to further thought,
a potential obstacle to seeing the new and appreciating the unexpected. Progress in science, I like to say, is impeded more by our

commitment to old knowledge than by our incapacity to acquire new knowledge.

As I have now outlined the traditional formulations that classify persistent preoedipal drives and the correlated ego-organizations that interact with these drives not only as "fixations" but, even more importantly, as "regressions," I must add that in the clinical material at hand these traditional formulations were not borne out. Despite my openness to discern the Oedipus complex in this patient's analysis and thus come face to face with the resistances that constitute clinical manifestations of the defenses against castration anxiety, I was unable to discover this classically pivotal configuration, at least not in its role as the nucleus of psychopathology. I was not only unable to find evidence of a pathogenic Oedipus complex in the material pertaining to the three dreams I am examining, but also in the material that preceded them and followed them right up to the end of the patient's long analysis.

Case Illustration: The Self Psychological Approach to Defense and Resistance

Having discussed at some length the drive- and ego-psychological approach to the specific defense-resistances of my patient, particularly in the context of the three key dreams I have singled out for consideration, I can now return to the mainstream of our inquiry by posing the following question: how does psychoanalytic self psychology approach the "defenses" and "resistances" of this patient?

In one respect, my response to this question will adopt a form analogous to my exposition of the drive- and ego-psychological outlook. Once again, that is, I will not dwell on the generalities of experience-distant theory, but will present the self psychological outlook as it relates to the specific case material at hand. In a second respect, however, the remarks that follow will not parallel my discussion of the drive- and ego-psychological outlook. To wit, my self psychological commentary will be at variance with the foregoing schematic depiction of individual defense-resistances by focusing not directly on the defenses, but on the patient's total personality as I came to understand it. Only secondarily, after outlining the overall psychological picture, will I offer a specific estimation of this patient's defense-resistances against the background of my understanding of his psychic organization as a whole.

Before resuming the clinical discussion of this case, I would offer the following caveat: my decision first to focus on the total personality of the patient and only subsequently to examine his defenses and resistances is not arbitrary but rather an intrinsic constituent of the overall stance of the self psychologist. Thus, what has by now become a deeply ingrained aspect of my own cognitive style—to construct first, however tentatively, a hypothesis concerning the structure of the patient's nuclear self, the outline of its central program, of the basic means by which the program is to be realized, and only subsequently to assess such details as psychic mechanisms against the background of this tentative overview of the personality—seems to be scientifically justified.

Experience undoubtedly plays a role in allowing the analyst to proceed in this way. Once he has mastered his repertory, the master pianist does not focus primarily on each detail, at least not consciously, but puts himself in the service of the mood of the piece he is playing, trying to communicate the artistic message of the composer with whose intentions he has become identified.[4] But even if we examine the question of whether to look for details of psychic functioning or to focus on the overall configuration of the self from the limited standpoint of one's increasing mastery, our answer can by no means be the simple one that we should first concentrate on detail and only later shift to overall configurations. Attention to detail and construction of a total picture should be taught from the beginning side by side, not one after the other. I therefore consider it a pedagogical error to direct the attention of psychoanalytic students at first only to mechanisms and to postpone the learning of how one goes about forming a picture of the patient's self until they have become more experienced. The student must from the beginning try to do both things at the same time. What does shift with experience is the *conscious* emphasis—the master will pick up the details effortlessly and without the glee of discovery; he will not jump at the patient's slip of the tongue, for example, or at his resistance to "insight." Such moves, to my mind, are evidence of inexperience.

Much more significant than the movement from the analysis of psychic details toward the attempt to trace the outlines of the nuclear self as an aspect of the professional maturation of the individual analyst is the cognitive relation that obtains between the whole and its parts in complex organizations. I am referring, in this context, to the relation that obtains between man's psychic organization and the products of his creativity. Disregarding very occasional exceptions to the rule, it is not the parts that explain the meaning and significance of the whole but the whole that explains the meaning and significance of the parts—or, at the very least, an understanding of the whole is more frequently helpful in grasping the meaning and significance of the parts than the other way around. Moreover, in those instances where the attempt to grasp the configuration of the whole (e.g., the nuclear self of an analysand; the basic purpose of an excavated struc-

ture of an unknown culture) is frustrated for some time and we are
reduced to describing the formal aspects of details in isolation, the
details will begin to make sense only when the overall purpose, design,
and destiny of the whole (the nuclear life program of a person; the
purpose of an excavated building [was it a factory? a dwelling? a
religious shrine?]) have been discovered.

It is in harmony with the last mentioned principle that I now return
to the examination of the so-called defense-resistances of my patient.
Specifically, I will examine the vicissitudes of this patient's self in order
to show that, without this knowledge, we cannot acquire an appreciation of the significance of the "defenses" in this man's personality
structure and of the "resistances" that he mobilized in psychoanalytic
treatment.

The Patient's Self Development

What can I report about this patient's personality? The firmly established thinking patterns of the analyst lead me immediately to the
childhood situation as I have been able to reconstruct it from the
observation of the transference and from the patient's direct memories.

The emotional milieu of this patient's childhood was overwhelmingly, though not completely, determined by his mother. She ruled
the family mainly by her silent presence—meaningful verbal communications not only between the parents and the children but also
between the parents themselves played an unusually small role in this
family—and her disapproval, unaccompanied by verbal threats but
clearly expressed in her face, was often followed by a severe (but
never sadistic) punitive action: spanking of the children; sudden and
irrevocable dismissal of household personnel of many years of service
who transgressed the rules by lying, being late, or covering up small
misdeeds of the children; removal of disobedient pets to whom the
children had formed emotional attachments; and the like. Emotional
coldness and joylessness pervaded the family as a result of the quasi-
military machinelike outlook on life imposed by the mother. But let
me move on to a few actions that will illustrate these general remarks
about the mother, more or less as my patient reported them to me at
various points in the analysis.

First I will briefly retell the patient's account of an episode—it may
have occurred several times with slight variations, perhaps when the
boy was between the ages of seven and nine—which we came to call
"the interrupted basement game." Although it had great significance
in more than one way—I will return to it in the context of describing
the patient's father and (maternal) grandparents as well as in describing those aspects of his mother's personality that surfaced briefly in
certain settings—I introduce it here mainly with reference to the

mother's personality and the nature of her influence on the family. As the patient described the incident, the father once played hide-and-go-seek with his two sons in the basement of their house. They were all apparently having a very good time, laughing and shrieking with delight, when the mother suddenly appeared and looked at them. According to the patient, she did not utter a single word but her wordless disapproval on learning what the laughter was all about was unmistakable. Although she left almost immediately and, as I mentioned before, said not a word, all the joy seemed to leave the three of them and, after listlessly playing on for a while, they stopped. The boys went to their rooms, and the father, as usual, went to his club.

Another episode is equally illustrative of the mother's personality and the way in which it manifested itself in her interactions with the patient when he was a child. One morning, probably around the age of four, the patient woke up from a nightmare. He had dreamt that he was falling off some high building. Still frightened, he ran to his parents, seeking protection, calming, and reassurance. His mother responded by telling him in an unemotional voice and with an expressionless face that he was to get dressed immediately. And she then took him, still frightened to death, downtown to the top of a skyscraper to teach him the lesson that there was nothing to be afraid of.

Finally, I want to mention the mother's attitude with regard to the patient's bowel functions. Concretely speaking, she had two strong convictions that determined her actions in this area. First, she was convinced that regularity was of paramount importance and that the bowels had to be moved every morning. Second, she was convinced that psychic disturbances in her children (including irritability, restlessness, fatigue, failure to concentrate on learning tasks, and the like) were due to the presence of feces inside the body and that, correspondingly, the cure for these disturbances was the elimination of the noxious substance. The vehicle of the cure was, of course, the enema, which the mother applied not only when the children were irritable and the like but in order to bring about the desirable morning evacuation instead of the undesirable evening one.

These three vignettes of the mother's actual behavior during the patient's childhood must for the moment suffice in creating a mental picture of her as she was remembered and described by my patient. She seems to have lacked warmth, was duty-oriented and moralistic (with a tendency toward the ritualistic), and on the whole created (exceptions will be noted later) a joyless, regimented life for her family. She appears to have lacked warmth and natural understanding for people in general and children in particular. In addition to these personality features, which my patient and I ultimately referred to as "American Gothic" (I supplied the term but the patient was familiar with Grant Wood's painting), there was also a good deal of evidence that the mother experienced a diffuse hypochondria, not so much about herself—at least we could not pinpoint any data that would have confirmed this supposition—but about her husband and, especially, her children. The patient believed her hypochondriacal worries were particularly focused on him. His mother became deeply concerned about the occurrence of minor colds and the usual childhood diseases which the children inevitably contracted—the patient never forgot his amazement when the school doctor made the terse diagnosis "healthy youngster" after examining him in first grade—but she was also quite pessimistic about their future. She counseled them to take simple, routine jobs that would give them security rather than undertake more challenging careers that would be more than they could handle.

The patient's father remained a somewhat vague figure in the analysis for a long time. At any rate, memories about him and emotions expressed toward him were minimal at first. In the analysis, his importance for the patient was at first as overshadowed by the importance of the mother as the mother had in fact overshadowed the patient's father during his childhood. His presence was only dimly outlined for a long time. In fact, he never became quite as clearly defined for me as the mother, even though his significance in the patient's childhood (and in the transference) was ultimately recognized. He seems to have been, potentially at least, a more joyful individual than the mother. He was quite successful in his career (he was a vice-president in charge of labor relations for a huge industrial concern) and during his college years had been an outstanding athlete who earned a number of trophies. Still, despite these masculine assets, the father was on the whole experienced by the patient and his brother as a distant and taciturn person who had little interest in them and who never spoke about his work or past achievements when he was at home. As I mentioned before, the patient's father was in fact not even much of a physical presence at home. While he shared the family dinner, a meal characterized either by silence or by conversation about a select number of almost pointedly meaningless topics (the weather, the food) in which the children were not allowed to participate, he would soon go out again.

Keeping in mind these psychologically significant facts about the patient's parents and the childhood atmosphere in which the patient grew up, I now turn directly to the task of providing an overall view of the patient's major personality problems. Readers familiar with self psychology will undoubtedly anticipate much of what I am going to say because, in many respects, this patient's problems were similar to the problems of other patients I have described, including, for example, Mr. X. (1977, pp. 199–219) and Mr. Z. (1979). Although there

are considerable differences between the personalities of these three
patients, the emotional constellation they hold in common was clearly
of the greatest significance for each of them. The patient discussed
here, like Mr. X. and Mr. Z., was exposed to development-thwarting
influences from the side of the mother, whereas his father, though
apparently possessing more healthy vigor and a greater capacity for
joyful living, withdrew from the home and from his sons both physically and emotionally. The result was the usual and predictable one:
an attempt to heal the self via the creation of compensatory structures,
or, expressed in dynamic terms, an attempt to turn away from the
mother and to heal the defect in the self via the potentially development-enhancing reactivation of the selfobject father.

Consider the patient's predicament as a child. He had a severely
pathological mother who harbored odd convictions about health and
who seemed, despite her apparent firmness (a near-paranoid rigidity
rather than true strength), to have been basically insecure and hypochondriacal. Like the father of Senatspraesident Schreber (see Freud
1911, 1953, 12:12 ff.), moreover, this mother enacted her convictions
not only by attitude but also through actions toward her son. The
psychic makeup of the boy's father, to repeat, appears to have been
basically healthier than that of the mother. He must have been an
active, outgoing, lively man in his business activities, relating easily to
people and free to show his enjoyment of life. His greatest shortcoming with regard to the son was that, intimidated by his wife and fearful
of being enslaved by her grim and utterly humorless outlook on life,
he was content to flee the home both emotionally and physically,
thereby sacrificing his fatherly instincts and abandoning his sons to
his wife's influence.

And how did the patient react to this situation when he was a child?
How did he manage to remain as relatively healthy as he did, retaining
the ability, despite problems and inhibitions, to become a reasonably
well functioning and clearly nonpsychotic adult? This is the crucial
question that I will now try to answer as directly and concisely as I
can.

Put in a nutshell: when this patient was a child, exposed to the
emotionally deleterious and self development-stifling situation I have
described, he still managed to keep a significant remnant of his nuclear
self alive, thus remaining at least potentially capable of responding
with renewed structure-building to new opportunities for further
growth. Expressed in technical terms, he remained potentially analyzable. Expressed in everyday, human terms, he never quite gave up
hope.

It is now our task to answer two interrelated questions concerning
the psychological problem at hand: (1) the predominantly genetic

question of *why* this patient was able to preserve his nuclear self, and (2) the predominantly dynamic question of *how* he performed the psychological feat of preserving this core structure.

The answer to the first question is twofold, in harmony with the complemental series of genetic factors (innate and environmental) of which Freud spoke (1953, 16:347).[5] We will first acknowledge the presence of congenital capacities promoting health and development; these capacities take the form of an innately present vigor of the nuclear self. This vigor, in turn, is tantamount to the nuclear self's resistiveness to disintegration and capacity to fight noxious influences. We cannot yet fully describe and explain this vigor and the resulting resistiveness to destruction in psychological terms.[6] But we can already take some steps toward defining some of its constituents via the discovery of the specific functions that the child mobilizes in order to maintain his nuclear self and thereby preserve the potential to fulfill its nuclear program and realize his specific psychological destiny. Thus, disregarding for the moment the extrinsic influences emanating from the environment—not an easy task for the psychoanalyst who thinks of genetic factors almost exclusively in terms of childhood experiences—I suggest that a simple way of bringing some preliminary order to the psychology of the intrinsic psychic equipment of the child is to view it against the background of the capacity to respond to the traumatization of the emerging self via the formation of (a) compensatory and (b) defensive structures.

In the specific case at hand, the patient's strength took the form of an innate capacity to maintain a hope for a satisfactory selfobject that would in the future enable him to consolidate the structures he had already formed, however weakly and tentatively, in childhood. As in the cases I have formerly described (for example, Mr. M., Mr. X., Mr. Z.), so too with our patient: he more or less relinquished the mirroring selfobject and attached himself to a potentially idealizable one.[7]

Concerning our patient's capacity to form defensive structures—structures used to *maintain* the remnants of the self, that is, to maintain the status quo, however unsatisfactory it may be—I will give only two illustrative examples. There were defensive structures that were clearly laid down to perform very specific self-remnant-preserving functions: the patient's "turning passive into active," for example, as evidenced in the transference dream of counterattacking the audience by unexpectedly snapping a picture of them at the very moment when he had received at least a moderate amount of the mirroring he needed. (This group of defensive structures was essentially retained in its original form and did not serve any function other than "self-remnant preservation.") In addition, there were defensive structures which, although originally serving the same simple preservative function, were later capable of a developmental forward move that allowed them to become an asset of the mature personality, particularly after the task of forming solid compensatory structures had been successfully advanced. In this latter category, we may mention the patient's early withdrawal upon himself, specifically, his thinking and reasoning powers with which he had been amply endowed ab initio. The further development of these powers (a process somewhat related to that comprehended by Hartmann's [1964, pp. 1–18] conceptualization of "secondary autonomy") later became a considerable asset to our patient. (For an earlier discussion of this same type of development, see Kohut 1977, p. 216.)

It is with a sigh of relief that I now turn from the innately given strengths in our patient's personality to those self-enhancing aspects of his environment that supported the preservation of a self, however weak and fragmented, along with the hope for an adequate selfobject that would strengthen and consolidate it. What in the childhood surroundings were the sources from which the patient drew at least that modicum of strength necessary to form a self that remained more or less cohesive as the center of initiative, albeit in very circumscribed areas of functioning, and, more importantly, a self that did not give up hope of someday being able to complete its development? In the following, I will discuss these sources by taking them up in the following sequence: the patient's father, his maternal grandfather, his maternal grandparents, and certain aspects of his mother. Although of some importance too, I will omit consideration of certain supports in the patient's later life, including particular high school teachers and one or two friends from that same period.

Let me begin by examining the positive contribution to the strengthening of the self that was made by the patient's father. As I have noted, he was a more vigorous, joyful, and less psychologically disturbed individual than the mother. The games in the basement with his children, the enjoyment he must have found in his work, and his former athletic prowess all support this hypothesis. Yet, after an analysis of many years, I cannot say for certain that the patient's remaining, marginal vigor was to any significant extent derived from his experiences with his father. The best one can say is probably that the father does not seem to have actively interfered with the patient's development, at least not in early life. Later on, the father seems to have knuckled under to the mother even more completely than when the patient was a child. I will not go into details here but will at least mention that he gave up his beloved job when the mother insisted that he devote himself to a task that *she* had set for him. This transaction occurred at the very point when the father himself could have advanced his career by becoming one of the chief executives within his industry. After this final capitulation to his wife, the father actively disapproved of important intellectual forward steps on his son's part, including his decision to become a lawyer. Where he had formerly failed to stand up for the boy against the mother, he subsequently allied himself with her and acted as her spokesman.

I will next turn to the examination of a figure that for a number of reasons was more invigorating to the patient's self than the father: the maternal grandfather. His significance is threefold: as the unsurpassed male figure in the life of the patient's mother, as a constituent of the life-affirming atmosphere in the grandparents' home from which the patient derived important psychological nourishment during several summer vacations in childhood, and as an available object capable of satisfying certain of the patient's idealizing needs.

There is little to be said concerning the first point since its meaning is obvious. The enormous persistent attachment of the patient's mother to her father, in particular her persistent idealization of him, resulted in her view of her husband—the patient's father—as second-rate. This low estimation prevented him from attaining the status in the home that the patient needed in his search for an idealizable selfobject in later childhood. It also seems possible that the mother's idealization of her father deprived her of the emotional capacity to display that development-enhancing maternal attitude toward her sons that is often, quite erroneously, referred to as "overestimation of the child." Instead of taking pleasure in their talents and envisioning their potential achievements with pride, she devalued their present strengths and future possibilities, crediting them only with the ability to be employees able to hold stable, risk-free, uninspiring positions in life. Still, in the face of all these deleterious results of the mother's attachment to her father, there was undoubtedly a positive aspect to it: the boy could at least see that the mother *was* capable of idealizing a man (albeit in the way a child looks up to a grown-up, not as the admiration of one mature person for another).

There is comparably little I need say about the second way in which the maternal grandfather was important to the patient, that is, as a constituent of the life-affirming atmosphere he found in the grandparents' home. The reason for my brevity here is that I must rely on memories that contained little if any detailed content concerning the interaction between his grandparents, but related only to the overall flavor of the atmosphere in their home during (perhaps) three summer vacations and to the immediate results that staying with them had on the patient. Thus, I have no specific information that the grandparents themselves accounted for these beneficial results. All I can report is that during the three summers which the patient and his brother spent with their grandparents (the father was not there, except for brief weekend visits; the mother spent perhaps half of one or two of these vacations with them), the boys were happy, outgoing, successful in sports, and able to participate in peer group activities.

I can provide more information about the grandfather's availability as a target for my patient's idealizing needs. His life story was a romantic one not only because it depicted a journey from comparative poverty to great wealth, but also because he had been a pioneering man in sparsely settled regions when he was young, had survived many dangers, and had led an altogether adventurous life about which he was by no means reluctant to talk. I will also add that, in striking contrast to the situation in the patient's own home, the grandmother clearly admired her man and, while apparently a strong and secure individual herself, did not compete with her husband and even encouraged him to be in the limelight.

Having to this point discussed not only the healthful influence of the patient's grandfather but also the atmosphere that both grandparents provided for the patient during several summer vacations (the patient was in lower school at the time of these vacations, somewhere between the ages of seven and eleven), I now return to the patient's mother. I wish to outline certain circumscribed areas of support she may have provided for the patient's self, even though her overall influence was unquestionably deleterious.

Positively tinged memories of the mother were supplied by the patient during the analysis, but for a number of reasons I would largely—though not wholly—doubt their validity. For one thing, the emergence of many of these memories was not accompanied by a mood of joy and satisfaction. Rather, they occurred in the context of the back-and-forth movements that characterized the patient's hesitant loosening of the ties that still bound him tightly to his mother. Specifically, he would gain some distance from the mother imago and begin to doubt the proper functioning of her mind. For a lengthy stretch of the analysis, however, every such move to gain emotional distance from her would be followed by a move back to her during which he would doubt the current functioning of his own mind and accuse himself of falsely accusing her. It was during such moments of emotional rebound that he would adduce the positive actions of his mother as proof that he must have been wrong in his preceding assessment of her. The second reason for my doubts about the validity of the development-enhancing memories of the mother (qua maternal selfobject) is that many of these positive memories emerged in the context of the summers with the grandparents, that is, they referred to times when mother and sons were staying with the grandparents. Although there is little doubt that the mother indeed behaved in a much warmer and more relaxed fashion toward the boys during these interludes, it seems to me that she did so more in the role of an older sister than of a mother. Like the boys, she benefited from the relaxed atmosphere of her parents' home and was supported by her own relationship with her parents, that is, the chronic sense of being over-burdened under which I believe she labored throughout her married life receded and she was able to bestow some genuine emotional gifts on her children.

Still, having expressed my doubts, I must add that there are also good reasons not to discount entirely the mother's role as a self-supportive agent. Although, as far as I could determine, she made a very minimal contribution during the major part of the year, she did seem to relax and offer more during vacations—even when they were spent apart from her parents. With regard to the patient, her most important activity was reading aloud to the boys during the evenings; she appears not only to have picked solidly boyish stories for them, but also to have read with a gusto that spilled over into the activities of the day. After reading a story about a boy and a dog, for example, they all decided—and actually carried out their plan—to get a dog and name him after the dog in the story. And reading for pleasure indeed became a source of genuine gratification for my patient in later life. Furthermore, I believe that the content of some of the stories that the mother selected for her readings—adventure stories in exotic faraway lands—contributed to another very gratifying adult activity of the patient: his undertaking adventurous, even daring, trips and his interest in exotic cultures.

But having said this much, I must not leave the impression that the positive, life-sustaining forces that prevented the patient from falling even more seriously ill than he did can be attributed to the mother. One fact above all leads me to this conclusion: the selfobject transferences, the analysis of which ultimately helped the patient, moved gradually away from the mother and toward the paternal symbols of grandfather and father. As the patient himself once summed it up when musing about the question of what the family of his childhood would have thought of his undertaking an analysis: his father probably would not have understood what it was all about, but would not have disapproved; his grandparents also would not have understood what was involved, but would have said: "If it helps you, go ahead!" But his mother would have understood—and been inexorably opposed to it.

The Patient's "Defenses" and "Resistances"

Now that I have outlined the dominant influences of the patient's childhood that thwarted or enhanced the firm establishment of his self, I can return to the defenses and resistances that could be discerned during his analysis. I will be neither systematic nor complete; my aim is not to give an encompassing presentation of this case, but to demonstrate the change in our perception of the significance of these phenomena, whether considered as endopsychic potentialities (defenses) or as potentialities expressed in action during the analysis (resistances). Still, since I want to provide a logical framework for my undertaking, I will proceed to discuss the defense-resistances of the patient in the order of their increasing psychological depth and significance as I evaluate them now. Specifically, and again in traditional terms, I will begin with the resistances related to the theme of sibling rivalry, turn next to those related to the patient's exhibitionism and voyeurism, proceed to those connected with anality, and finally discuss those resistances centering around homosexual and competitive-aggressive impulses broadly tied to the father relationship.

In view of the fact that "resistances" are often clearly related to the analysand's aggression directed toward the analyst and the analytic task, I feel that I should here digress for a moment and address the widespread misperception that self psychology, both theoretically and clinically, neglects aggression, that is, fails to assign it the significance it has in human life and fails to deal with it clinically by confronting the patient with its presence and encouraging him to acknowledge and experience it. In fact, nothing could be further from the truth, regarding both the theoretical formulations of self psychology and the self psychological clinician's responses to his analysands. As a matter of fact, as far as my own recent clinical experience is concerned, I have witnessed much more intense—and genuinely experienced!—aggression in my analysands than when I was working within the conceptual framework of traditional analysis.

With regard to our theoretical formulations about human aggressiveness and destructiveness, I can be brief since I have fully discussed these issues elsewhere (Kohut 1978b, 2:615–58). Suffice it to say here that I sharply differentiate between aggressions directed at objects (who stand in the way of cherished goals) and those directed at selfobjects (who have damaged the self). Notwithstanding the fact that the same attitudes or actions may contain both competitive aggressiveness *and* narcissistic rage, this distinction remains valid and important. I will add: (1) that there are many instances in which one type of aggression (especially narcissistic rage) obtains with no (or only minimal) admixture of the other type of aggression, and (2) that the social and endopsychic consequences of the two aggressive potentialities are significantly different. Aggressions directed against objects with whom we compete (or who block our pursuit of a cherished goal) cease as soon as the objects cease to be obstacles or as soon as we have reached our goal. In addition, these aggressions do not produce psychopathology; when they occur in childhood (e.g., in the context of oedipal competition or sibling rivalry), they do not become the nucleus of psychoneuroses. Narcissistic rage, on the other hand, cannot be satisfied via successful action against the offender—the injury lingers and so does the rage. It is narcissistic rage in childhood, therefore (e.g., against the parents or siblings as selfobjects), that does indeed play a significant role in the genesis of self pathology.

With regard to the criticism that we neglect human hostility in the clinical situation, I can also be quite specific in my reply. We rarely have the occasion to "interpret" the presence of object-directed aggressiveness; the conflicts evoked by this type of aggression (e.g., guilt or an unstable equilibrium between currents of fondness and anger) are not constitutive of psychopathology, however severe they might be, but part and parcel of normal human experience. The role of narcissistic rage, however, is keenly appreciated by the self psychologically informed psychoanalyst.

One illustration of this fact will be superior to a theoretical exposition. A colleague whom I had analyzed for a number of years told me, as he reflected on what he had achieved during the treatment, that it was "ironical" that while psychoanalytic scuttlebutt had it that self psychologists underplayed human aggression and hostility (supposedly by being too "nice" to their analysands), it was in the analysis with me and not in his training analysis with an analyst who repeatedly and insistently confronted him with the evidence of his hostility (especially in the transference) that he had for the first time experienced—deeply and fully—an intense wish to kill. And he told me, in retrospect, of an analytic session long ago (I believe it was about a year or two into his analysis) when he experienced this wish for the first time—at least for the first time with unmistakable intensity. It occurred in the aftermath of the analysis of a dream—not a "self-state dream," I should note, in view of another set of misapprehensions about self psychology that has come our way—on which we had been working for several sessions. The dream in question had taken place in a city block not far from my office. The patient observed a frail man walking along the block that led to a broad boulevard where a statue of a husky, muscular, proud warrior on horseback stood. As the patient watched the man walking along slowly, unsteadily, and weakly, he noticed that the man was not real but some kind of straw doll. Overcome with anger, the patient plunged a knife several times into the straw doll man. To his amazement—there was no evidence of guilt or horror about the deed in the dream—thick red blood flowed out between the straw.

The patient remembered that he had had analogous dreams during his previous analysis and that the analyst had always, after listening to his associations, interpreted oedipal hostility against the father (i.e., the wish to belittle him and kill him) and encouraged the patient to get in touch with these emotions, especially in the transference. And the patient also remembered how frustrating it had all been: the evidence seemed clear-cut and incontrovertible, but his insight was only intellectual. In particular, he had been unable to experience a genuine wish to kill the analyst—only moderate conscious anger at the analyst for not being able to help him. And how, in treatment with me, could he for the first time get in touch with such a wish? The reason, as he saw it, was the following: I had never referred to his anger, never confronted him with the murderous intent depicted in the dream, and never talked about defenses against emotions that would have to be experienced in order to make the insight psychologically valid, genuine, and meaningful, as his former analyst had done. Instead, against all his expectations that my response to the dream would parallel the response of the former analyst, I had on the whole listened quietly for several sessions to the material that emerged after the dream, partly via direct associations to the dream elements and partly in seeming independence of the dream. And when I finally responded, I focused neither on the dream in isolation nor on the specific aggressive act depicted in the dream nor on the specific murderous wish he supposedly harbored and against which he defended himself by splitting off his emotions. What I concentrated on in my interpretation, according to his memory, was his disappointment in having a weak father, both in his childhood and now in the transference (it was *my* physical frailty that the straw doll exhibited). It was in response to my interpretation—that in the analysis he was still trying to get to a strong father (the statue of the man on horseback) and that he was disappointed and frustrated because I was not such a father—that he began to talk not only about the small event in the hour preceding the dream that triggered the dream but also about his early life. These recollections—that he was the last-born child of by then aging and overburdened parents; that he grew up in an atmosphere of retrenchment, depression, and withdrawal; that his father was chronically ill, dying when the patient was eleven—fleshed out my skeletal interpretation and ultimately led to his full awareness of the intensity of the rage associated with his wish to get rid of the sick and depressed father. Unsurprisingly, it was not the father's physical weakness that enraged him but his lack of emotional vigor; and the same held true in the transference. The former analysis had in essence come to grief, not because the analyst had been physically weak but because he was unable to understand why the patient attacked and belittled him. It was his lack of in-tuneness that had made him a straw doll. When, however, the patient in his rage and frustration attacked me, real blood was finally forthcoming.

To return to the mainstream of this inquiry and thus to the resistances of my lawyer patient as they clustered around his three dreams. As I said, I will discuss his defense-resistances in the order of their, in my evaluation, increasing psychological depth and significance. In traditional terms, I will speak first of those related to sibling rivalry, then of those related to anality, and finally of those that may be seen as opposing the revelation of passive homosexuality and oedipal competitiveness, that is, those that concern the father theme. To begin with those defensive aspects of his personality and the correlated resistive aspects of his behavior during his analysis embedded in a sibling rivalry complex, there is no doubt that his younger brother played an emotionally important role in his childhood. He maintained that the brother was physically superior to him—in particular, better coordinated—and by virtue of both his physical grace and his compliance was preferred by the mother. The specific characterological defense that the patient instituted in response to this situation was an attitude of chronic superior withdrawal. In object-instinctual terms: fearing the trauma of having his libidinal wishes frustrated because his mother loved the brother but not him, he denied the presence of the drive-wish and withdrew into narcissistic isolation—the term "narcissistic" here being used in the traditional pejorative sense—feeling "superior" and contemptuous of the brother, whom he saw as compliant and accommodating. This attitude also played a significant role during the analysis, especially at first. Whenever the patient felt understood, he would invariably withdraw. Other patients (i.e., the brother) might accept my interpretations and be glad to have found someone responsive to them. The patient, however, did not wish to be understood and was indifferent to my ability—and the ability of analysis as a whole—to understand and help him. Thus, after proudly reporting to me that he had behaved maturely toward his wife and, in his dream, receiving recognition from me (albeit shared with a brother) of his progress, he suddenly turned the situation topsy-turvy and, raising the camera and exposing me to the painful limelight, denied having asked for a self-confirming mirroring response from the mother-analyst.

I see that in this last formulation I have already slipped into the vocabulary of self psychology—and so be it. Clearly, what is involved here is not a struggle for object love but a need for self-enhancing reflection: to be looked at, approvingly and admiringly and, with this self-confirmation, to be able to go on with the further firming and development of this core of our being.

And what is the self psychologist's response to this "defense-resis-tance"? A touch of censure cautiously phrased and gently expressed? An explanation that the attitude stands in the way of analytic progress, constituting a rejection of the analyst's help? The analytic demon-stration of a deeper wish (i.e., the wish to shine) covered over by the frozen attitude that opposed the reactivation of the conflict? Yes, all these are invoked to varying extents, as I pointed out long ago (Kohut 1978*b*, 2:547–61).

But there is also a good deal more. The decisive step that we un-dertake—to say that self psychology "advocates" this step does not adequately acknowledge the fact that, once the broad principles of self psychology have been adopted, the step is taken spontaneously as a natural part of the analyst's attitude toward his patient—is cor-related with our understanding that the so-called defense-resistances are neither defenses nor resistances. Rather, they constitute valuable moves to safeguard the self, however weak and defensive it may be, against destruction and invasion. It is only when we recognize that the patient has no healthier attitude at his disposal than the one he is in fact taking that we can evaluate the significance of "defenses" and "resistances" appropriately. The patient protects the defective self so that it will be ready to grow again in the future, to continue to develop from the point in time at which its development had been interrupted. And it is this recognition, deeply understood by the an-alyst who essentially sees the world through his patient's eyes while he analyzes him, that best prepares the soil for the developmental move forward that the stunted self of the analysand actively craves. Such recognition serves the patient better than anything else the an-alyst can offer, however deeply ingrained his traditional "realism" may be at such moments.

But why do we continue to have difficulty acting in accordance with this principle? There are two reasons, one of lesser and one of greater, even decisive, importance. The lesser one is the analyst's narcissistic vulnerability, his frustration at seeing his help rejected, as it were. And being narcissistically wounded, we tend to become enraged and then to rationalize our counterattack in scientific, moral, or, most frequently, morally tinged scientific terms. The more important rea-son is that we are steeped in a morality-tinged theory about the ther-apeutic centrality of truth-facing that is interwoven with a comparably morality-tinged scientific model about the need to make the uncon-scious conscious. In terms of this model, anything that opposes "mak-ing conscious" or "becoming conscious" is a resistance. In the self psychological outlook on the psychoanalytic process, this model, al-though retained and clearly useful in explaining certain details of the psychic process observed by the therapist (e.g., when he begins to analyze a dream), becomes subordinated to the theory of thwarted and remobilized self development responding to self development-thwarting and self development-enhancing selfobjects.

Specifically, with reference to my lawyer patient's dream of stunning his audience by taking its picture (dream 2), we can see how he safe-guarded his self against the intrusions of a mother he had come to appreciate as "a little crazy." And he frequently saw analysis in just this way: as a system that, although seemingly rational and scientific on the surface, was also "a little crazy," that is, more committed to demonstrating that its theories are correct and that psychic reality is explained by them than to learning open-mindedly what is going on in the patient's mind. It was in the context of our increasing under-standing of this patient's attitudes toward theories that are imposed on reality that we began to see that his "contempt" for his brother's "compliance" vis-à-vis his mother was not as comparatively simple a phenomenon as we had initially suspected. Specifically, it was not contempt and the resolve not to compete with the brother that made him adopt a stance of superior isolation, although this was the way he himself had always understood his attitude. Rather, the isolation was the product of his early recognition, however dimly formed, that his brother was being irrevocably damaged by the mother because, unlike the patient, he could not maintain the integrity of his self against her oppressive demands and expectations. And this brother who had been the mother's favorite did indeed emerge as much more damaged in later life—he became a drifter with multiple unstable relationships, unsuccessful, and unwilling or unable to seek thera-peutic help.[8]

Only one more word before we turn to the other defense-resistance clusters of my lawyer. It bears stressing once more that the whole concept of defense-resistance belongs in essence to a psychology—traditional analysis as it bears the imprint of Freud's preoccupations—that sees progress and lack of progress, success and failure, against the background of a cognitive orientation. To know or not to know, that is the question scrutinized by traditional analysis. Self psychology, on the other hand, with its background of a self-state orientation, would express its preoccupation in closer approximation to Shake-speare's sweet prince and, having in mind the self and its existence, ask the questions concerning progress and lack of progress, success and failure, as a to be or not to be. To be, in other words, the main-tenance of even the diseased remnants of the self is preferable to not being, that is, to accept the takeover of another's personality rather than his actively elicited responsiveness. The cognitive axis applies well, as I said before, to the mechanics of mental processes. But this knowledge has now become preconscious, second nature to the analyst who devotes his attention to observing the vicissitudes of a patient's self. Occasionally, rarely, he might for a moment pay attention to the details of a mental mechanism that may be discernible—like a master pianist who will for a moment think of finger positions and the like. But on the whole, this is not the self psychologist's interest any longer. Like the pianist who devotes all his attention to the conception of the work he performs and to the artistic message it transmits, so also the experienced self psychologically informed analyst: the details recede as he scrutinizes the gradual strengthening of his patient's self and the selfobject factors that enhance or hinder this development.

Having examined in detail my patient's defense-resistances as interwoven with the theme of sibling rivalry and having reevaluated their significance from the vantage point of self psychology, I can now take up more briefly those resistance clusters that relate to the exhibitionism-voyeurism theme, the anality theme, and the theme of oedipal competitiveness. I can be brief not only because all these themes are interwoven with one another and, by implication, have already been discussed to some extent in the foregoing, but also because I am only interested in demonstrating a principle which, I trust, has already been delineated with sufficient clarity not to require much further elaboration. The operative principle—one might call it *the principle of the primacy of self preservation*—will be further illustrated in the discussion of the other three resistance clusters referred to above. I will only mention here, as an aside, that the old self psychological formulation of the separate developmental lines of self and object proves again to be useful. Self preservation as a technical self psychological term is unrelated to such sociocultural, value-laden terms as selfishness, "narcissism," egotism, and the like. Successful self preservation is not only compatible with the full flowering of investment in objects; it is, for many individuals, though significantly not for all, a precondition for "object love."

Concerning the exhibitionism-voyeurism theme, I will begin by reiterating that the patient naturally needed to be "mirrored," that is, to be looked upon with joy and basic approval by a delighted parental selfobject. The needs of his mother's defective self, that is, her need to include the sons in her own hypochondria and to control them rigorously—not only their physical functions but also their thoughts[9]— and the unavailability of a father who would take pride in his sons deprived the patient of these self development-enhancing responses. Whenever his need for self-enhancement through mirroring increased, therefore, he felt intensely painful shame and embarrassment (see Kohut 1978b, 2:440–42 for an explanation of these sensations in the terms of traditional metapsychology). But instead of relinquishing his self to the total control of the selfobject as the brother had done, the patient was able to preserve the integrity of his self by mobilizing his aggression, that is, by turning passive into active. In this way, he became a sadistic voyeur, exposing the selfobject or its substitutes and making the selfobject ashamed and embarrassed in its exposure. The move from the dream of being naked in public (dream 1) to the dream of suddenly taking a picture of the analyst-audience (dream 2) demonstrates this sequence, as does the manifest content of the camera dream itself.

And the defense-resistances pertaining to his anality? Instead of elaborating on this theme and approaching it comprehensively, I will be anecdotal and demonstrate my point of view through a single clinical vignette. The topic of anality, that is, the topic of (prohibited) anal eroticism—credited by his former analyst with the truly causal role, the theme of the mother's hypochondria and control via enemas being secondary and peripheral to it—had not been especially prominent during the patient's analysis with me. As I pointed out, however, the patient frequently referred to his former analysis and, perhaps comparing the former analyst with me, repeatedly recalled during the first year of treatment with me that the former analyst had often confronted him with his anality, both during his childhood and as it was manifested in the transference. It seems that the former analyst thought that the patient and his mother enjoyed the enemas, that he resisted evacuation in order to prolong the pleasure, and that, ultimately, he gave way and produced a large volume of feces, thus reaching some kind of anal orgasm. The subsequent interpretation of the former analyst, clearly expressed, was that the patient was unwilling to reveal this forbidden pleasure to himself or to the analyst, just as he had kept it hidden in childhood. It was this unwillingness to face his clinging to a regressive pleasure aim that caused his "resistance" to "analyzing" this set of experiences, that is, to understanding them as traditional analysis explained them.

A good and cohesive story, I thought, but there was one inconsistency. One would have expected the patient to be relieved that I did not press him with regard to this topic, and, correspondingly, one would not have expected him to pursue it himself as a recurrent memory concerning the former analyst. And yet he did, not so much as a dutiful report or, ultimately, as a means of comparing the former analyst with me, but for its own sake, as it were, and with obvious *conflict-free* relish. In fact, the driving force that motivated my patient to recall the anality theme from the first analysis was neither his own anality (which indeed played only a very minor role in his personality) nor some resistance-type wish to play out the first analysis against the second. In fact, the patient's underlying motivation actually pertains to the last of the four so-called defense-resistances I am reinterpreting:

the father complex. In a word, the patient's reference to the anality interpretations of the former analyst referred to the *way* in which the analyst had expressed himself in offering these interpretations. When we finally found the way to the solution of the problem, the patient realized that it was the comfortable warmth that the former analyst exuded whenever he discussed the anal theme with the patient that had a simply magical effect on him—not because of the content of the analyst's interpretations but because of the tone of voice he adopted at such times, one that communicated aliveness, enjoyment of life, deep emotionality, and vitality. "First you are holding back for all you're worth," the analyst used to say to him, "but then you are making a b-i-i-i-g production." It was especially these last quoted words that the patient cherished as a memory, the analyst's enjoyment of the punlike ambiguity of his phrase and the comfortable, life-affirming, broadly "mirroring" enjoyment of an activity of the patient not only when he was a child but also in the present. It was at such moments that the patient's deepest need elicited an inadvertent response, a need I will discuss further in connection with the resistances against the father complex but one that is already understandable to the self psychologically informed psychoanalyst in view of the joyless atmosphere of the patient's childhood that I described earlier as prologue to my discussion of the resistances.

And now, even though I have already to some extent anticipated myself, I turn to the fourth and last of the so-called defense-resistances to be discussed. I will provide a reinterpretation of the psychic constellation that is traditionally associated with the male child's oedipal competitiveness vis-à-vis the adult male, with his partly reactive passive homosexuality, and with his defense-resistances against both of these interrelated drive-motivated unconscious wishes.

Again, as with my reinterpretations of the other traditionally conceived defense-resistances of my patient, I will attempt to "prove" neither that the self psychological interpretations are correct and the traditional ones wrong nor that the former are "deeper" than the latter, that is, that they focus on the more basic psychic constellations.[10] My aim is to present an alternative to the traditional view in the hope that it will be adopted by those analysts willing to suspend disbelief for sufficiently long periods to apply the alternative view, and thereby test it, in their own clinical work.

To begin with, let me say that the father theme, although it had temporarily appeared fairly early in the analysis, occupied center stage only much later, after, to return to traditional concepts, the brother conflict and the preoedipal mother attachment had been analyzed. And, continuing in this traditional vein, the attempt to explore the patient's feelings in this area evoked "resistances" that were even more intense than those that were mobilized vis-à-vis the attachment to the mother.[11] Still, after the mother theme had been analyzed for a long time and after he had come to discover that his mother had been "a little crazy," his feelings about the father emerged, both in the transference and in the transference-correlated memories from childhood about his father and maternal grandfather.

What emerged was, in brief, not a death wish against the father and a defense against it, but a yearning for a strong vital idealizable father-analyst. The clinical material, in this respect, paralleled the understanding of dream 3 at which the patient and I ultimately arrived. In the dream, it will be recalled, the revival of the father-analyst who had a heart attack seemingly invited interpretation in terms of a death wish and reaction formation against it. In reality, however, the act of resuscitation expressed the patient's wish to transform the analyst from an old, sick, dying man into a living, vital, and responsive ideal. This interpretation was supported by associative material about the analyst, the father, and the maternal grandfather.

That the mother had prevented the son from idealizing a strong and vigorous father should be self-evident from the material I have already reviewed; the frustrated hide-and-go-seek games in the basement that I described illustrate adequately the central childhood atmosphere in which maternal joylessness and prohibitiveness proved strong and paternal playfulness and vigor proved weak. It may come as some surprise, however, that the mother's outlook also put obstacles in the way of the boy's idealization of his grandfather, even though she herself idealized her father and, at any rate, used him and his successes in order to debase the father.

Instead of describing again how the boy's self-confidence and athletic performance improved and his social shyness diminished during the summers that he spent with his maternal grandparents, I will focus only on one memory, which emerged late in the analysis at a pivotal point preceding the patient's recognition that he secretly idealized and admired me. The specific way in which the mother had prevented the boy from reaping full benefit from his contact with the grandfather had been to burden him with a vastly exaggerated sense of the latter's physical frailty. Yes, the grandfather had been a pioneer and great man in his younger years—during the years that in a way belonged to his daughter—but heart disease had practically turned him into an invalid who could not exert himself and was likely to die at any moment. The memory in question concerned an evening in town when the grandfather had invited the boy, who must have been thirteen or fourteen at the time, to have dinner with him at his exclusive club. Only the patient and the grandfather would dine; it would be a man-to-man get-together with a great deal of enjoyable

meaning for both grandson and grandfather. What the patient remembered, however, was not the substance of the occasion itself but
a seemingly trivial detail. They had been driven to the club by a
substitute chauffeur who let them off one steep uphill block from the
club building and then drove off before they noticed the mistake.
Even though it was a cold, windy, snowy night, the grandfather, without any hesitation, went up that long steep block in vigorous strides
until they arrived happily, and without any discomfort on the grandfather's part, at their destination. The emotions the boy felt at the
time were, in a sense, a repetition of what he had felt much earlier
on receiving the school doctor's diagnosis of "healthy youngster" that
contrasted so completely with his mother's image of him. Yet, it is
significant to point out that, in analysis, the patient's decisive rise in
self-esteem was associated more with the availability of an idealizable
selfobject than with experiences of direct mirroring (as constituted,
for example, by the school doctor's diagnosis). His development, in
other words, had resulted in the permanent establishment of activat-
able compensatory structures to which he had turned after the decisive
failure in obtaining the selfobject responses needed to consolidate the
primary structures.

It is here, with regard to the father and grandfather theme—more
so than with the themes of sibling rivalry, voyeurism and exhibitionism, anality and mother attachment—that the self psychologically informed analyst's attitude toward the set of phenomena referred to as
"defense-resistances" gives the appearance of lying within the theoretical framework of ego psychology. Much as we might wish to say
that here, finally, even the self psychologist analyzes resistances in
order to do away with them, we are obliged to admit that our position
remains essentially different. We cannot, in other words, abandon our
conviction that it is the self and the survival of its nuclear program
that is the basic force in everyone's personality and that, in the last
resort and on the deepest level, every analyst will finally find himself
face to face with these basic motivating forces in his patient. We cannot,
in other words, accept the dictum that we are primarily engaged in
a battle to increase knowledge and that everything that impedes progress toward "becoming conscious," and toward sharing liberated cognitive content with the analyst via the analysand's communication of
his free associations, is to be considered a "resistance." However great
the analyst's wish to submit to the time-honored inclination of Western
man to place knowledge values at the pinnacle of his value hierarchy
(the primacy of knowledge values can indeed be traced to Plato's
Socrates; see, among other works, *Lesser Hippias, Phaedrus, Protagoras,*
and Plato's own *Republic,* especially books 6 and 7), he cannot do so
without abandoning his conviction that value-primacy is relative and

that, in our time at least, the struggles of the self and its attempt to safeguard its potentialities have clear priority. Thus the "resistances" that I described with regard to sibling rivalry, voyeurism, anality, and mother attachment must be interpreted by the self psychologically informed analyst as healthy psychic activities, in all their ramifications, because they safeguard the analysand's self for future growth. And even with regard to the father theme the self psychologist and the ego psychologist remain far apart. Not only are their interpretations of the basic dynamic constellations widely divergent (sexual drive-wishes for the mother motivating oedipal rivalry with the father versus the need for a strong idealizable father in order to strengthen the self), but, even disregarding these differences in content, the self psychologist cannot agree that he is dealing in this instance primarily with a "resistance" of the analysand.

To be sure, even after disabusing himself of the (to him) misleading and distorting prejudice—unfortunately at times a self-fulfilling prophecy—that the childlike patient is unwilling to face the truth, the self psychologist may yet be tempted to consider the analysand's reluctance to idealize the analyst (qua father) as a resistance; it is after all an attitude that stands in the way of exposing the self to the firming, cohesion-producing experiences that the patient needs and, on a deeper level, therefore, wants. But the self psychologist's acknowledgment that "on a deeper level" the patient "wants" to idealize a father figure in the transference must not be confused with the repetition compulsion of which the drive-wishes of traditional analysis are taken to be an expression, whether their aim is pleasure (lust, love: *Eros*) or suffering (pain, destruction: *Thanatos*). The "he wants" of which the self psychologist speaks is the expression of the healthiest aspect of the patient's personality; it is an expression of his enduring wish to complete his development and thereby realize the nuclear program of his self. And what of the "resistances" that are correlated to this central thread of the personality? Is the patient's hiding of the needs of his defective self as they become activated in the transference analogous to the way in which the traditional analyst sees the analysand opposing the pain and anxiety that he would have to face if he allowed his drive-wishes (libidinal and hostile-destructive) toward the father-analyst to emerge? Decidedly not. Just as was the case with the "resistances" vis-à-vis sibling rivalry, exhibitionism, and anality, so also with regard to the paternal selfobject. All these so-called resistances serve the basic ends of the self; they never have to be "overcome."[12] When Mr. Z. "attempted to close the door to keep the father out" (1979, p. 8), an ego psychological conception of his move might be that the ego, motivated by the anxiety aroused by libidinal (passive homosexual) and libidinal-destructive (to kill the rival and retain sole possession of the mother) urges, was putting up resistances, resistances that would reemerge when the old situation became reactivated in the transference. The self psychologist's perspective, however, is a different one. He believes that Mr. Z.'s throwing his weight against the door is an action that substitutes for the gradualism and modulation that he needs. An intruding father loaded with identificatory gifts is psychologically different from an available idealizable father. Our confusion of the two situations is an outgrowth of mechanistic, non-psychological thinking. "Intrusion" is unresponsive to the child's needs; it is not guided by empathy with the child. "Availability," in the psychological sense in which I use the term here, is responsiveness; it *is* guided by empathy. When Mr. Z. closes the door, or acts in analogous ways vis-à-vis the analyst, he demonstrates what is needed. And he will do so as long as the analyst is unable to supply it. And the same can be said of my lawyer patient and his "resistances" against the emergence of the need for the idealized father in the transference.

I realize that I have left many loose ends in the fabric portraying the self psychologist's outlook on defenses and resistances that I have tried to weave in the foregoing. And I can also say that I do not feel apologetic about not having tied up neatly all the loose ends, because I sincerely believe that good writing should always leave a task yet to be performed. In other words, it should provide the opportunity for active participation via the synthesizing ability of the reader, even at the risk that he might reach conclusions that I, myself, had not anticipated.

In my presentation then I will not try to summarize and, in this way, to safeguard my message from possible distortions. There is only one dimension of my reevaluation of the defense-resistances of the case of the lawyer-patient whose analysis has furnished me with paradigmatic illustrative material that I have neglected in my discussion up to now and which I will take up briefly at the end to round out the picture. My having focused on individual defense mechanisms, that is, my having used the traditional approach as my starting point, has prevented me up to now from making some comments on a broader issue—an issue, by the way, that is related to one I raised in a different context (see Kohut 1977) when I said that the traditional attitude of straitlaced reserve may (accidentally?) have been appropriate for those who as children had suffered the unempathic overstimulation by adults, whereas this attitude now would be unempathic and traumatic if it is perceived as an actual repetition of early understimulation and emotional distance.

Starting with a brief description of the overall wholesome personality changes that my patient was able to achieve during his analysis, I will say that he was at first extremely reserved, suspicious of free emotionality, and unable to relax (either socially or in the analytic situation), but that, gradually, his personality became more loose, he developed a sense of humor and the ability to laugh, and he spoke more freely and expressed emotions more openly—in short, he became more warmly human than he had ever been before.

I am mentioning these facts (which not only were clearly noticeable in the analysis but also were remarked upon by the patient's colleagues and acquaintances and finally acknowledged gradually by himself) not in order to proclaim a specific singular success of an analysis conducted along self psychological lines but because it gives me the opportunity to demonstrate that certain clinical formulations, although apparently satisfactory in their explanatory power, are in fact in the service of the maintenance of the status quo, while others which may seem to be based on overly experience-near theory upset the pathological balance and invite change.

My patient was indeed much inclined to think of his psychic life in terms of mechanisms and dynamisms, and he had on the whole felt more comfortable with his previous analyst than with me, at least during the first year or two of his analysis with me. I did not point out defenses against drive-wishes as the previous analyst had done—and the patient did not fail to mention this to me and to confront me with the reproach that I was not as scientific in my approach as the former analyst.

It is easy to become defensive at such junctures, but, after some faulty moves, I recovered my equilibrium and began to see that it was intrinsically the patient's personality that made him prefer the interpretation of the active mechanisms (though, I hasten to add, as employed by the previous analyst, always phrased in human terms, that is, as wish and resistance rather than as drive and defense) to the broad genetically based reconstructions of chronic attitudes to which I always tended to turn in order to explain his behavior, whether in treatment vis-à-vis me or elsewhere.

What I could finally see—and explain to the patient—was that he was "intellectualizing." But I also saw, indeed I knew immediately, that this was not a defense-resistance impeding analysis but a great achievement of his early life and an invaluable asset of his personality. His thought, his tendency to think independently, to doubt what was presented to him, the habit of being utterly objective about reality, whether physical reality or human experience, had successfully protected his self against his "a-little-crazy" mother's attempt to take him over. Formulations and terms of simple mechanisms were therefore much more in tune with his habitual mechanistic thinking than were my overall reconstructions. Indeed he thought of himself as a "thinking machine" as we could finally ascertain and it was this conception of himself—

that often independently active, logical computer—that protected him against intrusive craziness, illogic, and unempathic selfobject responsiveness, and safeguarded the maintenance of his self, however great the loss in vitality and range of experience.

The establishment of this, and similar, connections is surely of some significance in our own evaluation of the mechanistic trend in classical theory (macropsychology) and explains perhaps to some extent why the shift from the classical transference neuroses to the disorders of the self—of conflict pathology versus self pathology—has been paralleled by a shift to self psychological theory (micropsychology). But be that as it may, my lawyer's intellect-dominance was not exposed and overcome as a resistance by me but approvingly recognized as the safeguard that had preserved his feeble self for a reactivation of its development should the circumstances allow such a step. That the intellectualizations ultimately receded somewhat in his personality, although his intelligence remained always his highest asset in life, was not achieved in consequence of our overcoming a resistance to treatment but as part and parcel of the general developmental forward move achieved gradually as treatment progressed, especially in response to his recovery of the need for an idealizable father.

In the transference his fear was not, as I had erroneously believed for a while, that he could never match my achievements but, on the contrary, that I would knuckle under when belittled and attacked by those who disagreed with me just as his father had knuckled under when the mother belittled him during the patient's childhood. He wanted me not to hide my strengths and achievements but to display them proudly and openly—just like the maternal grandfather who had built his house in a conspicuous place on a hilltop prominent among the houses in the neighborhood. It was one of the most touching sessions in this man's analysis when, at an advanced stage in treatment, he admitted to me that he had been secretly proud of me all along even though he had felt the need to cover up his admiration by belittling me. And the same, needless to say, had been true in childhood regarding the father, even though he could then never admit to it.

8

Reflections on the Self-analytic Function

Our inquiry into the nature of the processes that lead to a psychoanalytic cure remains only partly complete. Thus, even though we have made considerable progress in arriving at a self psychological understanding of the therapeutic effect of psychoanalysis along with the role of "resistance analysis" in this process, many questions remain unanswered. I believe that a summarizing statement at this point concerning two major assumptions made by self psychology will help us on our way.

The first concerns the functional yield that self psychology anticipates from the therapeutic expansion and firming of the psychic structures of the self. We think, as I have stressed before, that this yield is optimally threefold: (a) that the analysand's capacity to make efficient use of selfobjects will be increased; (b) that at least one sector of the analysand's self, from the pole of ambitions to the pole of ideals, will be able to function effectively; and (c) that the analysand will be in a position to devote himself to the realization of the nuclear program laid down in the center of his self.

The second self psychological assumption I would like to stress at this point is the genetic one I have frequently adduced in a variety of contexts. Self psychology holds that we can best understand psychoanalytic cure in analogy to successful early development; we define therapeutic progress toward mental health not primarily by reference to expanded knowledge or increased ego autonomy, but by reference to the laying down of permanent self structures via optimal frustration.

I believe a variety of questions will be answered almost automatically if we hold fast to these two major self psychological assumptions about the psychoanalytic movement toward cure. It will be clear, for example, that the more accurately our theories correspond to the psychic realities that underlie our patients' disturbances, the closer our interpretations will come to providing for the patient, in an adult setting and in an adult form, the optimal frustrations that were not forthcoming from the imperfect selfobject responses of early life. Should an ill-disposed critic again claim gleefully that he has caught me redhanded, that once more I have openly admitted that—*horribile dictu*—we are indeed providing "corrective emotional experiences" for our patients, I could only reply once more with "So be it!" I would add, however, that the only way by which we could avoid gratifying the patient's need to be understood would be by consistently confronting him with erroneous, inaccurate, or untimely interpretations. And I know that no analyst, however great his desire to downplay the structure-building effect of the particular corrective emotional experience which the analyst provides via optimally frustrating correct interpretations, would go so far as to assert that we must not spoil our patients by trying to grasp their psychological problems as accurately as we possibly can. I will reiterate, in passing, that we can speak of a correct interpretation only as long as the analyst is open-mindedly responsive to the actual experiences of the patient at any given time. His theories, to give my meaning in more specific terms, must function as suggestions or proposals, not as commands or laws. Thus, on the one hand, the analyst must avoid falling prey to the misguided insistence that a patient see him as a selfobject when in fact the patient wants to possess him sexually or do away with him. Correspondingly, he must not cling at all cost to the interpretation that he is a drive-object for a patient when the patient needs him as a selfobject in order to strengthen his self.

Our formulations also explain, and without invoking the power of suggestion, that jack-of-all-trades in the realm of psychic causality that Glover explored long ago (1931): why successes can be achieved, and in fact have been achieved ever since psychoanalysis came into being, even when the theories that inform the analyst's interpretations are in error—when, for example, the analyst confuses the emergence of primary narcissistic needs with defensive narcissism (Kohut 1978b, 2:547–54). I have no doubt that in some of these instances pseudosuccesses were and still are being achieved via the patient's compliance, that is, that instances exist for which Glover's explanation that the patient knuckles under when exposed to the suggestive pressure exerted by the analyst is correct. I am equally convinced, however, that the majority of successes achieved in the past and still achieved today via the use of erroneous theories are not of this type. In these latter instances, we are dealing not with *pseudo*successes resulting from the patient's compliance but with incomplete successes resulting from the fact that the analyst's correct understanding of the patient could only be expressed in a distorted way because of his commitment to an erroneous or irrelevant theory.

In order to illuminate from yet another direction the self psychological formulation that the gradual acquisition of wholesome psychic structures via optimal frustration is provided by correct interpretations, I turn now to an examination of a well-known phenomenon: the former analysand's postanalytic use of the so-called self-analytic function (M. Kramer 1959). This phenomenon has been rightly adduced (Schlessinger and Robbins 1974) as an indication of the fact that psychoanalytic treatment has come to a successful conclusion. The following inquiry about the occasional employment of self-analysis by a former analysand, however, does not deal with the practical or pragmatic aspects of the phenomenon under scrutiny but with its significance in the context of my previous explanation of the nature of the psychoanalytic cure (the laying down of psychic structure). When examined from this standpoint, we will find, paradoxically, that the occasional recourse to self-analytic activity during periods of stress not only betokens the pragmatic success of a preceding analysis, but indicates that, in principle, the working through part of the analysis was never completed, that the ideal goal of analysis had not been reached. Clearly, we are not in search of perfection, neither as an outcome of normal development nor as an outcome of that belated developmental move that occurs during analysis. It is therefore appropriate to consider an analysis to have terminated with a thoroughly satisfactory result if it has led to a reliably maintained life of well-being, creativeness, and inner balance, but one in which the former patient supports himself during times of stress by activating the self-analytic function.[1]

But, as I have pointed out, I am not focusing on the self-analytic function as a practical issue—that is, as one of the criteria on which we base our satisfaction or dissatisfaction with the clinical results of a given analysis—but as an issue of principle. How can we shed light on the significance of self-analytic activity during periods of postanalytic crisis with the aid of the insights of self psychology? We can do so by observing that the presence of self-analytic activities indicates that the process of working through, particularly with reference to selfobject transferences, had not been completed. Specifically, such activities indicate that the selfobject imago of the analyst had not been transmuted into smoothly functioning psychic structures during the course of the analysis, that it had, at least in part, retained a quasi-external separateness within the analysand's psyche. We must not forget that the self-analytic activity, however rational and beneficial—and all analysts, of course, employ this activity when, in the clinical situation, they attempt to analyze their countertransferences—involves a rein-statement of the analytic situation and frequently proceeds along the same lines as the past analysis had been pursued by the analyst. What I am pointing to is neither more nor less than a principle that has been known for a long time in psychoanalysis with regard to normal development: the transitional phenomenon of only partially inter-nalized structures. As Anna Freud likes to point out, there is a stage in the child's life when the injunctions of the superego are experienced neither as completely part of the inner world, nor as coming com-pletely from the outside. A little girl may be overheard talking to herself as she is tempted to take some cookies from the cookie jar, telling herself, with her mother's intonation, that she must not give in to her greed. And she may even reinforce the power of the verbal prohibition by wagging her finger at herself. Under normal circum-stances this phase passes and the child's morality concerning everyday temptations, such as the impulse to steal, functions silently and outside of awareness.[2]

The psychoanalyst, however, encounters many patients for whom the developmental process of early life could not be completed because the "termination," so to speak, was premature. One of my analysands, for example, not only was overly strict with himself but also tended to be excessively harsh in his disapproval of the transgressions of his children and subordinates. This man, who had lost his father in pre-adolescence, remembered with the greatest clarity an incident that occurred when he was four. On the way home from a children's party, his father, who had picked him up, noticed that he carried a toy that did not belong to him. The boy admitted that he had taken one of the gifts that had been given to the child whose birthday was being celebrated. Although they were by then some distance from the lo-cation of the party, his father insisted that they turn around and that the boy return the gift with an apology. This memory, which became a symbol of the fact that this patient's psychic development had not been completed, was cherished by him. In it the father was still alive, the father whom he had suddenly lost when he was eleven and whom he had reinstated in a series of relationships to idealized men through-out his life. During periods when he was sustained by a relationship to a benign father figure—the first one in late adolescence, followed by several others in adulthood, including, finally, those periods during the analysis when the idealizing selfobject transference was in balance—he always became less harsh with himself and others. During periods when an idealized selfobject was not available to him, however, the structural weakness caused by the father's sudden, premature death became evident. Not having gone through the ultimate phase of internalization during adolescence and not having worked through the important shift in intergenerational feelings that occurs at this time, his self-critical attitude lacked smoothness; he did not possess the ability to keep his feelings of guilt and the resulting self-reproaches within moderate limits.

I have not presented this case vignette in order to illustrate the well-established relationship between parental prohibitions and the setting up of an internalized conscience. Instead, I adduced my patient's memory of his father's insistence that he return the stolen toy in the context of evaluating the significance of a self-analytic function after the termination of an analysis. Why did my patient remember this incident so clearly, why did he return to it repeatedly in the course of his analysis, and why did he treat it like a treasured possession? For a long time I believed that his recall of this incident served defensive functions. Specifically, I assumed that it would turn out to be a screen memory—that behind the joyful mood that accompanied the recollection of his father's insistence that he be honest and return the stolen toy with an apology, his fear and hatred of a threatening father who interfered with his pursuit of pleasurable goals would emerge. But despite my alertness to what I then considered the most likely explanation for the vividness of his childhood memory (i.e., that it buttressed a denial), nothing took place in the course of the analysis that supported my original conjecture that we were dealing with a screen memory. On the contrary, all the accumulated evidence pointed in the opposite direction. The memory, in other words, indeed referred to an important symbolic moment in his life; the memory of his father's firm but friendly insistence that he return the toy was joyful, not painful. We shall see that this "cherished symbolic moment" has implications for the explanation of the self-analytic function that follows.

These reflections about the recurrence of certain childhood memories are not only of theoretical value—for example, the contribution made to analytic theory by demonstrating an analogy between incomplete development in childhood and a specific incompleteness of the analytic cure. They also assist us in the clinical situation when, as therapists, we face the task of explaining the significance of certain emerging memories to the patient.

One of my patients, for example, a man in his mid-forties who had been in analysis with me for a number of years (his second analysis,

I should add, the first one having led to a result he felt was unsatisfactory), reported again, as he had done on three or four previous occasions, a childhood memory I always considered of great poignancy. I had always felt quite moved by it. What I did not understand, however, and what made me increasingly puzzled, was why the memory kept coming back. To compress my account as much as possible, here are the most important data. The patient had been a very lonely child, especially when, after a decisive alteration in the external living arrangements of his family (which curtailed the love of a doting extended family in a small town), the parents moved to Chicago. Following the move, both parents pursued business and professional activities that kept them away from home all day. Thus, the patient, an only child, was alone for many hours at the age of four or five, deprived of the lively company of adults and children who had surrounded and supported him during his earlier life and having no one but sitters, maids, and cleaning women for company. What made the situation emotionally worse was the fact that, even in the evenings and during weekends and holidays, the patient's parents appeared to remain at home as little as they possibly could. Evening meals were eaten in a hurry, and, as soon as they were over, the child was told to go to bed while the parents either went out or pursued their own interests with business friends or contacts at home. In the present context, I need not concentrate on the child's depressive response to the emotional deprivations to which he was exposed or describe his attempt to escape his depression via masturbation and compulsive eating. As I want to focus only on a single, recurrent memory, I provide the foregoing information not primarily to give an account of certain aspects of the genesis of my patient's personality disturbance, but rather to serve as a background for my understanding—which, in fact, was at least a partial misunderstanding—of the childhood memory under scrutiny. I will add, however, that, in contrast to the patient's first analysis, which had essentially interpreted his complaints as elaborate defenses against confronting his oedipal disappointments and his oedipal rage at being excluded from the parental bedroom, the analysis with me had focused patiently and in detail on his experiences of lonesomeness, on the emergence of his (still persisting) hypochondria and depression, and on his remedial attempts to keep himself stimulated via masturbation and addictive eating.

The recurrent memory in question consisted of a single, vivid image of his mother. Dressed up as Madame Pompadour, she was giving him a quick goodbye kiss—a "peck," as he called it—carefully avoiding closeness so as not to disturb her elaborate makeup and wig, and then leaving him quickly for a costume ball despite the fact that he was quite sick with high fever and the measles that evening.

Needless to say, I felt a stirring of compassion every time this memory emerged, and I communicated my emotions to the patient on one
occasion in the belief that he needed this direct expression of my
emotional understanding in order to take a step forward in overcoming an old sense of abandonment. But why, even after my expression
of compassionate understanding, did this memory continue to emerge?
Was he using it to lull me into compassion so as to avoid the deeper
conflicts of the oedipal triangle? Were we, in other words, dealing
with a screen memory which, covering the unconscious memory of
the primal scene and his sexual and aggressive drive conflicts, was
designed to protect him against the crucial psychoanalytic task of
analyzing his Oedipus complex? Ultimately, we made some progress
in understanding the memory. It came not primarily because of any
new insight concerning the patient or the significance of the recurrent
memory of the mother's goodbye "peck" when he was ill—that came
secondarily. Rather, it followed my shift of focus from the analysand
to myself. Why had I felt compassionate? I asked myself. And why
had I, disregarding my own injunctions against confusing empathy,
an objective data-gathering instrument, with sympathy or compassion
(see, e.g., Kohut 1971, p. 300; 1977, pp. 304–5; and 1980, pp. 458–
59), apparently done just that and expressed my compassion to the
patient?

When I finally began to look at my patient's recurrent memory with
a fresh eye—that is, when I focused again on the direct data of observation or, to express myself more accurately, when I only used the
most experience-near theories to order my observations—I began to
perceive new aspects of the meaning that I had formerly not perceived
or, more precisely, that I had perceived but disregarded. I began to
notice retrospectively, and again when it emerged one final time, that
the memory was very vivid,[3] that it stood out in bright colors, so to
speak, against my gray-on-gray dreariness of his accounts of lonely
childhood masturbation and of masturbatory eating.[4] And I was also
able to notice that the patient's mood and tone of voice were not
depressed when he told of his mother's hurried leaving. On the contrary, he described her in her exciting costume and the waiting father
in his knight's outfit with a degree of vitality and pleasure that was
completely absent from the accounts of this otherwise dreadful period
of his life when the nucleus of his adult psychopathology, while it was
not created at that period, jelled into the form that provided the basis
for his later suffering. What I learned now—and the correctness of
my new understanding of the significance of this memory was supported not only by the confirmatory associations with which the patient
immediately responded to my interpretations, but also by virtue of
the fact that the memory did not occur anymore—was that we were

dealing with a cherished memory, with a moment in his life from which he tried to derive strength and vitality, not a moment that bore witness to his early emotional deprivations. What the patient experienced when he told me about this scene, what he had *always* experienced when the memory emerged during the analysis with me—I could not, in other words, console myself by saying, in the spirit of Freud's view of the manifest dream content, that the memory was overdetermined and now expressed a different meaning—was that his parents were young, active, vital people who, while not enjoying him or seeking his company, at least enjoyed life. That he was the child of such fun-loving, enterprising parents gave him some access to health, provided some outlines of a nuclear self, and allowed the analysis ultimately to lead to a result that I can without hesitation characterize as an analytic cure.

And why, to round out my inquiry, did the memory not emerge again after I had interpreted it correctly? The answer to this question is fully in line with the long-established theory that pertains to one aspect of the analytic process. It did not recur because a decisive shift from the traumatic past to the here-and-now present of an analytic transference took place. The twofold nature of the parental imagoes—the father dressed up as a knight proved to be a much more important aspect of the memory than I had ever suspected, I might add—was transferred onto the patient's transference experience of me. It was with the aid of analysis of the transference—the working through of his feeling rejected by me versus his drawing idealized vitality from me—that the old developmental stalemate was ultimately overcome.

But let us now return to my opening claim that in one important respect the significance of recurrent memories such as the two I have just discussed and the significance of the self-analytic function after an analysis are the same. I believe, in a word, that both phenomena are indicators that a process has not come to the ne plus ultra of its completion. Thus, I would venture the guess that the memory of the first mentioned analysand would have faded away had his father been alive during his adolescence whereas the memory of the second would not have emerged again and again if parental vitality had been more available to his developing self in childhood. After a developmental course has been carried to completion, the functions of the individual links of the long chain of events that sustained the total forward move are dissolved. Our mind has no more use for them; they sink into oblivion via processes that are unrelated to repression—just as, at the end of a truly successful analysis, the patient is not burdened by memories of the numerous interventions and responses from the side of the analyst that assisted him in reaching a state of reliable self-cohesion or in resolving structural conflicts. If an analysis has been successful, in other words, most memories concerning the analyst fade away and the functions that the analyst had assumed—his understanding and explaining—have become unnecessary and are discarded. Normal mental functioning, whether established in consequence of successful development in childhood or in consequence of a successfully completed analysis, rests on smoothly interacting psychological structures. Neither the selfobjects of childhood nor the selfobjects revived in the analytic transference should be expected to play an important role in adult or postanalytic life, respectively. In fact, the relative success or failure of early development and of analysis can be gauged by evaluating adult and postanalytic functioning against the question of the degree to which transmuting internalization has taken place. The "foreign protein" of the selfobject and of the selfobject's functions, whether in childhood or during analysis, becomes split up after being ingested; its constituents are then reassembled to form the self in accordance with those individual patterns that characterize the growing child's (or analysand's) specific psychic "protein." These individual patterns derive from influences emanating from inherited patterns insofar as the child is concerned—although there can be no doubt that the actual content and form of the nuclear self are often decisively determined by the selective responses of the parental selfobjects (e.g., by selective "mirroring")—and preeminently in accordance with the basic design of the nuclear self of the adult analysand as it has been outlined through the confluent forces of a specific biological inheritance and a specific selfobject milieu in childhood. It follows that under optimum conditions the resulting psychic structures are only partially patterned in accordance with the gross features of the parental selfobject and they should show no more than the faintest traces of any of the gross features of the transference selfobject of analysis. And the same also holds with respect to the way in which, by comparison with the selfobjects of childhood and the selfobject of analysis, the adult and the postanalytic self perform the functions that the selfobjects had formerly performed for them. Not only do these functions become "depersonalized" (see Kohut 1971), but the specific way in which they are henceforth (internally) performed has few of the features that characterized the actions of the selfobjects of childhood and, under optimum circumstances, hardly any of the features that characterized the analytic selfobject. In addition, I will stress again, these functions are now largely performed outside of awareness.

Thoughts on the Training Analysis

As I emphasized earlier, the presence of the conscious exercise of a self-analytic function while, in principle, an indication of an incompleted working through process is, in practice—unless it has addictionlike features—quite appropriately evaluated as an indication that the analysis was a success (Schlessinger and Robbins 1974). But I am constrained to acknowledge at this point that certain aspects of the analogous phenomenon at the end of our training analyses cannot be evaluated with the same pragmatic disregard of the theoretical ideal. True, so long as it is a question of self-analysis per se, who would or could raise any objections? I do not believe that I would find much opposition if I ventured the guess that there is no analyst anywhere and there has never been such an analyst—I will not go so far as to claim that there will never be such an analyst in the future—who has not occasionally done a piece of emergency self-analysis, for example, when he sensed that something was out of kilter in his attitude vis-à-vis an analysand during a particular analytic session or, par excellence, when he realized that he was reacting inappropriately to one analysand after another on a particular day. All this is not only acceptable, it may indeed be termed desirable. I would venture the further guess, moreover, that most of my colleagues would, within limits, even be eager to report such experiences because they are proud of having acted at such times in just this way.[5]

A great deal can be said about the self-analytic activities of analysts, especially as they are occasionally employed during clinical work. In view of the fact that I have, pragmatically speaking, commented favorably on such activities with regard to our patients, should I not take the same attitude with regard to the members of the psychoanalytic profession? There is no doubt that I should—analysts, after all, are in no way essentially different from other people—and, up to a point, I do. But only up to a point. I will not hide my belief, for example, that the postanalytic adjustment of the psychoanalyst, the specific kind of psychic well-being and health that he achieves after his training analysis has ended, is inextricably interwoven with his professional identity as an analyst and with his functioning as an analyst. As I have observed elsewhere (1980, p. 497)—I expressed myself in a light vein, but some truths must first be expressed in the form of a joke—each person becomes "addicted" to his particular kind of mental health. What does the term "addiction" mean in this context? It indicates the presence of fear—the fear of the return of former insecurities and imbalances if the protective activity is given up or even relaxed. And it indicates, therefore, that activities which appear to be pure manifestations of health—realistic, adaptive, and socially useful—may, at least at certain times and in certain people, be pursued in ways that are overzealous, that lack the admixture of tolerance and wisdom of which I spoke years ago (Kohut 1978b, 1:427–60, esp. pp. 458–60) as one of the most significant transformations of narcissism.

A friend makes a slip of the tongue; a patient makes a slip of the tongue; an analyst makes a slip of the tongue. No one with any sense for the historical moment will deny the significance of Freud's discovery of what he called the psychopathology of everyday life. And yet on many occasions it is more "analytic," more an expression of the seasoned analyst's analytic wisdom, to pay little attention to such a minor manifestation of the unconscious than to concentrate on it and pursue it relentlessly until the underlying meaning has become manifest.

I am aware of the fact that critics will now appear who, removing this observation from its relevant context, will report to their colleagues that I am contending that slips of the tongue are unimportant, just as earlier critics claimed that I advocated dream analysis without an investigation of the patient's associations to the components of the manifest content. Since I know that benevolent fairness cannot be brought about by arguments, I will refrain from giving an anticipatory rebuttal. Not in defense, however, but simply in pursuing my own line of thought, I will say that experience has taught me that it is best in the great majority of instances to follow the direction in which the analysand is leading us via his spontaneously emerging thoughts and not to sidetrack and hamper him by imposing tasks that have become important to us mainly because of their significance in the historical development of analysis—a development of which we feel ourselves to be a part. It should be reiterated, in this connection, that the experience of taking part in the historical development of psychoanalysis, of identifying with it, may for many analysts constitute a force that plays an important role in buttressing their psychological equilibrium and sense of well-being. To conclude my reflections on the attitude of analysts toward slips and other similar manifestations of the unconscious, then, I offer the opinion that the well-adjusted analyst is not quasi-addictively forced to pursue these incidents—whether vis-à-vis his friends, his patients, or himself—but has the freedom to decide whether or not he should do so on the basis of the potential fruitfulness of the undertaking.

There is, however, a related issue that has vastly greater significance for analysis than the addictionlike application of certain technical rules and traditions during the analyst's clinical activity. However deleterious it may be to the results of a particular therapeutic analysis if the analyst, committed more to finding his theoretical convictions confirmed than to remaining open-mindedly able to accept the surprising and the new, misses the patient's psychological woods, seeing only the trees, there is a detrimental effect that is even more important for psychoanalysis as an investigative science. Let me start with a manifestation of this effect—the tip of a huge submerged iceberg of problems—that can be recognized without much trouble. This easily observable manifestation is given by the fact that in the largest number of instances a future analyst's training commits him, throughout his professional life, to a particular set of theoretical beliefs. With very rare exceptions to be discussed shortly, the analyst does not stray from these beliefs, which he comes to make his own. Rather, he defends them loyally, displaying hostility and contempt toward those who do not share them.

Why not? I will be asked by some. Why should we be surprised at these group formations and loyalties in psychoanalysis? Do they not occur in all sciences? Has Kuhn (1962) not demonstrated that in all sciences groups form around a central disciplinary matrix and work in its service, so to speak, until it is dethroned and replaced?

My answer to the first of these rhetorical questions is that I do not believe that groups whose members display such deep and unswerving loyalty to specific sets of theories are in fact encountered with equal frequency in other sciences. When similar schools are encountered in other sciences, moreover, they do not tend to persist for as long as psychoanalytic "schools."

In response to the second question, however, I would raise a counterquestion: why has Kuhn's theory—and Kuhn's theory, I might add, in a polemically distorted version[6]—been so enthusiastically embraced by psychoanalysts? (See, in this context, Gitelson 1964—to my knowledge the first of many analysts who gave Kuhn's theory a welcoming approval.) There exist, after all, other ordering principles—problem-solving ability, for example (cf. Feyerabend 1975; Laudan 1977; Ferguson 1981)—beyond the psychosocial one employed by Kuhn, that permit us to make sense of the development of scientific thought.

This is not the first time that I have puzzled about the issues surrounding psychoanalytic group loyalties (see Kohut 1978b, 2:511–46, 793–845). And I have often expressed my concern about the excessive conservatism of analysts and the morality-tinged stance they tend to take toward ideas suspected of being defensive or regressively escapist, and thereby of jeopardizing the hard-earned gains of the past. Since I discussed these topics earlier in this work and tried to illuminate some of the psychosocial factors that motivate the individual analyst's distrust of the new, I will here restrict myself to a brief look at this problem area from the vantage point of our preceding concern with the self-analytic function, now focusing more particularly on the training analysis of the future analyst. Are our reflections about the significance of postanalytic self-analysis and the return of positively experienced childhood memories of selfobject support of any help to us as we try to assess the group problem faced by the members of the psychoanalytic community? Although at first glance seemingly unrelated to these matters, these issues are indeed of assistance as we attempt to gain clarity about the complex and multifactorially determined[7] set of phenomena we are investigating.

The existence of the social phenomena I am describing is not difficult to demonstrate. Who could deny that these psychoanalytic groups exist, warring with each other, contemptuous of each other, and afraid of each other if their forces appear to be insecurely balanced? What I find more difficult to substantiate are my hypotheses: (1) that the existence of these groups and their unpleasant behavior toward each other is only one of several symptoms of a broader disease from which psychoanalysis is suffering, and (2) that it is the training analysis— the incompletely carried out training analysis, I hasten to add—which bears a large share of the responsibility for causing and perpetuating the disease, even though there are clearly other lesser factors that could also be adduced.

Concerning my first point I have little to add to what I have said earlier in the present work and elsewhere as well. Each of the psychoanalytic groups with which I am acquainted exhibits the symptoms of the same disease. Originally, the components of the scientific doctrine of a particular group—including its relevant point of view, its explanatory approaches, its meaningful definition of appropriate therapeutic goals, and its establishment of appropriate methods by which to achieve these goals—may have constituted tentative and testable hypotheses imbued with the joyful ongoing search of creative minds that are antithetical to fixed doctrine and dogma. Once a system had more or less jelled, however, its major outlines became dogmatic to adherents, who then needed to defend it vehemently against competing systems. The offshoot of this development was a deep-seated reluctance, even an inability, to suspend disbelief and seriously try out different points of view. Even though the claim of open-mindedness is always made—how could it be otherwise?—I believe that on the whole analysts do not study opposing viewpoints extensively, do not give wholehearted trials to new modes of depth psychological thought, and are unwilling even to shift their observational position to new vantage points from which to make the clinical observations that bear on alternative theoretical positions.

I realize that my perspective on this issue rests on my evaluation that I am indeed exploring a "disease." My use of this term clearly indicates that I have made a value judgment; I can do no more than acknowledge this fact. If the adherent of a particular school of thought within psychoanalysis would reply that the condition I am describing is not one of disease but, on the contrary, one of health—of scientists courageously upholding the truths they have discovered against the enemies of these truths—and add that my view is jaundiced because of personal disappointments, I could say little to make him change his mind. It may well be true that recent personal experiences have contributed to my alertness to the problem I am discussing. In fact, however, I have been interested in the warring groups within our field, and in the intensity with which theoretical beliefs are upheld by the respective members of these groups, ever since I became a student of analysis.

But let me return to the role played by the training analysis in bringing about the condition I am considering. Why is it that a therapeutic process which, in Freud's words (1923, 1953, vol. 19), should provide freedom for the ego, which, in Hartmann's terms, should give it *autonomy* (1964, pp. 113–41), and which, in terms of my own formulations (1971, p. 187; 1978*b*, 1:365–66), should bring about its *dominance*, leads in the professional field to the very opposite result? As I have said on a number of previous occasions, it is the incompleteness of the training analysis in the narcissistic sector that accounts for this fact, that is, for the fact that the training analysis, although personally beneficial in many instances, is a deleterious institution insofar as the intellectual mobility of analysts and thus the scientific progress of analysis are concerned.

Just as we approvingly view the recall of the development-enhancing functions of a selfobject from childhood, so with the revival of the function of the former analyst in the former patient's self-analytic activities: who would want to play the pedant here and insist that this occurrence is not indicative of the success of an analysis—and of early development—but evidence of minor failures? No, let us by all means continue, in a pragmatic sense, to number such occurrences among our blessings. But can we do the same with respect to the fact that training analysands continue to hold the scientific beliefs of their analysts, that they carry on their analyses in the same atmosphere in which they experienced their own? I think that we cannot, that we must not. Rather, our professional identities oblige us to look upon the training analysis with a different eye, to measure its result with a yardstick that differs from the one we employ when we measure the relative success or failure of an ordinary therapeutic analysis.

Yes, if the training analysis were to be judged in the same way as a therapeutic analysis, the former analysand's loyal commitment to the theories and techniques of the group of his training analyst could be viewed as part of that "addiction to one's own kind of mental health" to which I recently drew attention (1980). Furthermore, it could be positively evaluated in analogy to our positive judgment concerning the continuing vitality of the analyst's function in our former patients. But an analyst is not just a former patient, and the fear of the older generation of analysts that the succeeding generation might "become different" (see Terman 1972) has a significance which, if we take psychoanalysis seriously, vastly transcends the well-being of the individual analyst in any event. In the context of cultural progress, the individual's well-being must often be sacrificed—deep pain and deep anxiety often accompany such progress, the exhilarating joy of being an active participant in a pioneering enterprise notwithstanding.

Yes, the training analysand is undoubtedly a "patient" when he enters analysis; and, yes, the training analysis undoubtedly takes the form of a therapeutic analysis. When the training analysand has his analysis behind him, however, he is not only a former patient but an analyst as well. And the addiction to his particular kind of mental health will affect his capacity to change, that is, it will affect his ability to examine the new ideas, new theories, and new techniques to which he is subsequently exposed with an exhilarating feeling of open-minded curiosity rather than an anxiety and suspicion that well up because his insecurely established self feels threatened. This latter response, it goes without saying, is conducive to the automatic rejection of the new.

It is not the institution of the training analysis per se that is the culprit here; it is rather the incomplete training analysis, particularly the training analysis that disregards the primary narcissistic transferences of the training analysand, that is to blame. Since I have taken up this specific issue elsewhere (Kohut 1978*b*, 2:793–843, esp. pp. 803–4), I will not pursue the matter here, except to stress once more that the shift of the unanalyzed narcissistic transference (most frequently a primary idealizing transference that was mistaken either for secondary defensive narcissism, for the narcissistic component of object love, or for both) either to a personified ideal shared by analyst and analysand (such as Freud) or to the established body of analysis as a whole perpetuates the selfobject transference. Through the very self-sustaining support that this unanalyzed transference offers to the former training analysand, it stands in the way of his future ability to be freely creative, whether in the realm of creative learning, creative productivity, or both.

When I spoke of the former training analysand's postanalytic shift of his unanalyzed selfobject transference—often, as I have learned from my reanalyses of analysts over the last ten to fifteen years, the shift of an idealizing transference aiming to strengthen compensatory structures focusing on a paternal selfobject that failed in childhood without being irrevocably traumatic in its failure—to the established body of psychoanalysis as a whole, I am not only referring to that aspect of analysis that one might refer to as scientific doctrine. The strong father on whose selfobject support the analyst must continue to lean is represented not only by his scientific hypotheses and theories, but also by the much subtler moral climate that is the legacy of his scientific activities. What I am alluding to here can be characterized both as an inheritance from Freud's specific personality—his "Jewish sobriety"— and, not unrelated to the first, as an outgrowth of the moralistic conception of "Guilty Man," forever struggling to tame his drives. It is this admixture of archaic selfobject support that the analyst's self derives from being an analyst that has made analysis not only a science but also a "movement," or a number of movements if we consider the subgroups and schools within analysis. I believe this situation will begin to change only when training analyses begin to focus on the training analysands' self pathology and, correspondingly, to understand, interpret, and work through their selfobject transferences. Will such a shift do away with the future analyst's devotion to psychoanalysis and with his admiration for the great contributors of the past, including, of course, Freud himself? By no means. An analyst who has successfully worked through his selfobject transference might well come to recognize that qualities such as courageously facing the truth or being realistically pessimistic, to name only two sloganlike headlines, are securely established in him and do not deserve to occupy the top positions in his hierarchy of values. He might recognize, in other words, that his personality is constructed quite differently from the personified ideal of the analytic profession qua movement. But having arrived at this conclusion, I do not believe his devotion to his work, his feeling of kinship with his colleagues, or his admiration for the pioneers with whom he feels connected via a sense of historical continuity will subside. Indeed, his self will continue to derive strength and sustenance from the selfobject support that the sense of historical continuity and the feeling of group membership impart, more or less, to the members of all scientific and professional groups. As I have noted many times before, however, there is a decisive difference between the support of selfobjects that are sought after and chosen by a self in harmony with its innermost ideals—*sibi constat,* "to be consistent with oneself," as Horace's maxim states—and the abandoning of oneself to a foreign self, through which one gains borrowed cohesion at the price of genuine initiative and creative participation in life.

I will round out my reflections on the deleterious influence on scientific progress in analysis exerted by training analyses that bypass the training analysand's self disturbance by returning to a point to which I alluded earlier: that we must also account for the exceptions. There are, after all, analysts who do not espouse the ideas of their training analysts, and there are, from time to time at least, analysts who point out new directions to their colleagues and, riding roughshod over ingrained tool-and-method pride (see Kohut 1978*b,* 2:685–

724, esp. pp. 690–92), even advocate new techniques. It would be of the greatest interest, in this connection, to obtain detailed and reliable information about the analyses of analysts who later made original contributions that involved departures from the traditional ways. Not having access to these or other data relevant to understanding such exceptions, however, I must rely on the impressions, admittedly personal and unsystematic, gained from my observations of a number of colleagues who might be considered representative of this group. But before I turn to the genuine creative-productive innovator in psychoanalysis, I must stress that by far the largest number of those analysts who, on superficial inspection, seem to be acting in accordance with the foregoing description of inner freedom do not really deserve to be included among the innovators at all. For such analysts, the training analysis has not eventuated in a firming of the self sufficient to enable them to react creatively to their professional tasks; on the contrary, they remain in a state of chronic narcissistic rage that is either genetically predetermined (i.e., that may be said to have begun in childhood) or a reaction to narcissistic injuries inflicted on them by their training analysts. Most frequently, the narcissistic rage arises as the result of the confluence of both these factors. Analysts in this category, like narcissistically enraged adolescents, turn the parental teaching upside down, indicating by their very opposition that they have indeed learned the parental lesson but are unwilling to acknowledge that fact. But the outcome of such behavior in the nonprofessional sphere obtains in the professional sphere as well: with the passage of time the rebellion subsides and the basic submission to tradition becomes more and more overt. The rebel of yesterday is the conservative of tomorrow.

Leaving behind these representatives of pseudoautonomy, what of the analysts who show evidence of true intellectual independence and creative enterprise? And omitting issues of native and early acquired talent (a large omission indeed!) and restricting our focus to the influence of the training analysis, what accounts for the fact that these analysts, braving the disapproval of the large majority of their colleagues who are sustained by the maintenance of the scientific status quo, will think new thoughts and point out new ways of achieving scientific goals? Disregarding the fact that native and early acquired talent, favorably responded to in childhood, may set up a creative propensity of such vigor that it will express itself despite interfering external forces that would stifle others,[8] and, in our specific context, considering only the influence of the training analysis, what are the features of those training analyses that account for the appearance of creative mobility in the former training analysand? By way of responding to these questions, I will discuss a number of interconnected factors, all of them related to the personality of the training analyst. To begin with, it is my impression that if the training analyst can respond with genuine pleasure to his analysand's creativeness, then—independent of the analyst's overtly expressed convictions, that is, independent of the content of the interpretations that follow from his theories—the analytic process will not result in a commitment to the traditional system of thought that is at the expense of the future analyst's intellectual independence. It is my impression, furthermore, that analytic relationships of this type encompass an emotional situation that is akin to the situation of a child whose parents, although themselves deprived of the benefits of education and other cultural nourishment, strive to bestow these benefits on their child. Indeed, I believe that some great achievements grow on just such a selfobject soil. If a training analyst, although stifled in his own ability to realize his creative potential, is yet capable of shifting the sense of entitlement to be freely creative onto the next generation, then we may get the desirable results of which I spoke. Like the clustering of talent in certain historical periods, there seems to be a clustering of talent among the psychoanalytic offspring of certain training analysts—even though these training analysts themselves may not have been creative or, at any rate, may not have achieved the full flowering of their creative potential.

Finally, there are certainly instances in which the ability to pursue independent paths occurs as the result of appropriately conducted analyses in which selfobject transferences are allowed to unfold and then are understood, interpreted, and worked through. Do all such analyses lead to creativeness, to truly original thought in the former analysand? Of course not. Many other favorable forces must converge to produce such a result. But evidence of inner freedom, of joyful search, of the courageous ability to go one's own way can indeed be anticipated after such analyses. As is true with all human endeavors, we cannot expect optimum success every time. From time to time, however, to the great satisfaction of the self psychologically informed psychoanalyst who has conducted the treatment, we do get as gratifying results as that which one of my patients spelled out for me when, at the end of a long analysis during which there had been periods of gross identification with me, he said: "Now I am similar to you only in one respect: I am an independent person just like you."

I now briefly turn to a topic that is related to the preceding discussion and, especially, to our earlier observation that the process of transmuting internalization leads to a *silent* functioning of the psychic structures. I am referring to the relationship between the mode in which the analyst functions vis-à-vis his analysand in the clinical situation and the degree to which his theoretical knowledge is integrated

with the rest of his personality. (See in this context my remarks about
the qualities in prospective training analysts that demand special attention [Kohut 1978*b*, 2:853–59].) Just as the optimum experience
of selfobject responsiveness in childhood lays down silently functioning regulatory structures which in adult life function outside of awareness—that is, without the need to recall the personified imagoes of
the selfobjects of childhood—and just as the experience of optimum
selfobject responsiveness in analysis (the analyst's correct empathic
grasp of the analysand's needs and wishes followed by the correct
interpretation of the relevant transference context in its dynamic and
genetic dimensions) lays down regulatory structures which postanaly-
tically function outside of awareness—that is, without the need to
reinstate the functions of the selfobject analyst in the form of a conscious exercise of self-analysis[9]—so also with regard to the integration
of the analyst's theoretical knowledge with the rest of his personality.
Here, too, it is not a matter of conscious awareness of the invaluable
apparatus of concepts and theories that are at his disposal as he works
with his patients or investigates the nonclinical field, but of their silent,
preconscious use. An analyst, in other words, may be said to have
become a true master in his field—I am thinking here especially of
his clinical work—when his learning (i.e., his theoretical knowledge
and his clinical experience) has become so thoroughly integrated with
his total personality that he has ceased to be aware of it. Psychoanalytic
knowledge, in other words, should ultimately permit the analyst to
achieve the full expansion of his empathy, whether he focuses his
attention on the current (transference or nontransference) experiences of his patients or—via a mechanism one might call "regression
in the service of empathy"—on genetic material. Thus, as I have suggested before, the emotional reserve displayed by the classical analyst—however buttressed (rationalized) by the theory that by keeping
his activities to a minimum the analyst will optimally serve as a screen
for the patient's transferences—may very well have been the appropriately empathic response for patients who were overstimulated as
children and therefore in need of an environment that stimulated
them less. On the other hand, I believe that gifted analysts—whatever
their consciously held and openly professed theoretical beliefs—have
always, subtly or not so subtly, discarded their straitlaced reserve in
responding to those patients who, during childhood, were deprived
of the palpable emotionality of the selfobject. And they have thus
provided for these patients (e.g., via the vividness of their interpretations) that minimum of emotional responsiveness without which the

analytic work could not proceed optimally—just as normal mothers some decades ago continued to provide a lively emotional presence for their babies despite their lip service to the Watsonian principles of distant efficiency that had been impressed on them by their pediatricians.

9

The Role of Empathy
in Psychoanalytic Cure

The self psychologically informed response to the question of how
psychoanalytic treatment leads to a cure—a question to which, since
it involves consideration of the whole personality of the patient and
his psychic functions, there is no simple answer—can be condensed
into this formulation: The psychoanalytic situation sets into motion a
process which, via the optimal frustrations to which the analyst exposes
the patient through more or less accurate and timely interpretations,
leads to the transmuting internalization of the selfobject analyst and
his functions and thus to the acquisition of psychic structure. But what
exactly is the role of empathy in this process? Specifically, we must
ask two interrelated questions that have not been systematically addressed to this point: (1) Is the empathy of the psychoanalytic self
psychologist in essence different from the empathy employed by analysts before the advent of self psychology? (2) Do we achieve a cure
via a novel kind of empathy? In the following, I will attempt to explain
why my answers to both these questions are in principle in the negative.

I know that a number of my self psychological colleagues will not
agree with my negative answer to the question of whether the self
psychologist's empathy is different from the empathy employed by
analysts before self psychology came into existence. They will assert—
and I not only understand their propensity to adopt this view but
share it up to a point—that the empathy of the self psychologist is
qualitatively different from the empathy at the disposal of his analytic

predecessors. Specifically, they will make the claim that, with the advent of self psychology, the analyst is able for the first time to be empathic not only with the patient's transference experience of the analyst as a target of love and hate, but also with the patient's transference experience of him as a selfobject. Thus, through self psychology, the analyst acquires the ability to be empathic with the patient's inner experience of himself as part of the analyst or of the analyst as part of himself. These colleagues will further claim that in the clinical practice of psychoanalytic self psychology, in contrast to the clinical practice of traditional psychoanalysis, the analyst truly grasps the patient's perception of his psychic reality and accepts it as valid. This is tantamount to saying that the self psychologist does not confront the patient with an "objective" reality that is supposedly more "real" than his inner reality, but rather confirms the validity and legitimacy of the patient's own perception of reality, however contrary it might be to the accepted view of reality held by most adults and by society at large.

Before I spell out my reasons for questioning the adequacy of this overall judgment, I would like to comment on a specific issue that is related to the self psychological perspective on empathy: what is our estimation of the role of confrontation in the psychoanalytic process? Here, I would give voice to the opinion that the "confrontations" to which analysts expose their analysands not only are often trite, superfluous, and experienced as patronizing by the patient, but also may repeat the essential trauma of childhood in a way that is especially harmful to the progress of the analysis. By failing to acknowledge the validity and legitimacy of the patient's demands for development-enhancing selfobject responses, that is, the analyst fails the patient in the same way the parent had failed—often the more responsive parent to whom the child hopefully turned after the parent whose responses were even more flat, more severely distorted, and the like had failed him. That it may occasionally be helpful to an analysand, especially in the later phases of analysis, to hear from the analyst that old grievances, however valid and legitimate, must finally be relinquished, and that new and more responsive selfobjects must be sought in the present, goes without saying. On the basis of my clinical experience, however, including data gathered both from the period when I had not adopted my present stance and from present consultative work, I have come to the conclusion that confrontations should be used sparingly. They may shock the patient and momentarily enhance the analyst's self-esteem when he sees the patient taken by surprise, but they provide nothing that is not already provided by the realities of adult life. It is not the task of the analyst to educate the patient via confrontations but, via the consistent interpretation of the selfobject transferences, to cure the defect in his self. As the working-through processes concerning the psychic reality of childhood near completion during the late stages of analysis, then, the patient, in consequence of the new psychic structures that have gradually been acquired over the years of treatment, will be able to learn the lessons of realism from life itself.

But turning away from the narrow technical issue involving the relative desirability of confrontations, what of the broader theoretical assertion, in my opinion erroneous or at any rate overstated, that only with the emergence of self psychology can analysts be truly empathic with their patients, that only with self psychology can analysts truly accept the fact that, in the psychoanalytic situation, the psychic reality of the patient not only commands respect but is the only reality that matters?

I will not deny that these claims contain a modicum of truth. This pertains not only to the progression from nineteenth-century science with its sharp differentiation between observer and observed to twentieth-century science with its understanding of the observer and observed as a unit that is, in certain respects, indivisible (Kohut 1977, p. 68, and chap. 3). In the context of the psychoanalytic situation, it also pertains to those specific phenomena to which self psychology refers as selfobject transferences. Still, even though I accept the validity of these claims if their validity is applied to certain specific areas of psychological understanding (for an explicit statement on this topic, see Kohut 1977, pp. 63–69), I consider the claims erroneous when, as has happened at times, they are formulated without the necessary qualifications.

I believe that a careful distinction between the following three sets of functions employed by the psychoanalyst in the clinical situation— presented here in a condensed fashion but supported by references to previously published more extensive discussions—should make it easier to retain the essential truths contained in the statements of a number of my colleagues—I am thinking here especially of certain contributions by P. Ornstein (1979) and E. Schwaber (1981)—while avoiding conceptual and terminological inexactness. The three sets of functions that we must distinguish from one another are (1) the analyst's use of empathy, (2) the analyst's creation and use of theories, and (3) the analyst's move from understanding to explaining in his communications to the analysand. If we examine the question of whether self psychology has introduced a new kind of empathy to psychoanalysis against the background of a clear distinction between these three separate activities, we will see the question in a different light and be able to respond to it with a different answer.

1. Empathy is the operation that defines the field of psychoanalysis. No psychology of complex mental states is conceivable without the

employment of empathy. It is a value-neutral tool of observation which (a) can lead to correct or incorrect results, (b) can be used in the service of either compassionate, inimical, or dispassionate-neutral purposes, and (c) can be employed either rapidly and outside awareness or slowly and deliberately, with focused conscious attention. We define it as "vicarious introspection" or, more simply, as one person's (attempt to) experience the inner life of another while simultaneously retaining the stance of an objective observer. When defined in this general way (see, for example, Kohut 1978*b*, 1:205–12; 1971, pp. 300–307; 1977, pp. 298–312; 1980, pp. 456–69, 482–88), the claim that self psychology has introduced a new kind of empathy in psychoanalysis cannot be supported.

2. Although self psychology must not claim that it has provided psychoanalysis with a new kind of empathy, it can claim that it has supplied analysis with new theories which broaden and deepen the field of empathic perception. The greatest geniuses of vision, not to mention ordinary men, had not seen that objects appear to diminish as they recede into the distance and that parallel lines converge toward a single vanishing point until Brunelleschi demonstrated these pivotal insights in his famous architectural drawings. Should we therefore say that Brunelleschi improved man's vision, that he gave a new kind of vision to man, or rather that he gave us a new theory (supported by illustrations) which allowed us to perceive the world more correctly? I have no doubt that it is the latter statement, not the former, which describes Brunelleschi's contribution more appropriately.

I will now add an important qualification to my reference to Brunelleschi and his discovery of "perspective."[1] I said that Brunelleschi introduced a new theory. I could also have said—and perhaps this is the preferable way of putting it—that he disabused visual man of an old theory, or, one might also say, of previous established knowledge. In order to demonstrate convincingly the validity of this observation, I will shift from Brunelleschi and his theory of perspective to a related change in visual theory. Painters had always known (via previous theory or previously established knowledge) that objects (people, animals) retained their size whether they were close to the observer or far away from him. It was this theory (knowledge) that prevented them from seeing that objects become smaller as the distance from the observer increases and therefore from appreciating the need to render objects that were farther from the observer smaller on the canvas. Within the framework of our visual perception of the universe, however, the statement that a man in the distance does not appear the same size as a man close by is just as true as the statement that the size of a man will increase if he moves closer to us or we to him, or that he will appear larger to people close to him and smaller to people far away from him.

Does the lesson which the psychoanalyst can learn from these afore-mentioned facts still need to be spelled out? If a patient tells me how hurt he was because I was a minute late or because I did not respond to his prideful story of a success, should I tell him that his responses are unrealistic? Should I tell him that his perception of reality is distorted and that he is confusing me with his father or mother? Or should I rather say to him that we all are sensitive to the actions of people around us who have come to be as important to us as our parents were to us long ago and that, in view of his mother's unpre-dictability and his father's disinterest in him, his perception of the significance of my actions and omissions has been understandably heightened and his reactions to them intensified? Clearly, it is the second response that provides the patient with a more accurate as-sessment of that aspect of reality with which we deal in psychoanalysis. And to insist that we should tell him otherwise—that we should tell him with even the faintest trace of disapproval that he confuses the present and the past, that he mixes us up with his parents, and the like—is as misguided as to insist that our painters should go back to the medieval style and paint distant objects the same size as near ones.

But we must return now to the question in the service of which I introduced Brunelleschi's great lesson to the painter of the Renais-sance. Has self psychology given us a new kind of empathy or has it advanced a new theory that informs our empathy? Clearly, what I sought to underscore with the aid of my example was this: no more than Brunelleschi gave a new kind of vision to the art of painting has self psychology given a new kind of empathy to the psychology of complex mental states. In both cases it was a matter of introducing a new theory that permitted the observer (the quattrocento painter, the contemporary psychoanalytic clinician) to perceive formerly unrec-ognized configurations or, at the very least, to increase his awareness of the significance of configurations he had but dimly perceived.

3. The last of the three psychological action patterns in clinical analysis that we must consider in assessing the question of whether self psychology has introduced a new kind of empathy is the analyst's continuously repeated move from a position of understanding to a position of explaining. And it bears stressing that the analyst's essential activities in each of these positions—not only the first one—are based on empathy.

In the understanding phase, the analyst verbalizes to the patient that he has grasped what the patient feels; he describes the patient's inner state to the patient, thus demonstrating to him that he has been "understood," that is, that another person has been able to experience, at least in approximation, what he himself experienced, whether, for example, the experience in question is one of inner emptiness and depression or of pride and enhanced self-esteem.

In certain analyses, the analyst has no need to restrict himself to the understanding phase, even at the very beginning of treatment; rather, he can employ the total understanding-explaining sequence from the start. Furthermore, in many instances, either ab initio or later, there is no clear operational separation between the two steps. Even though the division between them remains valid in principle, the actual activity of the analyst combines them or oscillates between them so rapidly that the operational distinction becomes blurred even with respect to a single intervention. But during particular phases of many analyses, especially analyses of certain severely traumatized patients, the understanding phase of treatment must remain the only phase for a very long time (see Kohut 1978b, 1:85–88). Eventually, however, and to an increasing degree, the total two-step sequence can be employed without undue trauma to the analysand, even the analysand who, at the beginning of the analysis, was traumatized by any move from the side of the analyst that went beyond the simple communication of his understanding.

It cannot be stressed enough, it seems to me, that there are patients with whom respectable analytic results can eventually be achieved who early in their analysis, and for subsequent, increasingly delimited periods extending through years of treatment, are unable to tolerate any interventions from the side of the analyst beyond the communication of his understanding. Occasionally, despite the analyst's sincere attempts to grasp the inner life of such patients, they will initially react to the inaccuracies of the analyst's understanding or simply to the foreignness, the remaining otherness of the analyst, in alarming ways. At these times, only the analyst's willingness to be an attentive silent listener will be tolerable to the patient.

Responses of this type do not usually occur right away, and the analyst's narcissistic balance may be severely upset when, after an initial period during which his analysand has responded with outside behavioral improvement as well as with a degree of gratitude toward the analyst and his interventions within the psychoanalytic situation, he is suddenly confronted with a seemingly ominous worsening of the analysand's condition. Such deterioration is characteristically accompanied by a barrage of reproaches from the side of the analysand that the analysis is ruining him, that the analyst's inept, misguided, bull-in-a-china shop interventions are destroying him. Why is there this period of calm before the storm? Why can the patient at first tolerate the analyst's unavoidable mistakes and errors in empathy only to become suddenly intolerant of them? The answer is simple to the point of triteness, and every analyst, except at those times when he is himself traumatized and thus not at his best, should be expected to know it. What happens is nothing else but the transference clicking into place. Thus, during the calm before the storm, the analyst and the patient have jointly explored the patient's traumatic past, allied in the shared pursuit of a goal; once the storm breaks loose, however, the analytic situation has *become* the traumatic past and the analyst has *become* the traumatizing selfobject of early life.[2]

Clinical Vignette

I will illustrate the preceding insights about the vicissitudes of the understanding phase of treatment with the following vignette. A professional man in his late forties had attempted psychotherapy several times, including analysis with a colleague whom I knew to be a competent, well-regarded member of the profession. From what I could gather during the initial interview, the therapists, according to the patient, had all turned out to be grossly lacking in understanding and had reacted to his complaints of being treated incompetently either by attacking him—the analyst was quoted by the patient as shouting at him repeatedly that he was insane and belonged in a mental institution—or by withdrawing from him and suggesting that he seek the help of another therapist. The patient also spoke with great anger about his parents, especially his mother, a devout, bigoted Southern Baptist, blaming them both for his serious lifelong emotional disturbance. I will not go into details about either the nature of the patient's illness—a very serious narcissistic personality disorder with chronic painful feelings of being unreal—or the traumata to which he had been exposed in childhood—the mother, according to the patient's complaint, was totally absorbed with her church and treated her children in accordance with prescribed dogma rather than their own emotional needs; the father, on the other hand, was blamed for withdrawing from the family and giving insufficient emotional sustenance to the boy, who made some short-lived attempts to turn to him for help. I will only say that the treatment with me apparently developed in the same way as the previous attempts at therapy, with the only difference—a significant difference, indeed—being that the treatment with me was not broken off.

The patient, who is not a mental health professional, came to me after hearing a series of open lectures I had presented under the aegis of a university. As he listened to me, he reported feeling that my humane, simple, and direct attitude contrasted favorably with the narrow outlook and artificial behavior of his previous therapists and that he suddenly had the thought that, perhaps through treatment with me, he had yet another chance.

I felt uneasy on first hearing the patient's story when he came to me and requested treatment. Although there was nothing in his contact with me to indicate psychotic ideation, I wondered whether his history of failures with previous therapists and the almost monotonous similarity of his complaints about their emotional crudeness toward him or distance from him did not in fact point to a psychotic paranoid core in his personality. Still, reassured by the patient's actual behavior toward me and drawing courage from the fact that I was able almost from the very beginning of our contact to form, on the basis of his account of his childhood and his description of his parents' personalities, a plausible hypothesis concerning the nature of the transference that had caused earlier attempts at therapy to come to grief, I decided I would accept the risk and undertake an analysis.

The treatment, as I mentioned earlier, began in an atmosphere of friendly cooperation. In line with what every student of analysis is taught to expect and, especially, in view of the patient's account of his previous attempts to avail himself of psychotherapeutic help (i.e., the regularity with which he developed an intensely derogatory attitude toward the therapist and felt mistreated by him), I thought that I was emotionally and intellectually prepared for the fact that the analytic honeymoon would not last forever and that a complete change in his attitude toward me was to be expected. I was hopeful I could weather the impending storm once it broke loose. At first, however, the therapy indeed proceeded in a calm fashion—at least as far as I could then discern. (The patient taught me later to recognize the harbingers of his dissatisfaction with me when the latter, in a vastly intensified form, began to be expressed with little inhibition and became a searing blaze of attacks on me, mainly but not exclusively in the form of verbalized reproaches.)

During the interlude of calmness, I listened attentively and, after a while, began to share with the patient the understanding at which I had arrived by connecting his present experiences, including what had transpired in his previous attempts at therapy, with his childhood experiences. These interventions were, on the whole, accepted by the patient in a friendly fashion. The only indicators that the analytic peace was only precariously maintained by my analysand—realized more in retrospect than during this early period of analysis—were the severe headaches he frequently developed before his sessions (which would sometimes lessen as the hour went on, but would not infrequently either remain the same or get worse) and the fact that he was totally unforgiving in his criticism of both his previous therapists and his parents, especially his mother. Accordingly, the patient would become annoyed and impatient whenever he felt that I spoke of these people with a degree of objectivity—that is, whenever I looked upon them as transference imagoes rather than the real villains who, he unyieldingly insisted, tried to destroy him and were his hated enemies.

Still, apart from these indicators of the patient's uncompromising, undying hatred toward certain people in his past, the analysis on the whole went quite smoothly, with clearly discernible positive feelings toward me as being helpful and with clear-cut evidence that his functioning outside the analytic situation was greatly improved. The big change took place after about a year. I had been away for a vacation, and for several weeks following my return the situation seemed unchanged. But then some alarming developments took place which indicated the presence of a serious psychic imbalance. In the course of several weeks, the patient's headaches changed in character; he filled hour after hour with detailed accounts about how they felt to him without being able either to clarify to himself just what he was trying to understand about their nature or to make me understand what he was trying to communicate. The headaches that had formerly caused him physical discomfort were no longer painful in the usual sense of the word, but they caused him unspeakable discomfort to the point that he could think and talk of nothing else, especially during the therapeutic sessions. When he was away from me, the problem was at first not incapacitating. Gradually, however, he came to feel more and more upset about these sensations in the head during all his waking hours to the point that even his work began to suffer— even though, comparatively speaking, his emotional life outside the analysis remained much less disturbed than his life within the analysis.

My initial approach to the problem was twofold. At first I focused on the preceding interruption of the treatment and encouraged the patient to tell me his feelings with regard to that event. I reminded him, in this connection, of earlier experiences of feeling deprived of support and abandoned, and, in consequence of experiencing such loss of support, of suffering hypochondriacal concerns about body changes and failing health. The patient's response to my attempt to establish a dynamic connection between the vacation and the change in his condition was, as far as I could discern, a negative one. He complained that my theory seemed inapplicable in the present, even though, as far as certain analogous events of the past were concerned, it made good sense. But not now. He had, after all, been neither unduly upset while I was gone nor unduly upset for several weeks after I returned. In any event, he felt certain, without being able to prove the point, that what I said was not helpful, that I was completely out of tune with him, and that he was wasting his time in coming to see me. I listened to the patient's rejection of my observations as dispassionately and open-mindedly as I could, and, after the emergence of some associative material that appeared to point to another set of circumstances that were relevant to the change that had taken place, I offered an alternative explanation. I suggested that, paradoxically, the worsening of the patient's condition was part and parcel of his improvement, that he had opened himself more to emotional interactions with the world, inside and outside the analysis, and that, as a consequence of his increased courage and enterprise, he now faced a variety of tasks that exposed him to anxieties and tensions from which he had formerly protected himself. As a further consequence, I continued, he felt continuously traumatized and overburdened since he was unused to performing on this level of activity and, consequently, unused to the unavoidable traumatizations that impinge on all of us.

At first, and immediately, the patient responded very favorably to what I said. His facial expression, which to that point had been one of angry despair, brightened visibly, and he began to talk about a variety of tasks he had recently taken on that taxed him and made him anxious. But the good feeling that was engendered by my new tack in attempting to understand what lay behind the worsening of his condition was comparatively short-lived. After two or three sessions during which he pursued the possibility that he felt overtaxed, a contingency that I thought I had discerned in his associations, he turned away from this theme and began once again to accuse me of lacking all understanding and of ruining him; his psychic condition worsened alarmingly. At this juncture, he not only complained of the painful head sensations with which he had been preoccupied for several months, but also, in a quasi-paranoid fashion, began to blame different people in his environment for his symptoms in a variety of ways. It was, in particular, the offensiveness of their voices (a shrillness, a harshness, or a grating or rasping quality of their speech) that he suspected to be the cause of his suffering. And once, only once—I remember that moment as the peak of my concern about his state, a moment when I simply asked myself whether it would not be better to stop the treatment and send the patient to someone else to cool off, as it were—he not only harbored suspicious thoughts and told me about them, but proceeded to *act* on his conjectures. He believed at that moment that the sound of the television set in his house had become shrill and actually took it to a repair shop to ascertain that it had not been tampered with.

Yes, I became alarmed—but not as alarmed as I might have become and not as alarmed as, I believe, many of my colleagues would have become under similar circumstances. During the time I was treating this man I had already formed some of the notions that would later jell into a cohesive psychoanalytic psychology of the self (Kohut 1971); I had grasped, intuitively, that even serious states of self fragmentation, if they occur as an intrinsic aspect of that layer of the therapeutic action which I later designated the selfobject transferences, are less dangerous than they appear to be if—a crucial "if" indeed!—the analyst retains his analytic stance and, open-mindedly and nondefensively, attempts to resonate empathically with what the patient is experiencing.[3] I thus persisted in my efforts to understand my patient, tolerated his attacks on me as best I could—even including a temporary phase in which he bad-mouthed me openly to a colleague of mine with whom he became briefly acquainted at a reception. That my own reactions were imperfect, that I often became defensive under the barrage of attacks, is understandable since the patient always reproached me for real flaws in my emotional responses and intellectual performance. And I learned—again, of course, imperfectly—not even to respond by telling the patient that however germane his criticisms might be, they were exaggerated and disproportionate. The patient, as I finally grasped, insisted—and had a right to insist—that I learn to see things exclusively in *his* way and not at all in *my* way.[4] And as we finally came to see—or rather as I finally came to see, since the patient had seen it all along—the content of *all* my various interpretations had been cognitively correct but incomplete in a decisive direction. The patient had indeed reacted to my having been away; he had indeed felt overwhelmed by the traumatizations to which he was now exposed by virtue of his expanding activities, and he continued to react with prolonged, intense suffering as a result of remaining broadly engaged with the world. What I had not seen, however, was that the patient had felt additionally traumatized by feeling that all these explanations on my part came only from the outside: that I did not fully feel what he felt, that I gave him words but not real understanding, and that I thereby repeated the essential trauma of his early life. The task that the analyst faces at such moments—the crucial moment in which a "borderline" condition either will or will not become an analyzable narcissistic personality disorder—is largely one of self scrutiny. To hammer away at the analysand's transference distortions brings no results; it only confirms the analysand's conviction that the analyst is as dogmatic, as utterly sure of himself, as walled off in the self-righteousness of a distorted view as the pathogenic parents (or other selfobject) had been. Only the analyst's continuing sincere acceptance of the patient's reproaches as (psychologically) realistic, followed by a prolonged (and ultimately successful) attempt to look into himself and remove the inner barriers that stand in the way of his empathic grasp of the patient, ultimately have a chance to turn the tide. And if some of my colleagues will say at this juncture that this is not analysis—so be it. My inclination is to respond with the old adage that they should get out of the kitchen if they cannot stand the heat.

If the analyst *is* able to stand the heat, however, if he persists in extending his instrument of empathic observation to the patient rather than withdrawing from him by declaring him "unanalyzable"—as if this term connoted an objective reality in which the analyst himself was not included—then he may be rewarded by witnessing the way in which a borderline case becomes a narcissistic personality disorder. In the specific instance of this case vignette—one that I am adducing to illustrate what one might call "the principle of the relativity of diagnostic classification and the specific prognosis"—I was rewarded by a shift of the associative material into a new, unexpected, and at first not fully understood direction. The patient's sensitivity to noise began to subside. Simultaneously, his reproaches toward me persisted, even though they changed in character, becoming more specific than they had previously been. In view of the fact that this is only an illustrative vignette and not a case presentation, I will only say that the new material related to the patient's father and was a revival of frustrating experiences from a later period of the patient's childhood. The reproaches were directed at his father for not fostering his male development. Specifically, the reproaches were directed at a father who was a physician himself—like the father and yet beyond him, other than him. The father and I—through my originally erroneous transference interpretations—insisted on being looked up to and imitated. The son had wanted the father to respond to his own (i.e., the son's) potentials, suggestions, and ideas; he wanted to have the father's experience and knowledge as an aid in his own growth and in the realization of his own potential. It follows, then, that we had not, as I erroneously believed at first, entered a phase of an idealizing transference but had—analogous to the patient's similar move in childhood—entered a phase of mirroring needs vis-à-vis a different selfobject. The archaic mirror transference in which the seriously disturbed, unresponsive maternal environment of early life had been revived psychosomatically in the diffuse noise-hypersensitivity–headache syndrome was now replaced by the more focused syndrome of transference reproaches directed at the nonmirroring father who was preoccupied with his own self enhancement and thus refused to respond to the son's originality and talents. In terms of the dynamics of the sequence of selfobject transferences, one could say that the borderline state enacted via a "primary archaic mirror transference" had been secondary to the narcissistic personality disorder. The narcissistic personality disorder, on the other hand, was subsequently enacted via a secondary mirror transference at a higher level of self development and not via a secondary idealizing transference as I, repeating the trauma of the so-called latency period, had at first believed.

I will now break off the account of the analysis of this patient. I adduced this clinical material not to depict the course of the analysis of a patient with a severe but analyzable narcissistic personality disturbance, but to illustrate the claim that the concept of "borderline" pathology (which I define as analyzable cryptopsychosis [see 1971, p. 18]) is a relative one, depending, at least in a substantial number of cases, on the analyst's ability or inability (a) to retain his attitude of "empathic intention" despite the serious narcissistic injuries to which he is exposed and (b) ultimately to enable the patient, via the understanding of his or her experience of the world, to reassemble his or her self sufficiently with the aid of the selfobject transference to make possible the gradual exploration of the dynamic and genetic causes of the underlying vulnerability.

Empathy and the Explaining Phase of Treatment

Returning to the mainstream of our theoretical inquiry into the nature of the self psychological contribution to the psychoanalytic elucidation of empathy, we will now shift our attention from the understanding phase to the explaining phase of the basic therapeutic unit of psychoanalytic therapy. I will stress first of all that the explanatory phase— or, as it might well be more accurate to put it, the explanatory aspect of the analyst's interventions—is also based on empathy. But here, more so than was the case with respect to the understanding phase, the analyst's theoretical equipment—for example, his grasp of the theory of selfobjects as it pertains to the patient's experiences both in the transference and in childhood—will strongly influence the accuracy, breadth, and depth of his dynamic and genetic formulations. In a certain sense, therefore, it could be maintained that correct dynamic interpretations and genetic reconstructions provide no more for the analysand than further proof that another person has understood him.

It would seem to follow from the above that the explanatory phase of the basic therapeutic unit should be regarded as an extension and deepening of the understanding phase. But it would be erroneous to restrict our definition of the significance of the second part of the basic therapeutic unit in this way. The explanatory phase differs in an important sense from the understanding phase, not only cognitively but, more significantly, emotionally. The intensity of the archaic bond of an identity of inner experiences based on the analyst's ability to perceive the patient accurately and then to communicate what he perceives is lessened as the analyst moves from understanding to explaining. Yet, and this is the crucial point, while the archaic merger bond is lessened, an empathic bond on a more mature level of experience supplants what has been left behind. The empathic connectedness between patient and analyst is thus retained and, beyond doubt, even deepened in its scope via the analyst's imparting his dynamic and genetic insights to the patient. As he engages in his explaining activity, the analyst enables the patient to continue to feel supported by the fact that he, the analyst, retains his selfobject functions and, ipso facto, enables the patient to become more objective vis-à-vis himself and his problems. Formerly, the analyst had simply shared with the patient his grasp of what the patient experienced. Now, in moving toward the greater objectivity embodied in his explanations, however, the analyst provides the patient with the opportunity to become more objective about himself while continuing to accept himself, just as the analyst continues to accept him in offering the dynamic and genetic explanations. The movement toward greater objectivity during the analysis should therefore be seen as a sign of developmental progress; it parallels the replacement of one selfobject experience with another, namely, the replacement of an archaic selfobject experience by a mature one, the replacement of a merger experience with the selfobject by the experience of empathic resonance from the side of the selfobject.

The foregoing formulations about the change in the experience of the selfobject and its functions, and the maturing of selfobject needs, provide me with the opportunity to stress, as I have done for many years (see Kohut 1978*b*, 1:427–60), that archaic narcissism belongs to a separate line of development. This means that narcissism, like object love, evolves from archaic to mature forms and that, under certain circumstances, we find it useful to examine these two developmental lines and their relative levels of maturity by focusing first on the one and then on the other. In any event, the formulation that narcissism is replaced by object love—that narcissism is archaic and object love mature—is in error (see Kohut 1978*b*, 2:757–70).

Furthermore, as I have pointed out before (1978*b*, 2:741–42), the formulations about the maturing of the selfobject experience that results from each of the innumerable two-phase basic therapeutic steps taken during an analysis and that, via the cumulative effect of these recurrent fractionated forward movements, leads to the gradual and increasingly firm establishment of a mature selfobject experience and of mature selfobject needs of the patient are in harmony with the basic tenet that certain crucial psychic events of adult life can best be understood when evaluated from the vantage point of childhood development. In our specific case, this means that the forward moves, the progression of the therapeutic process toward a psychoanalytic cure, essentially repeats (though not in all details) the steps of normal childhood maturation—steps that had not been completed in early life but which can be brought to a degree of belated completion via the analytic process. Just as in normal childhood, so also in the analogous experiences of the adult analysand as the steps are taken from understanding to explaining, the physical distance between the self and the selfobject increases at the same time as empathic closeness is maintained.

Consider the following episode of early development. As a baby the little girl is picked up by her mother and thereby feels herself part of the omnipotent strength and calmness of the idealized selfobject. Later in childhood, however, when she walks away from her mother for the first time, the little girl will try to maintain the bond to her mother by turning around and looking back at the mother's face. If she is an emotionally healthy child who has been surrounded by a milieu of emotionally healthy selfobjects, she will do so not primarily because she is afraid and needs to be reassured that she can return, but rather to obtain the confirming reverberation of her mother's proud smile at her great new achievement. There is an analogue in analysis for the child's experience of increasing distance from the selfobject, particularly the child's developmental ability to replace physical merging with the selfobject milieu by a bond of empathic resonance with the selfobject; it is established as the analyst moves from an initial concentration on the understanding phase (the empathic grasp of the experiential state of the patient) to an increasing emphasis on the explaining phase (the empathic grasp of the dynamics of the transference interactions and their genetic precursors).

At this juncture, it may be advisable to return to a question that has surely arisen again in the minds of many readers: what exactly is it that constitutes normality? Is it really "normal," let us say, for a little girl to walk away from the mother and turn around not with a fearful glance which seeks reassurance that the mother is still there and available to reestablish the merger, but with a proud smile which expects and gets confirmation and support in the form of the mother's pride in her? I will not respond to this question with a simple yes or no answer, although, as I hope to show in the following, I would indeed say yes if I were pressed for such an unambiguous reply. Instead, I will examine this paradigmatic event from two points of view which, I must stress immediately, can be separated only at a price since the different images that emerge are in fact interrelated. The two points of view concern (1) the more experience-distant issue of the significance which should be assigned to the event by the evaluating observer (and I am speaking not only of the relevant childhood events but also of the analogous events during psychoanalysis) and (2) the more experience-near issue of the actual behavior of the child who moves away (or of the analysand who, for example, allows himself to hold views which, he believes, are not shared by the analyst or to engage in activities which, he believes, are anathema to the analyst).[5]

Why is it impossible to keep these two viewpoints entirely separate? The bond that unites them is given by the fact that the significance of the event of moving away is not only evaluated by the observer on the basis of experience-distant considerations; it is also felt, however vaguely and often nonverbally, by the principal actor in the drama, that is, by the child or the adult analysand. Specifically, the analyst and analytic child observer must realize that, in evaluating a developmental forward move, it is not only their objective theory-based opinions that count—opinions that are strongly influenced by their moral stance, by the values they hold—but also the opinion of the subject of the forward move, specifically, the precise way in which the child or the adult patient experiences such a move. In short, the analytic observer's empathic grasp of what the child or the analysand feels must be taken into account as he formulates a theoretical understanding of the significance of the forward move.

Having thus called attention to the necessary interrelatedness of the experience-distant and experience-near viewpoints (experience-distant theory, including the observer's values, influencing what can be perceived; experience-near theory, the configurationally organized data of the subject's experiences obtained through empathic observation, influencing the experience-distant theories the observer ultimately adopts), we will still find it useful to examine the significance of the forward moves under scrutiny from the standpoint of these two contrasting vantage points. We begin by posing the experience-distant question of the emotional significance that we should ascribe to the forward move. My answer is unambiguous: the forward move is in essence normal, and the normal response to this event is joy on the part of the self of the forward-moving subject (the child, the analysand) and the self of the observing selfobject (the parent, the analyst). In harmony with C. Daly King's definition that "the normal . . . is to be defined as *that which functions in accordance with its design*" (1945, p. 493; see p. 212), the significance of the forward move, to the degree that it manifests the actual readiness of the involved psychic structures for the move in question and is not in traditional terms, a "flight forward" undertaken to deny anxious insecurity, is that of a proud achievement. The psychic content of such a forward move— paradigmatically, of the child's walking toward some object that attracts him or simply walking into the open space[6]—is not appropriately described by saying that a separation of the self and the selfobject has taken place. The event is not tantamount to the breakup of (or the first symbolic move indicating the future breakup of) a relationship between objects (symbiosis), but embodies the shift in an essentially persisting self-selfobject relationship from one level to another. Psychic life is impossible outside of a milieu of selfobjects, at least not for protracted periods. When the child joyfully walks into open space or toward an object he is curious about or wants to grasp, the self-self-object unit with the mother is not dissolved; instead, the empathic resonance of shared joy (about a developmental achievement or a self-assertive act) has taken the place of physical holding and bodily merger.

But what of the experience-near viewpoint regarding the forward move in development, the new step into space? Is it not true that—unlike the young dog who chases a bird or a squirrel for the first time with all the signs of enjoyment since, in a manner of speaking, he is functioning in accordance with his design—many a small child will take a very cautious first step toward the pigeon or squirrel on that first spring day in the park only to look back anxiously to the mother to reassure himself that she is there and available for merger if need be? And is it not also true, with respect to both early development and the enactive process of analysis, that any response of the selfobject that either fails to see the child's (or analysand's) anxiety or, having seen it, denies its existence should be evaluated as a selfobject failure? The answer to both of these questions is, of course, in the affirmative.

The fact, the easily ascertainable fact, is that when we examine the situation at hand from the vantage point of experience-near theory,[7] we must acknowledge that failures can occur in either of these directions: (a) an analyst may fasten on an analysand's old fears and inhibitions when the preceding associations actually expressed the hope that the parental selfobject would finally respond with pride to the child's achievement, however great the anxiety that accompanied the act had been; (b) an analyst may fasten on an analysand's achievement when the preceding associations actually expressed the hope that the parental selfobject would finally shed the empty "go out and give 'em hell" faith in his child qua undaunted hero and acknowledge the anxiety that had remained unexpressed because the child knew the selfobject could not perceive this anxiety because of his or her own anxiety or intolerance of unpleasant emotions; and (c) an analyst may fasten on either achievement or anxiety instead of recognizing that the patient's associations had specifically expressed the hope that the parental selfobject would finally acknowledge that one can teeter-totter between pride in achievement *and* fear. I should clarify that this last contingency is a specific one. Thus, the routine response that we *always* experience both joyful pride in achievement *and* anxiety will, in those instances that fall under (a) and (b), be in error and experienced as selfobject failures.

I cannot stress enough how important it is to separate conceptually (1) the experience-distant general principle of what is normal in development—whether in early development or during the process that leads to cure—that is, what we should consider as functioning "in accordance with its design," from (2) the experience-near empathic grasp of what our patients (or, with regard to early development, our children) experience at a given moment. Our response must be to the latter, to the actual experience, whether it entails a prideful sharing of accomplishment and the expression of our understanding for the enjoyment that has accompanied a forward move or a readiness to share apprehension and fear. What is of decisive importance, however, is the fact that, however direct and strong and immediate our response to the emotions of the moment might—and should—be, our orienting comprehension of the baseline of experience-distant normality informs all our responses. It is this experience-distant notion, that is, which influences our reactions via the over- and undertones of our verbal communication as well as our nonverbal responses (e.g., our facial expressions and postural changes). This fact obtains whether we function as the selfobject of the small child who moves toward the pigeon in the park or, in the analytic situation, as the understanding-interpreting selfobject of the analysand who broaches a daring move in his profession.

If the emphasis of the analysand's experience, however cautiously expressed initially, is on his or her pride about a forward move, then the analyst's in-tuneness with the aforementioned experience-distant principle of normality will influence the way in which he acknowledges the patient's joy by the admixture of overtones contained in expressions such as "of course," "that's the way we are," "this is what we will experience under such circumstances"; such overtones, however faint, will prevent the analysand's joy from spreading unduly, from expanding into the land of manic excitement. And if, in the obverse, the analysand experiences anxiety and/or overburdenedness when he first begins to take more daring initiatives, resuming the developmental move toward the pigeon in the park that had been interrupted in childhood, the analyst's in-tuneness with the experience-distant principle of normality will influence the way in which he acknowledges the patient's fear by the admixture of overtones contained in expressions such as "yes, you are fearful, at first, and we can hardly be surprised when we consider how the selfobjects of childhood thwarted your naturally arising joy" or the like; and overtones of this sort, however faint, will prevent the analysand's discouragement about the inhibiting influence of anxiety from spreading unduly, from expanding into the land of depressive apathy.[8]

It is in the light of the preceding interpretation of the clinical significance of normality—understood, following C. D. King, as a functioning that is in accordance with structural design—that two other related phenomena must be evaluated: the overestimation of children by their doting parents and the functionally analogous overvaluation of analysands by their analysts. We have in general been taught to look upon these attitudes as misguided, as manifestations of the fact that our sober judgment has been led astray by our emotions. And analysts in particular have interpreted their tendency to think more highly of their patients—their talents, their achievements—than others who know them in everyday life as variants of countertransference, that is, specifically, as variants of an attitude that must be mastered and eventually dissolved by self-analysis and insight into the dynamics and genetics of such distorted judgments. To my mind, however, there is another dimension to this attitude that pertains to both parents vis-à-vis their children and analysts vis-à-vis their patients. I believe, in short, that this overvaluating attitude too is "normal," that it expresses the fact that, as parents and therapists, we are indeed functioning in accordance with our design and that an analyst who consciously eradicates this attitude and replaces it by cold objectivity (in accord with Freud's 1912 metaphor of the analyst as surgeon) is as misguided as the Watson-guided "objective" mother of half a century ago (see Watson 1925).

The obvious fact, the fact that practically goes without saying, is that we are dealing not with an "either-or" dilemma but with an integration of aims and attitudes. To put this more precisely in terms of the principle I enunciated earlier, we are dealing not with an amalgamation of at times conflicting attitudes and aims, not with syncretism, as Bertram Lewin used to maintain (1958; Lewin and Ross 1960, pp. 46 ff.), but with a variety of experience-near acts and attitudes that are informed by an experience-distant principle on a higher level of abstraction, however deeply rooted in our psyche this principle may be. It follows that we must never confuse the deep human response called forth in us vis-à-vis another human being's thoughts and emotions with sentimentality and companionship. Parents and analysts, respectively, will insist on the child's and the analysand's confronting unpleasant realities, including the limits that all of us have to recognize, but they will do so while simultaneously acknowledging the facts that all of us rightfully feel special and unique and that we cannot exist unless we feel that we are affirmed by others, including, and especially, by our parents and those who later come to have a parental selfobject significance for us. All meaningful human interactions, specifically those between parent qua selfobject and child and between analyst qua selfobject and analysand, are not only broad in the sense of applying to a variety of experiences, but deep in the sense of being in contact with early, and, in form, archaic, experiences. When a friend puts his arm around our shoulder at the moment we need to be sustained by him, he does not know that his gesture implies a willingness to let us merge with the calmness and strength of his body, just as the selfobject mother once provided us with this experience when she lifted us, anxious and fragmenting, and held us to her. And the same thing happens between analyst and analysand. However objective and limit-recognizing an analyst's interpretations may be, if they are preceded by understanding and deepen the analysand's recognition that he has been understood, then the old reassurance of a merger-bond, even on archaic levels, will reverberate, if ever so faintly, with the experience. Thus, whatever lip service some analysts may have given to scientific objectivity vis-à-vis their analysands, trying to "model themselves . . . on the surgeon" in accordance with Freud's advice of 1912, and whatever lip service some mothers may have given to the scientific regularity of their responses, trying to live up to strict behaviorist tenets, in healthy specimens of analyst and mother alike the old adage *naturam expellas furca, tamen usque recurret,* "nature may be pushed aside, but it will always return," will in the end prevail: in harmony with their human design, they will not interfere with their use as selfobjects by analysand and child, respectively.

10

The Selfobject Transferences and Interpretation

In this final chapter, we shift from the examination of the over- and undertones involved in the analyst's interpretations to the actual content of these interpretations. What is the main focus of the content of the analyst's interpretations? What does the analyst tell his patient that not only achieves cognitive accuracy in dynamic and genetic terms but also provides a bond of human understanding in the deep sense that I have discussed in the preceding pages? My answer, surely not an unexpected one for analysts, is as follows: since the essential driving force of the analytic process in the disturbances of the self is provided by the reactivation of the thwarted developmental needs of the self (Kohut 1978b, 2:547–61; 1971), since, in other words, the renewed search of the damaged self for the development-enhancing responses of an appropriately empathic selfobject always occupies center stage in the analysand's experiences during the analysis, it follows that the analyst's pivotal communications to the analysand are those that focus on the psychic configurations to which we refer as selfobject transferences. I will add immediately, in view of the fact that we now conceive of the self as consisting of three major constituents (the pole of ambitions, the pole of ideals, and the intermediate area of talents and skills), that we subdivide the selfobject transferences into three groups: (1) those in which the damaged pole of ambitions attempts to elicit the confirming-approving responses of the selfobject (mirror transference); (2) those in which the damaged pole of ideals searches for a selfobject that will accept its idealization (idealizing transference); and (3) those in which the damaged intermediate area of talents and skills seeks a selfobject that will make itself available for the reassuring experience of essential alikeness (twinship or alter ego transference).

It will not have escaped the reader familiar with my work that this classification of selfobject transferences deviates somewhat from that given in 1971. I have been led to these changes through the combined impact of both clinical and theoretical considerations, or, to express myself more accurately, by mixtures of clinical and theoretical influences on my thinking—mixtures in which sometimes the pressure of experience-near evidence and sometimes the need for theoretical consistency and clarity dominated. Changes in nomenclature—our decision in recent years to refer to certain recurrent sets of the patient's experiences in the analytic situation as selfobject transferences rather than narcissistic transferences and the present decision to posit three rather than two classes of selfobject transferences via the conceptualization of the twinship or alter ego transferences as a selfobject transference sui generis and not as a subgroup of the mirror transference—cannot be justified in isolation. Instead, these changes must be seen simply as the necessary outgrowth of our broadened clinical experience and our deepened understanding of the clinical phenomena that we observe.

The earlier of the two changes, that of nomenclature, is probably less in need of explanation. When I used the term "narcissistic transferences" in 1971, I was simply trying to pour new wine into old bottles, attempting to make new ideas appear less radically new and more acceptable not only to my fellow analysts, but above all to myself; because of shared training and shared tradition, that is, I shared my colleagues' reluctance to face openly the fact that our theories needed a radical change.

In addition, speaking of "selfobject transferences" rather than of "narcissistic transferences" enabled me to accommodate more easily a further change in thinking that has emerged since 1971, or, at any rate, an insight that has been more unambiguously formulated since then. I am referring to the fact that the need for, and the experience of, imagoes used for the creation and sustenance of the self undergoes a lifelong maturation, development, and change. Expressed differently, I mean that we must not confuse (1) the archaic selfobjects that (a) are the normal requirement of early life and (b) are required later on, either chronically in disorders of the self or, passingly, during periods of special stress in those who are free from self pathology, with (2) the mature selfobjects that all of us need for our psychological survival from birth to death.

The individual developmental lines of our three major selfobject needs should therefore be examined—and this task, I should add, is still largely undone—via a detailed investigation of the needs of man for the sustenance of his self in these three areas (i.e., his need to experience mirroring and acceptance; his need to experience merger with greatness, strength, and calmness;[1] and his need to experience the presence of essential alikeness) from the moment of birth to the moment of death. We have to date investigated the selfobject requirements of early life almost exclusively via transference reconstructions, and we have, through the observation of the changing and maturing selfobject needs of our analysands during successful analyses, formed some notions about the normal selfobject needs of adult life. But, as I said, much remains to be done; we need investigations of the special selfobject needs of adolescents and the elderly, for example, along with investigations of the selfobject needs that accompany specific life tasks including those shifts to a new cultural milieu that deprive a person of his "cultural selfobjects," during his mature years or when he has to deal with a debilitating illness, or the confrontation with death (Wolf 1980; A. Ornstein 1981).

Let me first focus on the developmental lines of our twinship or alter ego needs. I turn to this particular need first and will discuss it more broadly than our need for self-enhancement by a merger with ideals because the latter have become more familiar to us. They have, after all, been conceptually separated (as transference entities) for a good many years, while the recognition that our twinship or alter ego needs deserve a separate status and have a separate line of development has come only recently.

I believe that I simultaneously became aware of the significance of the need for alter ego or twinship experiences in two distinct transference forms, one pathological and one normal. Although different in external appearance, these two forms possess one thing in common: the relevant transference experiences are revivals of analogous experiences during that part of later childhood which, in conformity with the traditional drive-psychological terminology, we tend to refer to as early "latency." Even though I recognized the significance of these two phenomena simultaneously—that is, it was only the observation of both of them in the clinical situation that alerted me to their significance—I realize in retrospect that I had in fact observed the pathological form on a number of occasions, and its significance became clear to me only after I recognized that it was the regressive fantasied equivalent of experiences that normally contribute to the sustenance of the child's self via enactments with selfobjects responsive to the child's specific needs.

The transference revival of the pathological variant can take a broad spectrum of forms. In one woman patient, for example, it was via some quasi-fetishistic and quasi-obsessional preoccupations which occurred during a period preceding my summer vacation that my attention was first drawn to the phenomenon in question. Her manifest dreams and conscious daydreamlike associations began to deal with things rather than with people, and I noticed, in particular, the recurrent theme of covering things: putting the lids on jars, removing flowers from vases and putting something (a piece of cardboard or paper) across the top, putting corks into empty bottles, putting a glass plate over an empty aquarium, and the like. When I called the patient's attention to the changed content of her dreams and associations and, in particular, to her understandably depressed mood and (not yet understood) repetitive quasi-compulsive preoccupation with closing up hollow spaces, adding that these developments had come about after I told her about the lengthy summer vacation I would be taking that year, she responded with associations that led back to her childhood. Specifically, she associated to her protracted loneliness when she was about six or seven years of age. At that time, her family had moved to a new location, depriving her of the friendly closeness of grandparents and exposing her in a more concentrated way to her cold and distant parents. It was in pursuit of these memories from latency that she admitted, against great resistance, not only that she had had a bottle on her bureau that she always kept stoppered, but that she had imagined some person to be living in this bottle—"my genie," as she tried to joke—with whom she had endless talks during the period of her greatest loneliness. Despite the fact that the memory of these childhood experiences had always been available to her, she had never told me about them, ostensibly because they had never occurred to her during the analytic sessions but also, as she came to recognize with increasing clarity, because she felt keenly ashamed of them. The reason for her great shame—and thus for her intense resistance to talking about this topic—was that the symptom, if one can call it that, had persisted into her adult life and that, even now, she occasionally carried on talks with "the genie in the bottle" which were, as the psychiatric lingo goes, "borderline" in character. In fact, it was difficult to say whether she was actually delusional during such periods or simply engaging in daydreams and fantasies.

After this aspect of her inner life that was formerly unknown to me became shared knowledge between us, the patient felt much relieved. It was at this time that I ventured the guess that, since the topic had come to a head after I had announced that I would be away for several weeks, the captive in the bottle was none other than me—a transference revival of the maneuver in latency that followed the loss of the sustenance of her grandparents, in particular, of her beloved paternal grandmother. The patient's response to my interpretation, although given with great reluctance and embarrassment, was yet an unequivocal no. It was not the analyst who was the genie in the bottle, and it had not been her grandmother in childhood. Then as now the captive was a little girl, a twin, someone just like herself and yet not herself to whom she could talk, who kept her company and made it possible for her to survive the hours of loneliness when she felt that no one other than her companion in the bottle cared for her.

I will not expand further on the investigation of the nature of the alter ego of this patient except to note that the insights gained during the period in which she anticipated losing me also helped me to grasp the meaning of the transference that had been established *before* I informed her about my vacation. Formerly, I had misunderstood the essence of the transference by assuming that I was dealing with the patient's need for an approving and accepting mirroring selfobject. But, as I now came to understand, unlike Miss F. (see Kohut 1971, pp. 286–87), this patient did not want me to repeat what she had said, to reflect her moods, to confirm her being present and alive, that is, to concentrate entirely on her. Her self was sustained simply by the presence of someone she knew was sufficiently like her to understand her and to be understood by her. As long as the transference had been in balance, as it had been, more or less, until I told her I would be going away, her self had indeed been sustained by my simple presence, by my allowing her to experience me as, in essence, just like her self. The perfect selfobject for Miss F. had been the one that repeated and confirmed what she had said, that had no function other than to vitalize via emotional participation and reflection what the patient had experienced but was unable to feel as real. This patient's need, by contrast, was for a silent presence. She would talk to the twin, but the twin did not have to respond to her. As a matter of fact, just being together with the twin in silent communion was often the most satisfactory state. This interpretation of the beneficial effects of silently being together, in essence given by my patient rather than by me, illuminated the significance of the long periods of silence that had occurred earlier in the analysis—silences that my intellect told me must be "resistances," even though I had always tolerated these interludes easily without impatiently urging the patient to communicate her thoughts. The interpretation further clarified the meaning of the benefit that the patient had to this point in treatment derived from seeing me, at least as long as she could maintain the twinship experience.

But I also learned another very important lesson from this patient, one that derived both from a deeper understanding of the dynamics of the twinship transference and from the scrutiny of the genetic precursor of the sequential transference experiences. Let me say first of all that, at the time I treated this patient, I had already formed a vague notion of the decisive difference between instinctually cathected objects who are the targets of our drives and selfobjects who maintain the cohesion, vitality, strength, and harmony of the self. And although the distinct formulations that I at present employ were not available to me then, I still knew, in essence if not by name, what a mirroring selfobject was. In fact, the crux of my confusion at the time was not between a love object and a selfobject but between a mirroring and an alter ego selfobject. And what I learned from this case, apart from obtaining a first insight into the meaning and significance of psychological twinship, was—as I have said many times since in various ways—that the archaic selfobject need did not proceed from the loss of a love object but from the loss of a more mature selfobject experience.[2] Although analytic insights about our patients are usually first obtained via the scrutiny of the ongoing transference, an important point that applies, I believe, in general to new insights in depth-psychological research, this case was one in which the pivotal discovery of the precursor of the pathological experience, of the normal counterpart of the genie in the bottle, was drawn from genetic material. I will dispense with the details of the process that led to the crucial memory and proceed immediately to the end result. The memory—never repressed as to its content but never before appreciated with respect to the emotional significance of the content—was that of being in her grandmother's kitchen (perhaps at the age of four) while her grandmother kneaded dough, and she too silently kneaded dough on a little table next to the big one on which her grandmother was working.

"What an anticlimax!" the reader may well think. Indeed, what a seemingly insipid, everyday occurrence compared to the drama of the primal scene, of the child's sexual excitement and death wishes, that Freud wrested from the unconscious. Perhaps so, but I would point out that dramatic excitement and truth value do not necessarily go hand in hand. The self sustenance that a little girl might get from silently working in the kitchen next to her grandmother, that a little boy might get from "shaving" next to his daddy or from working next to his daddy with daddy's tools in the basement—these are indeed undramatic everyday events. The drama ensues or, more correctly, the tragedy ensues when a child is chronically deprived of such experiences—unless, of course, his self receives its primary sustenance in the areas of mirrored ambition and merger with idealized goals. It is then, after the self has fallen apart, that those dramatic events occur that we have so often in the past taken for the deepest, drive-fueled sources of pathology. In fact, they are secondary developments, transitions between the nuclear pathology (the injured self) and the surface manifestations of the disturbance in adult life.

But I must return to the context in which I introduced the foregoing clinical vignette. One of my purposes in adducing this material, indeed the most important purpose, was to justify a change in our classification of selfobject transferences by which we add a twinship (alter ego) transference to the mirror transference and the idealizing transference, thus positing the existence of three major selfobject transferences. This is tantamount to postulating three separate lines of selfobject development rather than subsuming the twinship transference under the mirror transference and dealing only with two developmental lines of basic selfobject experience.

Clearly, the discovery of important pivotal points at the ages of, say, four and six in this supposedly separate line of selfobject development is not sufficient to warrant the change in our classification. We need additional data—obtained through either observation, introspective thought experimentation, or both—indicating that important twinship (alter ego) experiences are self-sustaining events not only, let us say, from the age of four to ten (when events like those which my patient reported when she was four are easily ascertained in many instances), but throughout life. It is not a question of looking for point-by-point replicas of the little girl's kneading dough in the kitchen or the little boy's working next to his father in the basement; we must find experiences that provide emotionally analogous support, however greatly the content of the experiences may differ from the content of the preceding clinical vignette.

Are there such analogous experiences both earlier and later in life? I cannot give an affirmative answer with complete confidence, but the evidence clearly points in this direction. As one would expect, it is difficult, if not impossible, to reconstruct from the transference experiences of our analysands those states of early psychological life that correspond to, or are precursors of, the common experiences I have just discussed. Again, it is not external resemblances that we are looking for, but identity of significance, similarity of function.

When a friend puts his hand on our shoulder when we are troubled, this symbolic gesture indicates without a doubt that a self-selfobject relationship is being established, that our fragmenting, weakening, or disharmonious self is made more coherent, is being invigorated, or is having harmony restored via the friend qua selfobject. But can we determine with confidence whether the restoring function emanates from a mirroring selfobject, an idealized selfobject, or an alter ego selfobject? Clinical experience, self-observation, and reflection tell me that the situation I am describing is not likely to be one of twin-ship—the gesture (i.e., the touching of the shoulder) seems to speak against such an interpretation. But is the gesture a symbol for a merger with a mirroring selfobject or with an idealized selfobject? Or, to put the question into the more specific terms that lead us back to the context of our present reflections: is the shoulder-touching move a mature replica of a merger with an archaic mirroring selfobject or an idealized selfobject? Although on the basis of clinical experience, in-trospection, and thought experimentation I am inclined to say that in most instances the gesture indicates that the experience of a rela-tionship to an archaic idealized selfobject is being enacted, a reliable decision can only be made via the detailed examination of just what the participants in our little scene are experiencing. It is most likely, as I said, that the disturbed recipient of the friend's touch senses this gesture as a replica, however distant, of times when, as an upset baby, he was lifted up by his mother and thus able to merge into her calm-ness and omnipotent strength as he was held close to her body, suf-fused by the sense of merger with her and by the sense of participation in her perfection. But must it always be that way? Is it not possible that the same gesture, perhaps enacted in a way that differs ever so slightly from what we have just described, could also be the repetition of a merger with an archaic mirroring selfobject? In this case, the touching would signify approval, an expression of confidence in our innate power and in our resilience; it would constitute an expression of admiration for us even in our present state of disturbance. I have no doubt that this could be the case, and I will further admit that occasionally, though rarely, the same situation may relate to early twinship support. In any event, I believe that an inquiry of this sort, apart from the specific context within which it is being undertaken here, would inevitably lead to results that support, and even make inescapable, the conclusion that we must speak of selfobjects not only with respect to early childhood and the regressive states of later life, but in the context of the normal experiences of support, indeed, the continuous stream of supportive experiences that we need to maintain the self during all periods of life: in later childhood, in adolescence, as adults, in old age, and ultimately in death.

But now, after this, I believe, necessary digression, let us return to the question of whether there are precursors to the easily observable and comparatively well-known "chip off the old block," alter ego re-lationship of later childhood that I adduced. Here we are entering a territory that is difficult to explore. In later childhood we clearly see that it is the intermediate area of skills and talents—the girl kneading dough, the boy working with tools—that is the leading contact point in the twinship; the archaic precursors of these experiences, however, cannot be formulated in such clearly defined terms. Still, I have had the increasingly strong impression that we do encounter important self-affirming and self-maintaining experiences in early childhood that can be classified in terms of neither the mirroring needs of the self nor the self's need to merge into ideals of calmness and strength. Why do I associate these experiences with archaic alter-ego relationships? I can best put my impression into words by saying that—parallel to the older child's sense of security as he feels himself to be a cook next to a cook or a craftsman next to a craftsman—the young child, even the baby, obtains a vague but intense and pervasive sense of security as he feels himself to be a human among humans.

Some of the most painful feelings to which man is exposed, unforgettably described by Kafka in *The Metamorphosis* and observable during the analyses of many people with severe narcissistic personality disorders, relate to the sense of not being human. The awareness of such a central distortion in the personality stems, I believe, from the absence of *human* humans in the environment of the small child. The mere presence of people in a child's surroundings—their voices and body odors, the emotions they express, the noises they produce as they engage in human activities, the specific aroma of the foods they prepare and eat—creates a security in the child, a sense of belonging and participating, that cannot be explained in terms of a mirroring response or a merger with ideals. Instead, these feelings derive from confirmation of the feeling that one is a human being among other human beings. To be sure, the specific features of these early impressions vary—explaining, for example, the reassuring magic of hearing one's mother tongue on returning from foreign language excursions—but they all point to something that human beings have in common: an overall alikeness in the capacity for good and evil, in emotionality, in gesture and voice. These aspects of our basic alikeness are signposts of the human world that we need without knowing we need them so long as they are available to us.[3]

And twinships later in life? I believe that our observations inside and outside the analytic situation supply us with numerous data that support the hypothesis of a line of development of twinship transferences and other self-sustaining twinship experiences. Homosexual relationships, for example, can easily be classified in accordance with the predominant selfobject need that is fulfilled by either passive or active enactments. The younger partner (whether or not actually younger in years is irrelevant; he enacts the child) looks up at the father in admiration; the father feels confirmed by the approving admiration of the young partner. But there are also homosexual relationships in which each partner is the mirror image of the other, the other's alter ego or twin—not only in the emotional sphere but in the area of sexual practices as well.[4] Nonsexual friendships between members of the same sex can also be classified in accordance with this schema, as can heterosexual relationships, determining marital choices and the favorite forms of sexual enactment. The special requirements of artists are good sources of information in the present context. When I first described a "transference of creativity," I particularly had in mind the creator's need for a merger with an idealized selfobject while he was engaged in the most taxing creative tasks and the subsiding of this need after the daring creative step had been carried out.[5] But mirroring needs (e.g., of Proust and Celeste; O'Neill and Carlotta Monterey) are by no means rare, and twinship relationships (e.g., of Picasso and Braque, as described by M. Gedo 1980, especially p. 84) also occur side by side with the other forms of transference that fulfill the needs of certain creative individuals.

But I cannot remain with the subject matter of the twinship transferences and other twinship relationships any longer. I only wanted to supply sufficient evidence to support the viewpoint that it deserves to be investigated separately and regarded as one of the major self-object needs of man. And I adduced the foregoing material in particular because I wanted to demonstrate that the basis of my proposal is not the compatibility of such a conceptualization with the model of the self with which we are now working—specifically, the assumption that we have three areas (the pole of ambitions, the pole of idealized goals, and the intermediate area of skills and talents) to which the three major selfobject needs may be said to correspond—but the fact that our introspective and empathic immersion into the inner life of man provides us with data that are most unforcedly classified when we subdivide them into the three aforementioned groups.

Although I am not quite ready yet to let go of the subject matter of the classification of selfobject transferences altogether, I will interrupt my discussion of this topic for a moment in order to stress the fact that, however important the classification of the basic selfobject transferences may be, in and of itself, I am discussing it here mainly to emphasize what should indeed go without saying: (1) that the self-object transferences arise spontaneously and without any active encouragement from the side of the analyst and (2) that their analysis lies in the center of the analytic task. The selfobject transferences arise, in other words, in consequence of the fact that certain developmental needs were not responded to adequately in childhood but, on the other hand, were not frustrated completely. Owing to the fact that at least one of the selfobjects of childhood was not totally unresponsive to the needs of the childhood self, in other words, hope was kept alive, and given the hope-activating import of that specific set of circumstances which we call the psychoanalytic situation (i.e., the patient's experience of being the focus of the empathically listening analyst), this hope is intensified and leads to the unfolding of a transference. Still, while my treatment of the transferences in this chapter aims primarily to underscore these two aforementioned points, I will proceed to a few additional reflections about the specific classification of the transferences I have just proposed.

Specifically, I want to point out that classifications, whether of so-called disease entities or syndromes, of personality types, or—our present hope—of the various genetically preformed patterns of childhood needs and/or wishes that we call transferences, are always artifacts (see Kohut and Wolf 1978 for a critical discussion of psychoanalytic typologies). Although classifications can never do full justice to the complexity of the phenomena that the analyst is studying, we still need classifications to give us a degree of cognitive mastery of our complex field, and we further need terms that refer to various classes of psychic phenomena in order to discuss our findings with colleagues. Our subdivision of selfobject transferences, however strained and oversimplified it may often seem, enables us to refer to the specific thwarted need of the analysand's self in childhood and to the specific person from childhood whose archaic selfobject responses the analysand tries to elicit again from the analyst. In other words, it enables us to conceptualize the various genetic clusters of thwarted developmental needs, independent of the specific pathological state of the self that supervened as a result of the selfobject failures of childhood and independent of whether the self became predominantly prone to fragmentation, enfeeblement, or disharmony, or of which mixture of these different propensities characterized the resulting self disturbance. The ability to differentiate between various types of selfobject transferences also gives us the opportunity to study in greater detail the developmental line characteristically associated with the archaic form of a particular self-selfobject relationship—from the archaic state that is revived at the beginning of the transference to the mature state which, as a result of the systematic and patiently pursued working-through process, may be attained at the end of successful analyses.[6]

But however helpful classifications in general, and the classification of selfobject transferences in particular, may be, the conceptual categories of any classificatory system become a hindrance rather than a help when, rather than alerting us to the occurrence of preponderant clusters of genetic and experiential importance, they become concrete entities, demanding that we force the data we observe into the rubric of an unalterable scheme. My own attitude toward the classifications I have proposed has always been that they are temporary, changeable, improvable—in short, that they will cease to be useful if we are unwilling to alter them in order to accommodate new insights or facts. And this is an attitude I have especially taken—to the discomfort of those colleagues who look, alas in vain, for reliable and enduring guidelines for their observations and thought—with regard to the classifications of the selfobject transferences. True, we can differentiate between the three major functions that our selfobjects performed for our childhood self, the three functions that create a self that we experience as cohesive, firm, and harmonious. And true, our selfobjects may traumatize us by failing us selectively in one or two of these functions. But there remain important issues that our classificatory procedure, in and of itself, cannot at present resolve. Turning to the endpoint of development—and to the endpoint of the successful analysis of a patient with a self disorder—people may ultimately be sustained from all three directions, that is, all three constituents of the self will receive emotional support from the mature self-selfobject relationships that result from normal development or successful analysis. But this desirable result is by no means always achieved via a uniform distribution of the three kinds of sustaining forces. There are certainly great variations within the spectrum of normality or maturity. Certain people are predominantly creative and self-expressive, and their creative selves are sustained by the actually occurring, or at least confidently expected, approval of the selfobject milieu in which they live. Others are predominantly sustained by feeling uplifted by ideals—all the sustaining forces which our culture puts at our disposal at any given time and place, that is, our current cultural selfobjects belong here. Culture, in other words, can indeed function as a selfobject—as differentiated from civilization, which can be defined as the sum total of the drive-taming institutions of society—whether it is via a multiplicity of diverse functions or through the personified embodiment of a single cultural hero–ideal such as, in the case of most psychoanalysts, the idealized image of Freud. Finally, there are still other people who derive the sustenance that maintains their selves mainly from feeling surrounded by alter egos. They feel strong and cohesive as members of a group of people whom they experience as being in essence like them, doing similar work, sharing similar biases and predilections, and the like. Anyone who has been away from his usual surroundings for some time—in a foreign country, for example—will remember the strengthening feeling of again being surrounded by other people who are like himself, a feeling, I will add, which is not to be confused with being mirrored by these people or with having the opportunity to idealize them.[7] Still, having considered this explanatory limitation of our present classificatory schema, I remain convinced that this schema has much to recommend itself, that it is helpful, and, at present, perhaps even indispensable in our work. There are many occasions when we can indeed distinguish quite clearly one or the other of the three types of selfobject transferences, when, for example, after making observations or interpretations that presume one type of transference, our analysand's reactions indicate unequivocally that we had misunderstood him. In particular, there are many occasions when we can clearly determine to which one of the three selfobject needs the childhood milieu had been especially unresponsive (thus traumatizing the self) and, last but not least, to which of these needs it had responded with at least a modicum of understanding (thus imparting a degree of structure to the self, though unable to endow it with firmness, vigor, and harmony). It is often the analyst's understanding of the last-mentioned set of childhood experiences that becomes pivotally important when the analysand's transference begins to turn to the analyst qua that childhood selfobject which, although not sufficiently responsive, had still been the best one available. It is this selfobject transference that becomes the crucial one, because it is around this less traumatic selfobject that the analysand's movement toward health now attempts to organize itself.

Our clinical material is replete with relevant data—there is hardly a case of self disorder in which the analysis of the transference would not provide supportive material—bearing on the "principle of the formation of compensatory structures" (see Kohut 1977, pp. 3–6) that I enunciated in the preceding paragraph. Someone[8] will gradually appear in the patient's memories from childhood who, differing from the hypochondriacal, anxious, nonsustaining member of the family, was, or at least had once been, strong and idealizable. Within the context of the transference, an outline will gradually come to light of a person for whom the patient's early existence and actions were a source of genuine joy; the significance of this person as a silent pressure, as an alter ego or twin next to whom the child felt alive (the little girl doing chores in the kitchen next to her mother or grandmother; the little boy working in the basement next to his father or grandfather) will gradually become clear.

One lesson to be derived from the foregoing considerations is clear: the classification of selfobject transferences—and this obtains for all our concepts and theories—must remain our helpmate and not become our master. So long as it assists us in our work, so long as it aids us in bringing order into the profusion of seemingly incoherent data we encounter in clinical and nonclinical fields, so long will we be willing to overlook minor inconsistencies and shortcomings. But the defects of our theories (and classifications are de facto theories) become significant if explanations based on them cease to be in harmony with the clinical and nonclinical data or cease to be relevant to large areas of the field under investigation. In either of these eventualities, they must be replaced by better ones.

Fortunately, I feel certain we have not reached this latter juncture with respect to the classificatory schema of the selfobject transferences. On the contrary, the formulations that can be derived from the schema are, as repeated observation has taught us, in harmony with the clinical data; moreover, they are able to guide us successfully when we investigate new material, in particular the emerging transference, during the analysis of new patients. It is only with the aid of our classification, for example, that we can, on the basis of clinical evidence involving the sequential unrolling of selfobject transferences, recognize that disabling disorders of the self come about only when at least two of the three constituents of the self have serious defects because of flawed or insufficient selfobject responses in childhood. On the basis of the data supplied by the selfobject transferences that establish themselves in analyzable disorders of the self (i.e., the narcissistic personality and behavior disorders), we can further ascertain that the selfobjects' inability to respond appropriately to the developmental needs of *one* of the constituents of the self will bring about an intensified attempt to obtain adequate responses to the developmental needs of the *two others*. In such instances, a health-providing sectorial continuum in the self may yet be established if the circumstances are favorable. After prolonged attempts to obtain even minimally adequate selfobject responses for one constituent of the self have failed, in other words, another constituent of the self, supported by sufficiently sustaining selfobject responses, will grow with special vigor. In so doing, it is potentially able to provide the psyche with that new sectorial continuum—we speak of "compensatory structures" in this context—which, given at least adequate opportunities, will allow the unfolding, the flowering, and the ultimate fruition via creative-productive action of a person's central life program as shaped by his particular ambitions, talents, and ideals. If earlier mirroring responses are badly flawed, for example, the child will intensify his search for the structuring presence of a selfobject that is experienced as an alter ego or for the uplifting, self-organizing experience that comes from the availability of a selfobject that is idealizable. Just as a tree will, within certain limits, be able to grow around an obstacle so that it can ultimately expose its leaves to the life-sustaining rays of the sun, so will the self in its developmental search abandon the effort to continue in one particular direction and try to move forward in another.

We believe that we have to date learned two specific lessons about these developmental vicissitudes of the self. The first lesson, as I noted before, is that the self will be seriously impaired only if, after one of the selfobjects of the child has failed to respond, the attempt to acquire compensatory structures via the adequate responses of another self-object has also come to grief. The second lesson—I realize that I am repeating myself, but I believe these statements bear repetition—is that in a properly conducted analysis, that is, an analysis that does not block the spontaneous unfolding of the transferences, the basic and pivotal selfobject transference that ultimately establishes itself will frequently be organized around the *less* traumatic aspect of the self-object milieu of childhood or, as we can often put it, around the less traumatic of the two selfobject parents.[9] It is the working-through process mobilized by the analysis of this central selfobject transference that, as clinical experience has taught us, ultimately leads to the strengthening of that compensatory area of the self, insufficiently established in childhood but yet not hopelessly defective, which brings about the analytic cure.[10] Whether this pivotal transference is a mirror transference, an alter ego transference, or an idealizing transference, it is the repetition of the two-step interventions of the analyst—the experience, over and over again, of understanding followed by explaining—that leads to structure building via transmuting internalizations.

Just as in normal development the baby's need for the direct and immediate mirroring by the empathic mother is gradually replaced by the more mature expectation that others will appreciate his achievements; just as in normal development the baby's reassuring awareness of being surrounded by the voices and smells of a human environment leads to the older child's sense of strength (as the little boy plays at shaving while his father shaves, or the little girl works in the kitchen next to her mother), and subsequently leads to the adult's reassuring experience of being surrounded by other persons who are (nationally, professionally, etc.) essentially identical[11] to him; and, finally, just as the baby's archaic merger-idealizations of fusing with the calm body of the adult who picks him up gradually lead to the reassuring and self-organizing experiences embodied in our admiration for great political leaders, artists, scientists, and their inspiring ideas—so also in analysis. Time and time again in the course of analysis, the basic therapeutic unit is brought into play when a disruption of the selfobject transference, be it of the mirroring, twinship, or idealizing variety, is understood and explained and a potential trauma is transformed into an experience of optimal frustration. And, in consequence of these optimal frustrations, the needs of the analysand gradually change as, via imperceptible accretions of structure, his damaged self is increasingly able to feel enhanced and supported by those selfobject responses that are available to adults. And just as young children who walk away from their selfobjects for the first time retain the need for the selfobjects' empathic responses—their pride in the children's growth, the silently present example of their own grown-up existence in a milieu of selfobjects, their goal-setting ideals—so also with our analysands. With each step forward there is the anxious question of whether the selfobject analyst's empathy will follow them on the new level they have reached, and of whether he will respond with the correct interpretation of their transference needs. Perhaps more important still, each time the analyst's interpretations are wrong, inaccurate, or otherwise faulty, there is the anxious question of whether the selfobject analyst, often in contrast to the parental selfobject of childhood, will be able to recognize his mistake and thus transform a potential trauma into a development-enhancing structure-building optimal frustration. And, as the analysis ends, the patient's ultimate step toward health may again require the analyst's acknowledgment— if the patient invites this endorsement—that however exhilarating the experience of a self that has become a center of independent initiative may be, the maintenance of such a self will always require a responsive selfobject milieu which one must learn to find and secure.

As I near the end of the section of this book dealing with the nature of the psychoanalytic cure and, more especially, with how self psychology sees the movement toward cure in analogy to the movement which, under favorable circumstances, takes place in early development, I will return briefly to a question that I considered in the preceding chapter: has self psychology introduced a new kind of empathy into analysis? I trust that my preceding discussion of the difference between empathy, the theories that inform it, and the two-step sequence of our clinical interventions has clarified my reasons for answering this question in the negative. Should someone still insist that the new theories have enriched our capacity to observe the inner life of man to such a degree that quantitative change has become qualitative, I would not engage in an unrewarding argument with him. Certainly, if someone were to advance the claim that Brunelleschi gave a new vision to man, who would take issue with the assertion? But I would insist nonetheless that such a statement is more poetry than science—a claim which does not deny that poets may at times express certain psychological truths more poignantly and, within certain limits, more relevantly than we scientists are able to do.

Concluding Remarks

I have now come to the end of my inquiry regarding the self psychological theory of the therapeutic action of psychoanalysis. Although the self psychological theory of analytic cure, in harmony with the self psychological outlook on man—that is, the expanded focus that allows us to acknowledge the significance of the problems of tragic man and to study these problems with scientific seriousness—is clearly different from the theory of cure propounded by traditional analysis, I do not consider it a deviation from traditional theory but an expansion of analytic understanding, however tentative, incomplete, and in flux the new insights may be.

Self psychology does not advocate a change in the essence of analytic technique. The transferences are allowed to unfold and their analysis—the understanding of the transference reactions, their explanation in dynamic and genetic terms—occupies, now as before, the center of the analyst's attention. Where the self psychologist deviates from the classical model, from Eissler's (1953) "basic model technique," he does so not because he strays from the basic principles which, to his understanding, underlie analysis (e.g., by introducing "parameters" [cf. Eissler 1953]), but because he seeks to adhere to them even more closely than those who prescribe strict adherence to the traditional rules of analytic technique. We believe that the theory of drive primacy and drive taming and the theory of the movement from dependency to autonomy and from narcissism to object love are—or have gradually become—part of a supraordinated moral system in scientific disguise; we therefore believe, verbal disclaimers to the contrary, that the actual practice of analysis is burdened by an admixture of hidden moral and educational goals. Self psychology, by contrast, holds that it is consistent with the guiding principles of a scientific psychology of complex mental states to say that we are dealing with drive experiences and not with drives; that, if the self is healthy, the drives are experienced not in an isolated fashion but as an immanent modality of this healthy self; and that, under these circumstances—even when we set ourselves up against our aggression and lust—pathogenic conflicts will not arise, however great our pain, however absorbing our struggles. Self psychology further holds, again in contrast to traditional theory, that the conception of a powerless baby, seen as existing outside a sustaining selfobject milieu, creates an artifact and that the theory derivative to this erroneous conception—that normal development proceeds from helpless dependence to autonomy and from self-love to the love of others—is therefore misleading. Self psychology asserts that normality is properly defined by positing a meaningful sequence of changes in the nature of self-selfobject relations throughout the course of a person's life; normality is not tantamount to the claim—the unrealistic claim—that the need for selfobjects is relinquished by the adult and replaced by autonomy and object love. We see a movement from archaic to mature narcissism, side by side and intertwined with a movement from archaic to mature object love; we do not see an abandonment of self-love and its replacement by the love for others.

It is against the background of this shift in outlook that we must understand the claim that the essential result of an analytic cure is the taming or relinquishment of the patient's infantile drives. In fact, this result is not the patient's abandonment of dependency relationships and becoming strong and autonomous, and it is not his turning self-love into the love of others. A good analysis will have explained to the patient how the shortcomings of the selfobject milieu brought about the deficits in his self structure and how, in consequence of the absence of the joy that results when the self feels welcomed and supported by its selfobjects, the drives became isolated as a depressive self attempted to maintain itself through joyless pleasure seeking. And a good analysis will have explained to the patient, furthermore, that the anxious clinging to the archaic selfobject and its functions was not due to a childish reluctance to give up old gratifications; instead, it was a welcome indicator that the striving to complete the development of the self had never been totally given up. And finally, a good analysis will have explained to the patient how the stalemated development of the self led to the emergence of the persisting—and, again, in essence welcome—demands, often deeply buried in the personality, that the selfobject ultimately respond adequately so that development may proceed to completion.

A good analysis, we believe, leads to a cure only by its employment, in countless repetitions, of the basic therapeutic unit of understanding and explaining, that is, via interpretations, the analyst's only active function in the analytic process. True, we must not be perfectionists; we accept the fact that a modicum of psychotherapeutic impurity will often if not always be present, even following analyses that have been satisfactorily concluded. Such impurity will be found alongside the structural changes effected by the analysis, essentially grafted into the fully transmuted new structures that have been acquired. Although the self psychologist knows that self psychology, by allowing the analyst to recognize and analyze the selfobject transferences, has enormously reduced this psychotherapeutic admixture, he also knows that the ideal zero-point of such admixtures is still out of reach. (This recognition probably means no more than that there are still transferences—probably varieties of selfobject transferences—that have not yet been discovered and which, therefore, remain unanalyzed.) Still, while we are justly proud of the advances that analysis is making in the therapeutic realm, we will not, to repeat, be perfectionistic. As exemplified by our acceptance of a self-analytic function in certain former analysands, we will not fault either traditional or self psychologically informed technique for such harmless impurities in its results. We cannot be equally indulgent, however, with regard to terminations in which the analysand's recovery is inextricably interwoven with certain permanent restrictions—especially with restrictions in his freedom to employ his creative mobility—and, as I have explained in detail, we are deeply dissatisfied with the results of our training analyses in this respect. Here we indeed see results that deviate grossly from the analytic ideal: a state of psychic well-being which, uncomfortably resembling the beneficial effects of commitment to religious dogma and to personified symbols of salvation, is achieved via the permanent espousal of a set of basic beliefs and an unbroken attachment—in submission or rebellion—to an idealized leader figure.

Self psychology is at one with the technical principle that interpretation in general, and the interpretation of transferences in particular, is the major instrumentality of therapeutic psychoanalysis. We believe, however, that interpretation can only be truly analytic, that is, will ultimately allow the analysand to live in harmony with the patterns of his own nuclear self, if it is given without the hidden moral and educational pressure that is unavoidable as long as the traditional emphasis on drive primacy, the infant's helplessness, and the pejorative connotation of the concept of narcissism are retained. Only if the analyst is able to grasp more or less accurately the experiences of his analysand, present and past, will he, via his interpretations, set up a working-through process that re-creates in the analysis a situation that provides protracted, development-enhancing exposure to optimal frustrations. It is this opportunity, insufficiently provided to the analysand in childhood, that is offered once more by analysis.

Notes

1. As I said before, all value judgments are to a certain extent self-fulfilling prophecies, and the procedure employed by the psychology of the self, i.e., its positing of
the reliable continuousness and cohesion of the tension arc of the self as yardstick with
which to measure health, is no exception. It is no exception because we, too, first claim
the validity of certain evaluative standards and then apply this yardstick to data that
are themselves correlated to the values of which the yardstick is composed. There is
no doubt that we are doing this; indeed there is no other way. In questions of health
and cure the choice of an axiomatically posited set of values must be made. But there
are two important arguments that can be made in support of our approach. The first
is that our value system is based on a claim that rests on empirical data and can therefore
be either proved or disproved by observation. The claim in question is that human
beings may have the experience that they are leading—or, toward the end of their lives,
that they have led—meaningful, joyful, fulfilling lives despite the absence of pleasure
and despite the presence of physical and psychological (including psychoneurotic)
suffering. Stated in the obverse, the claim in question is that human beings may have
the experience that they are leading—or, again, have led—meaningless, joyless, empty
lives despite their success in obtaining pleasures and despite the relative absence of
physical and psychological pain. The second argument in support of our approach is
that, given our definition of a desirable human existence as sketched out in the foregoing, we may still investigate, and by adducing empirical data prove or disprove, the
claim that the presence of an essentially cohesive self, the existence of an energic
continuum between ambitions and ideals, is the sine qua non of the capacity to lead
such a fulfilling life. It is certainly possible, for example, that we may in the future
discover certain specific discontinuities in the self that do not stand in the way of a
fulfilling life—a finding that would necessitate a revision of our theory.

2. The following discussion of the psychoses and borderline states is undertaken entirely from a psychological point of view. The fact, however, that instances exist in which periods characterized by the perfectly organized functioning of important and vigorously active compensatory structures not only *alternate* with periods of psychotic disorganization but may even be maintained *during* periods of psychotic disorganization seems to me to defy psychological explanation and require the positing of an etiologically decisive organic element. I cannot see, for example, how an utter distortion of reality such as the one that held sway over Van Gogh during the time of his self-mutilation could be compatible with the profoundest perception of reality achieved by the artist during the same period if the disturbance responsible for the reality-distortion was primarily psychological. To my mind, it is only the presence of a decisive organic factor that can explain the simultaneous preservation of an undamaged creative sector—a continuum from the depth of creativeness over the perfection of skills to the synthesizing powers of the artistic ideals—with utter disorganization, impulsiveness, and gross disorder of thinking.

3. As an aside I will mention here, in an attempt to diminish the misgivings of colleagues who feel that our communications should always be conceptually exact, that I am aware of the fact that the expression "distant, understimulating parental selfobjects" is inexact and inconsistent. To be fully precise, I would have to speak of "the specific unavailability of those functions of the parents that we call selfobject functions—an unavailability that, in experiential terms, can be characterized as 'distant' and that, in interactional terms, can be referred to as 'understimulating behavior.' "

4. More research should be done on the varieties of selfobject failures at various phases of development including illustrations of the difference between selfobject failures during the oedipal stage, e.g., the personality disturbance of a mother who needs to include the child as support for her fragmenting or weak self and imprisons the child, prevents him from being with other children.

Chapter Two

1. In this context it behooves us to ponder C. Daly King's statement that the "average may be, and very often is, abnormal. The normal, on the other hand, is objectively, and properly, to be defined as *that which functions in accordance with its design*" (1945, p. 493). We may or may not choose to use King's definition of normalcy, and we are also free to dispense with the value-laden principle of normalcy altogether. Still, if we need to choose a baseline from which to measure degrees of deviation, King's concept strikes me as a very felicitous one for this purpose. It is in this sense, for example, that my statement that "the baby is born strong, not weak" has to be understood. The baseline used in this maxim is informed by my assumption that the baby's adult parental environment is, to apply King's definition, functioning "in accordance with its design" when it reacts with empathic responsiveness to the baby. Assumptions that babies will survive psychologically when they are provided with "good enough mothering" (Winnicott 1965), or that all babies feel helpless and develop defensive, hallucinatory, wish-fulfilling ideations (Freud 1900, 1953, 5:565–67) along with a belief in the omnipotence of their thoughts and wishes (Ferenczi 1916), or that babies are all basically depressed and paranoid because they feel abandoned and mistreated (M. Klein 1932) are undoubtedly based on empirical data, the statistical frequency of which may perhaps become determinable some day. I do not object to these claims per se; I do find them objectionable and misleading, however, when, as has happened to a greater or lesser extent with all these assumptions, they become basic to the definition of psychological man, to the essence of man's psychological condition. My assertion that the human baby is born into a milieu of empathic-responsive selfobjects, on the other hand, can

be properly taken as a baseline of normal psychological experience—the baby *is* strong—just as his being born into a milieu of oxygen can be properly taken as the baseline of his physiological functioning—the baby *is* healthy.

2. For the sake of completeness and in order to express myself as exactly as possible concerning the significance of the oedipal phase, I will admit here that the division between internal response (the child's own pride) and external response (the pride of the parental selfobjects) is a concession to entrenched thought patterns and conventional language. In fact—in *psychological* fact, that is—the two experiences are two facets of the same central constellation inasmuch as the indivisible self-selfobject unit, while undergoing many changes from infancy to old age, continues to exist as the essence of psychological life from birth to death.

3. For an illustration of parental joy and pride in a child's aggressiveness, see Kohut (1978*b*, 1:438).

4. I intentionally did not say "the most intensive anxiety" because the degree of anxiety that an individual actually feels is influenced by many factors. But I would not hesitate to state unequivocally that disintegration anxiety is not only man's deepest but also, *potentially,* his most severe anxiety.

5. While there is some truth in the statement that all the forms of anxiety enumerated by Freud, and especially the one he designated fear of loss of love of the love object, contain admixtures of disintegration anxiety, the attempt to establish a conceptual equivalence between Freud's categories and disintegration anxiety as understood by self psychology results in a tour de force with ambiguous results. A meaningful equivalence might be established if we specified, vis-à-vis Freud's "fear of loss of love," that we are dealing not with the fear that the love object will withhold love (thus leading to a blockage of libidinal discharge and a catastrophic increase in libidinal tension) but with the fear that the selfobject will cease to sustain the child's self.

6. I will not repeat my account here but trust that the reader will refresh his memory by perusing the passage in question.

7. Some aspects of this analysis, though not this dream, have been reported before (see Kohut 1977, pp. 55–58, 79–80).

8. Rendered schematically, the analyst first took the place of the fetish; later he was increasingly experienced as a responsive, optimally frustrating selfobject; then—and this is the juncture at which the dream occurred—at the time the patient began to think about leaving the analysis, the usual pretermination regression occurred and the analyst again became the fetish of Mr. U.'s childhood whose presence had protected him from disintegration.

9. I discovered the material about Bismarck's relationship with Schweninger in Pflanze (1977). For a general discussion of the selfobject significance of eating and food, see Kohut (1978*b*, 2:789–90 and 845–50).

10. In the present context I would like to draw attention to two passages in my work (Kohut 1978*b*, 2:706–21 and 908–14) in particular the anecdote concerning the wish of the astronauts to be "reunited with earth," which affirm and illustrate the fact that disintegration anxiety rests on the fear of being permanently deprived of "human meaning, human contact, human experience" and that this fear is even greater than the fear of death. Furthermore, although on two previous occasions I did not express myself as explicitly on the differentiation between two types of anxiety experience as I am able to do now, the two above-mentioned comments (see also Kohut 1977, pp. 103–8, where I first expanded on the topic under scrutiny) approach the issue from a somewhat different angle and might thus be of assistance in deepening the grasp of the significance of the differentiation.

11. I am fully aware of the fact that most analysts have traditionally maintained—though not all of them (cf., for example, the remarks of Freud 1930, 1953, 21:103,

and Eissler 1963, p. 1403, on the lack of genuine creativity in women)—not that the male sex organs *are* more desirable, but only that they *seem* to be more desirable to the child (and, by extension, are responded to as less desirable by the archaic layers of the adult's mind). I have come more and more to the opinion that even this benign view of the genesis of the belittling of the female is in error. I do not believe, in other words, that a child's low self-esteem, in general, and low body-self-esteem, in particular, are in essence gender-related. For the little boy no less than for the little girl, such disturbed self-esteem is a pathological state with genetic roots in the flawed mirroring responses of the selfobjects of childhood (see Kohut 1978*b*, 2:776–77).

12. With regard to the nature of the evidence capable of confirming the theories of the depth-psychological researcher, see especially Kohut (1978*b*, 2:737–70, and 1977, pp. 140–70).

13. I will from now on speak (1) of the oedipal *stage* when I have in mind the joyfully experienced step of normal development, the proudly achieved forward move of the oedipal child whose selfobjects respond to their child with the pride and joy that testifies to the presence of a firmly established empathic parental self; (2) of the Oedipus *complex* when I refer to the pathologically altered experiences of the child whose selfobjects feel (preconsciously) sexually stimulated by their child's qualitatively changed and intensified affectionate attitudes and actions and/or endangered by their child's qualitatively changed and intensified assertiveness; and (3) of the oedipal *period* when I refer to neither normal nor pathological development but am simply talking about the time-limited phase in the life of the child when the normal or pathological experiences of either the oedipal stage or the Oedipus complex are in evidence. (I may, occasionally, also employ the term oedipal *phase* when I want to stress the developmental-maturational regularity of this period without, however, specifying whether it has or has not become abnormal.)

14. See in particular the differentiating comparison between Freud's early seduction theory and the self psychological theory, p. 11.

15. The question that needs to be answered is really this: are traces of the self-disturbance that leads to oedipal neurosis more frequent than traces of the self-disturbances that lead to narcissistic personality and behavior disorders and to borderline states and psychoses? I cannot answer this question conclusively; I can only say that on the basis of my own clinical experience the answer would have to be in the negative. To be more exact, these traces are ubiquitous with reference to all developmental stages, and in my experience there is little evidence for the predominance of parental failure that is more or less restricted to the oedipal phase. Indeed the clinical evidence available to me points the other way. Yet, wherever the emphasis might now be placed, why should traces of an Oedipus complex not be present in every human being? The need to be mirrored, to be proudly included with the idealized selfobject are great after every developmental spurt—one might speak here of a principle of the vulnerability of new structures (see Kohut 1971, p. 44, where I refer to Hartmann 1964, p. 177). It thus stands to reason that the little girl and the little boy experience new expansive feelings of affection and assertiveness at the beginning of the oedipal phase and that the oedipal self demands proud and pleased confirming responses and reacts with disastrous fragmentation to serious shortcomings of the selfobject milieu. Could it be, one might speculate, that the tendency toward minimal shortcomings in the oedipal selfobject milieu was selected into our own species over millions of generations because the children exposed to such shortcomings fared better in life—because they stimulated the "transmuting internalization and creative change" of which I spoke—while children who remained *totally* untraumatized developed only their primary psychological equipment, having no need to develop creative compensatory structures?

16. The full weight and extent of the influence which the theoretical views outlined here have on the clinical practice of psychoanalysis—in particular with regard to the all-important shift in the ambience of psychoanalytic sessions—will become apparent in chaps. 5 and 6, which examine the nature of the therapeutic action of psychoanalysis.

17. A male patient, for example, whom I analyzed many years ago, remembered that as an oedipal child he had had a nightmare of being attacked by a lion. When he told his mother about it, she responded with cold reason to his fears and took him to the lion house in the zoo to demonstrate to him that one need not be afraid of lions. It will come as no surprise to the self psychologically informed analyst that the analysis of this patient went beyond the Oedipus complex and finally focused on the severely distorted personality of his bizarrely unempathic mother and on the unavailability of his more emotionally accessible father who had volunteered for military service and was away from the family for several years. What was decisive to this patient's analytic cure, in other words, was not fear of the stronger competitor's revenge, but the absence of healthy psychological structures that would have prevented the spread of his anxiety. The mother's lack of compassion and inability to soothe the child along with the father's unavailability as a model of idealized courage and calmness, in other words, were responsible for the psychopathology, not the ubiquitous situation of childhood competition with a stronger rival. For the sake of completeness, I should add that another mother's taking her child to the zoo after a similar nightmare might have to be evaluated quite differently. If a healthy responsive mother, grasping her child's fears, first responds to this fear with soothing compassion and then, after the child's anxiety has subsided, suggests a trip to the zoo together, the secure overt act would then simply be a specific detail of the overall pattern of a wholesome selfobject milieu. No single act—and this dictum holds also mutatis mutandis for the analyst's responses in the analytic situation—can be judged in isolation.

18. I have unfortunately not analyzed a phobic woman during the past fifteen years, i.e., since I began to adopt the viewpoint of self psychology; I am therefore relying on therapeutic experiences that I had many years earlier. I realize that these data are less than optimal, and I hope that others who have the opportunity to analyze patients with agoraphobic symptomatology will reevaluate the clinical material in the light of self psychology, report their findings, and either confirm, amend, or contradict my hypotheses.

19. As an aside, I will mention that the effectiveness of psychopharmacology in agoraphobia, particularly the use of tricyclics, might well be understood psychologically within the framework of self psychology, which sees the deficiency of soothing, anxiety-curbing, idealized structures as the central illness. The drug, like the accompanying woman, takes the place of the precursor of psychological structure, i.e., of the archaic idealized selfobject into whose calmness and strength the self can merge. In view of the fact that neither coping strategy activates working-through processes, however, calming structures are not laid down and addictionlike dependence on either the drug or the accompanying woman persists.

20. Nor, to emphasize my point more strongly, does the sexual wish for the father constitute the more severe pathogenic pressure. On the contrary, it is the need for the selfobject mother that constitutes the nucleus of the psychopathology. It is the very severity of the structural deficit in the sphere of the anxiety-curbing functions that makes it impossible for the patient to fight against the need. As is the case with the analogous dependency of the addict, the personality has to bow to the pressure of the need in order to survive.

21. For a previous discussion of selfobject failures vis-à-vis specifically intense or unusual demands, see Kohut (1977, pp. 25–29), where I discuss a selfobject's relative failure in the face of an especially trying task—the failure of Mr. M.'s mother vis-à-vis her child's excessive demands. In this case, I should note, the extra burden that the

mother was unable to carry was not due to the baby's congenital shortcomings, but to the fact that the baby had been adopted after having spent the first three months of life in an orphanage. But the considerations regarding the relationship between self-object failure and the extra demands placed on the selfobject are probably quite similar in cases of congenital defect and early traumatization.

Chapter Three

1. It may be fruitful at this juncture to compare my statement about the significance of the experience of being listened to in order to be understood with the following terse statement of Freud's: "When are we to begin making our communications to the patient?" Freud asks. And he replies: "Not until an effective transference has been established in the patient, a proper *rapport* with him. It remains the first aim of the treatment to attach him to it and to the person of the doctor. To ensure this, nothing need be done but to give him time. If one exhibits a serious interest in him, carefully clears away the resistances that crop up at the beginning, and avoids making certain mistakes, he will himself form such an attachment and link the doctor up with one of the imagos of the people by whom he was accustomed to be treated with affection" (1913, 1966, 12:139–40). I believe that in this statement Freud refers, tangentially and in a few word to the area which self psychology has come to consider the most central and significant in the analytic process, an area worthy of intensive and detailed study. As I noted above, the major part of the present work examines this aspect of the analytic process. At this point, I would only like to stress, as I have done and will do again, that it is the self psychological shift in emphasis—from the centrality of biological drives to the motivating force of the psychological need for a milieu of empathic selfobjects—that accounts for the fact that a constellation of psychic forces Freud considered of only small significance and treated in a rather cursory fashion has now become central for us. This constellation of forces, which we conceptualize in terms of the selfobject transferences, has been, and will continue to be, the subject matter of our continuing investigations. It is noteworthy, however, that Freud, in the obiter dictum just quoted, refers to a *positive* experience of the past, albeit, of course, within the framework of the libido theory (he says "by whom he was . . . treated with affection" where we would say "whom he experienced as a not *completely* unsustaining selfobject"), thus establishing a link between his work and the work we are now pursuing.

2. With regard to the opposite potential shortcoming of the psychoanalytically informed psychohistorian, his inability to think himself accurately into the personalities of those who participated in historical events that took place long ago because the gap between his cultural milieu and that past era is too great, see Kohut (1978b, 2:910–13, 917–19).

3. For a discussion of the reason for my present adherence to the term "transference neurosis" despite the fact that patients suffering from narcissistic personality and behavior disorders also establish analyzable transferences, see Kohut (1980, pp. 525–26).

4. The self that ultimately emerges as the result of a successful analysis of a patient with a narcissistic personality or behavior disorder is never a self that is created de novo by the treatment; what emerges is a structure that in its outlines was already determined in childhood. This is the case whether the self was built up of incompletely consolidated primary structures or, as is more frequently the case, of incompletely consolidated compensatory structures. The latter structures were incompletely laid down when, following the traumatic failure of one selfobject, the child turned to another which, though better able to respond to the child's needs, was still not able to provide the child with a firmly consolidated self. The most frequent reason for this failure, according to my clinical experience, is that the second, less pathological parental figure

could not assert itself sufficiently against the more pathological one. As a result, the structure that the child acquired from the less pathological parent went into hiding and was deprived of the opportunity for consolidation and growth. Although there are instances in which the personality of the analyst, or his or her personality-determined selection of interpretations, determines which of two (or more?) potentialities concerning the content and shape of the self is ultimately consolidated in a successful analysis (see Kohut 1977, pp. 262–66, for a discussion of such an instance), the occurrence of these instances does not contradict the dictum that analysis does not create, as in childhood, a self de novo but only a strengthening of preexisting structures. The fact that a reconsolidated self may ultimately express its program by either one or another action pattern, in other words, is due to the fact that these potentialities had been almost evenly balanced in the patient *before* he entered analysis.

Chapter Four

1. I was referring to the statement that "self-selfobject relationships are present from birth to death" which I had introduced as a prototypical example to serve as a point of departure for my argument.

2. When I refer here to the formulations of traditional psychoanalysis in order to contrast them with those of self psychology, I do not have in mind Freud's general statements about neurosogenesis in childhood—here he did indeed stress from early on the influence of environmental factors and acknowledge their influence via his references to the complementary effect of inherent (hereditary) factors and traumatization by the environment (i.e., the "complementary series"). There is no question, however, that having felt befooled by the seduction stories of his hysterical patients, Freud henceforth concentrated not on the influence of the childhood milieu, but on the patient's contributions to his illness. To the end, in other words, he maintained that when the deepest drive-related experiences had been mobilized, analysis had penetrated as far as it could, had reached biological bedrock (see Freud 1937, 1953, 16:252).

3. In theory, any value could cease to exist. If man's propensity to react with anger would vanish, for example, even nonaggression values, such as those on which the Sixth Commandment is based, would become irrelevant.

Chapter Five

1. It is in the same context—i.e., in the context of my argument against assigning curative primacy to verbalizable insight—that my discussion in chap. 7 of the significance of the presence of a self-analytic function after termination should be viewed. While I agree that, for practical purposes, the posttermination appearance of the ability to employ a self-analytic function is to be welcomed, I insist that, in principle, it is an indicator that the analysis has remained incomplete. Simply put, its appearance not only indicates in many instances that the patient has had a good analysis, but also that even in the best analyses the working through of the selfobject aspects of the transference has led to only imperfect results. Analogous considerations apply, mutatis mutandis, to the developmental processes that take place in the matrix of a childhood milieu of appropriately responsive selfobjects. The recurrence of certain childhood memories, in particular memories of instances when the selfobjects of early life provided us with self-cohesion-enhancing support, must not be taken as necessarily signifying the presence of a defensive screen against the recall of traumata. Such recurring memories indicate instead that the transmuting internalization of the wholesome milieu had not been completely achieved.

2. I will mention here that my own earlier statements regarding "the mechanisms which bring about therapeutic progress in psychoanalysis" (Kohut 1971, pp. 196–99), while correct in terms of the conceptual framework that was at my disposal at the time, were incomplete. They were incomplete because they were restricted by the conceptualizations of ego psychology, i.e., they were based on the erroneous theoretical conception of the adult personality as an autonomous organization—an organization that had relinquished its ties to selfobjects, that had overcome the need for a nurturing selfobject milieu.

3. An examination of the analytic process described with regard to several of the cases reported in *The Psychology of the Self: A Casebook* (Goldberg 1978) could, for example, be undertaken to adduce support for the hypothesis offered here. Some material about postanalytic adjustment from an analysis that I described extensively (1979) could also be reexamined to serve at least as an illustration in depth. Finally, I would like to report that I have been able to help via analysis a number of individuals whose most important symptom was an inability to realize their full creative potential. In each case—one involving a world-famous scientist whose successful therapy, unfortunately, cannot be reported—the reactivation of creative ability was reached indirectly and only after the passage of some time following the termination of treatment. In the case of the scientist, for example, the crucial link in the causal chain that led to his great professional success about four years after the termination of therapy had not been discovered while he was still in treatment. It was after the analysis that this patient provided himself with—or, I should rather say, provided his self with—the support of an empathically responsive selfobject: he married a woman who fit his needs in every respect. Through the marriage, he thus created a milieu in which his creative mind was able to perform at full capacity. (Compare, at a somewhat lower level of achievement, the patient described in "The Two Analyses of Mr. Z." [1979] and also my remarks about the comparably ameliorative effect of Eugene O'Neill's third marriage [1980, pp. 493–94].)

4. It is clearly too restrictive to equate "the analyst's failures" with his flawed "interpretations," as I have just done. What constitutes a failure cannot be defined in terms of the analyst's performance considered in isolation. Just as the adequacy or inadequacy of a mother's or father's selfobject functioning must be evaluated with reference to this or that specific child, i.e., with reference to the specific selfobject response required by a particular child (cf. Kohut 1977, p. 29), so also with the responses of the analyst. With some patients it may indeed be adequate to equate the analyst's failure as his flawed "interpretation." With other patients, however, the emotional reverberations that accompany the analyst's interpretation—communicated via his tone of voice and by other means as well—are as important as the verbal message that he communicates. Even a correct and accurate interpretation, in other words, can be flawed if the patient senses that the analyst offered the interpretation in an emotionally flat, preoccupied, or disinterested way. It goes without saying that such faulty responses become grist for the mill of the analytic process if the patient's subsequent retreat elicits an interpretation of the dynamics of the transference and the reconstruction of the genetic factors that are the basis of the patient's specific sensitivity.

5. I am referring here only to the narcissistic personality and behavior disorders and am disregarding the fact that I believe the oedipal neuroses, too, should be viewed as self-disorders in a wider sense (see chap. 2).

6. To this most general description of the gradual change (from merger to empathic resonance) in the nature of the bond between the self and its selfobjects that takes place as the child grows up, I must add this qualification. During periods when a person's self is exposed to severe stress, his ability to avail himself temporarily of archaic modes of narcissistic sustenance via archaic self-selfobject processes of support is an

asset of his personality organization and a quality that is not only compatible with, but specifically characterizes the mature self organization of some of the most successfully creative-productive individuals. This is another appropriate place (see note 1 above) to acknowledge that sensitive, psychologically gifted analysts have always silently assumed that the capacity to which self psychology now refers as "mature selfobject resonance" is implied in the concept of mature relations with a love object, and they may be inclined to protest that the self psychological conceptualization of a changing matrix of self-selfobject relations is unnecessary. To this objection, I would reply that self psychologists, in their conceptual and terminological originality, remain truer to the spirit of drive psychology than analysts who, unwilling to make the necessary theory changes, twist the concepts of libido theory to the point where its creator would not be able to recognize them anymore. The sexual drive which cathects the love-object imago can be sublimated via the maturation of the drive-processing structures of the ego, but it always remains nondirectional as far as the object is concerned. Only the conceptualizations of self psychology allow us to transcend the limits imposed by a system that rests on the basic assumption of the primacy of drives and drive discharge. Only when the self is placed in the center of the psychological system, that is, can we examine in an unforced way the need for selfobjects that enable the self to maintain its cohesion, strength, and harmony, including its ability to enjoy drive experiences and to engage in assertive action. Correspondingly, only when the self is seen as psychologically central can we fully understand its fragmentation, weakness, disharmony, and the ensuing emergence of drive fragments and disturbances in assertiveness.

7. Although I generally do not get overly excited by issues of classification and nomenclature, I believe I should here say a word about the usefulness of the conceptual differentiation between severe narcissistic personality disorders and borderline states that I have recommended (Kohut 1971). My proposal is based on dynamic-structural considerations and not on the assessment of the patient's symptomatology or behavioral disturbance. Certain patients with severe narcissistic personality disturbances may temporarily suffer from frank delusions (see, for example, Kohut 1971, p. 136), and certain patients who, according to my classification, are "borderline" (see, in particular, my discussion of the "schizoid personality" in Kohut 1971, pp. 12–14) will neither suffer from any troublesome symptoms nor exhibit abnormal behavior. My differentiation is based on the assessment of the specific dynamic-structural conditions that characterize the patient's personality. Specifically, the question we must ask ourselves in arriving at a differential diagnosis is whether or not the patient is able to develop a selfobject transference when the opportunity to reexperience the selfobject of childhood is offered to him in the psychoanalytic situation. If the answer is yes, we will diagnose the patient as a "narcissistic personality disorder"; if the answer is no, we will diagnose him as "borderline." The line, as is generally true for the differentiation between neurosis and psychosis, is not an immovable one. It may depend, for example, on the skill and special gifts of the therapist or on the special psychological fit between a given patient and the personality of a given therapist. A psychosis or borderline state in one situation may be a severe narcissistic personality disorder in another. As this last judgment suggests, I am a diagnostic relativist up to a point. I say "up to a point" because there are many instances when the confluence of severe early trauma and congenital vulnerability lead to such severe impairment of the ability to fit into a responsive selfobject milieu that no therapist, at least with the psychotherapeutic tools that are currently at our disposal, would be able to provide a milieu in which the would-be analysand could develop a selfobject transference (see Brandchaft and Stolorow 1982).

8. The nature of my practice has not in recent years provided me with the opportunity of studying the return to a healthy oedipal stage at the end of successful analyses of

structural neuroses. Retrospectively, however, I can recognize this development as having occurred in patients whom I analyzed many years ago.

9. In view of the fact that I have defined "empathy" as "vicarious introspection" (Kohut 1978b, 1:205–32), my use of the phrase "the patient's empathy with himself" might seem to be strangely inconsistent at first glance. Still, if one considers our ability to step away from ourselves and look at ourselves as objectively as possible, i.e., as if we were another person, the differentiation between "introspection" (the directly perceived experience of one's inner life) and "empathy with oneself" (the indirectly perceived experience of one's inner life) will make sense.

10. But see Kohut (1978b, 1:233–53, esp. pp. 240–43) for a discussion of secondary processes outside the realm of language and verbal thought.

11. Extensive studies of the great variety of selfobject relations that support the cohesion, vigor, and harmony of the adult self need to be undertaken, ranging from the cultural selfobjects (the writers, artists, and political leaders of the group—the nation, for example—to which a person feels he belongs; the events that increase the sense of support one receives from these cultural selfobjects during repressive crisis situations, or the uplifting admiration one feels for cultural heroes during temporarily increased uncertainty of self cohesion as it occurs during periods of transition and change, such as in adolescence) to the mutual selfobject functions that the partners in a good marriage provide for each other. Concerning the latter—an extremely important topic that awaits detailed investigation from the vantage point of self psychology—I used to quip for many years that "a good marriage is one in which only one partner is crazy at any given time." (Compare Shakespeare's beautiful depiction of the perfectly mutual self-selfobject relationship in the words of Othello: "She lov'd me for the dangers I had pass'd; And I lov'd her that she did pity them.") It is only now, however, with the aid of self psychological understanding, that I can grasp the meaning of my own joke. The truth to which it alludes is that a good marriage is one in which one or the other partner rises to the challenge of providing the selfobject functions that the other's temporarily impaired self needs at a particular moment. And who can potentially respond with more accurate empathic resonance to a person's needs than his or her marital partner? And, conversely, who—as every analyst has ample opportunity to observe—can traumatize a person more than a wife or husband who, like the traumatizing parental selfobject of childhood, responds with flawed understanding or, feeling overburdened, refuses to respond at all? This is indeed the stuff of which the breakup of marriages accompanied by the undying hatred of the marital partners for each other (chronic narcissistic rage following chronic disappointments) is made.

Chapter Six

1. I know of one analysis, for example, which, after making steady progress with a severely traumatized patient for two years, came to grief because the analyst insisted on changing the position of her chair in order to prevent her patient from continuing to glance at her face at certain crucial moments. The analyst tried to justify this move to the analysand by telling him that the rules of analysis prohibited this kind of gratification—that gratifying him by making her emotionally involved face available to him would be an obstacle to "remembering" and "working through." She thereby repeated the chronically cold attitude of the patient's schizoid mother who had imposed bizarre rules of behavior on the child from the time he was born and had been unable to respond to him with natural warmth and concern. The analysand felt unable to tolerate this change and ended treatment. Could an analyst have done what this one did and still made it possible for the patient to continue treatment? Perhaps so, i.e., if the analyst had been able to convince the patient with all her available warmth that she understood

the intensity of his need, his almost unbearable sense of isolation that craved relief at certain decisive moments, and further, if she could have reconstructed, with similarly deep involvement, what his despair had been as a child, how enraged he had become in analogous situations, and the like. Under these circumstances, the patient might have been able to tolerate the unavailability of her face and to replace it with verbal understanding from her side. But one wonders why an analyst would feel obliged to instigate such a contest of wills in the first place. In my clinical experience of the past ten to fifteen years, I seem to have avoided such impasses entirely; I did, however, encounter them infrequently during my earlier years as an analyst. It is not that my gross behavior toward my analysands has changed—I still sit behind them in the conventional way. But on the basis of the deepened understanding of certain dimensions of my analysands' personalities afforded by self psychology, I have come to feel freer and, without guilt and misgivings, to show analysands my deep involvement and concern via the warmth of my voice, the words that I choose, and other similarly subtle means.

2. I will take up this theme more extensively, especially with regard to the reinterpretation of the dream of the return of Mr. Z.'s father, in chap. 9.

3. In the example I am discussing, suggestibility may, however, play a role in the analysand's not noticing that her jaw muscles are tight or remembering that they had been tight. Suggestibility, in other words, may play a role in the patient's compliance with the analyst's theoretical outlook and ability to supply the analyst with concrete data to support it. In the case of our example, one would have to know many details about the interactions between patient and analyst that preceded the incident under discussion. Had the analyst, for example, transmitted her pleasure and approval when the patient supplied her with confirmatory data? And had she, however subtly, expressed disapproval of the analysand upon the emergence of contradictory material?

4. I am stressing this, I assume, self-evident truth to underscore once more that conceptions of the therapeutic process in psychoanalysis are selected, refined, discarded, and replaced on the basis of scientific and not moral considerations. Values of courageously-facing-the-truth or of bravely-confronting-the-biologic-(drive)-bedrock-of-human-nature should play no role in determining which methods of therapy are the most thoroughly helpful and reliable. Comparably, such values must not be invoked as arguments, either pro or con, when changes in psychoanalytic theory and technique are being advanced.

5. Since my own psychoanalytic knowledge and experience was obtained almost exclusively under the aegis of classical analysis (see Kohut 1978b, 2:931–38) and since an adequate appreciation of my work is impossible without a thorough knowledge of traditional theory and practice, I have often regretfully pondered the question of why the classical tradition has disregarded those "crucial experiences" of today to which I make reference. After all, classical analysis, and especially ego psychology, some crucial errors in theory and practice notwithstanding, continues to be the most significant and respectable organized branch of scientific depth-psychology, and my own long-standing emotional commitment to the traditional approach has not ceased to exist. My tentative answer to the question of why traditional analysis has neglected these experiences—specifically, why it continues to look on psychopathology almost exclusively from the viewpoint of structural conflict and the Oedipus complex—is as follows: in harmony with the popular saying that "a half truth is the worst enemy of the truth," the half truth of Freud's early experience-distant formulations about libido regression and fixation allowed analysts to protect themselves against empathic immersion in the analysand's diseased self and prevented them from arriving at the experience-near formulations of self psychology that are relevant to the psychic miseries of our time. Specifically, the availability of the classical theory of regression and fixation, particularly in the form of a complementary series, has been able to cover up the fact that one of

the most important clusters of human psychic disturbance remained de-emphasized. To put it still differently, the regression-fixation theory now leads some critics of self psychology to maintain that the self psychological field of inquiry was explained long ago by Freud and the ego psychologists. For these critics, the old theories are satisfactory and do not require the complementary insights of self psychology. The security that these claims have provided for us has, up to now, prevented us from perceiving what many of our patients have been trying to tell us for a long, long time: that the issues they are facing cannot be joined in earnest as long as our theories dictate an ultimate focus either on the drives, genital or pregenital, as the biological bedrock of our personalities, or on the ego, mature or infantile, as the central organ of a mental apparatus that mediates between biological drives and the curbs imposed on them by reality.

6. Having made this statement, I should immediately add that the contribution of self psychological theory to the understanding phase of treatment is not to be underestimated. Aspects of the theory may only be *spelled out* to the patient in the explanatory phase, but accurate understanding is still facilitated by the ease with which the empathic bond between analyst and analysand is reestablished—and this latter task is aided by self psychological theory. To be sure, even analysts who subscribe to "incorrect" theories can eventually achieve empathic understanding of their patients, but the more accurate their theories the easier this task and the more adequate and encompassing the cures they can hope to achieve.

Chapter Seven

1. [For a fuller discussion of these concepts and their influence on the analyst's attitudes toward cure, see vol. 3 of *Search* (in prep.) for a letter from Kohut to a colleague (E.) which has been somewhat condensed for this book.—E.K.]

2. [For an elaboration of self-state dreams, see the letter to E. in vol. 3 of *Search.*— E.K.]

3. I am unfortunately unable to reveal the details of the clever device that the patient used in law school since I would thereby endanger his anonymity.

4. In this context a remark by Mozart demonstrates that even a genius may remain aware of the fact that previous work was necessary to move beyond conscious attention to detail. "Whenever I play for Richter," he wrote once, "he invariably looks at my fingers, and one day he said, 'My God! how I am obliged to torment myself and sweat . . . and for you, my friend, it is merely play!' 'Yes,' said I, 'I had to labor once in order not to show labor now.'"

5. It is significant to recall that Freud applied his complemental series principally to the ordering of factors that bring about pathology, whereas the self psychological outlook is at least equally interested in examining, identifying, and defining the health-enhancing factors.

6. When we turn to such concepts as "biological equipment," "biogenetic inheritance," and the like, we have not turned to the biological bedrock on which psychology rests, but simply switched from one exploratory framework to another. To clarify my meaning with the aid of the opposite approach: we can examine the activity of ganglia and perhaps in the future obtain as yet unforeseeably detailed knowledge about them. But however far the researcher may penetrate into the secrets of ganglionic activity, he will not in this way participate directly in the thoughts, feelings, and experiences of an individual. The psychologist of the future, for his part, may undertake introspective-empathic investigations that lead to observations and discoveries that have a profound impact on the biological research of the future. But he would comparably have no right to speak of the "psychological bedrock of biology," even if he were inclined to make so bold an assertion. We are simply dealing with two different ways—the introspective-

empathic and the direct and indirect extrospective one—of exploring a sector of reality. And reality, as I have often stressed before, is in essence unknowable. We can only describe what we discover as the result of specific investigative operations.

7. There are unquestionably instances in which the continued search proceeds in the opposite direction or remains with the primary mirroring selfobject. In the case of a woman whose analysis with a colleague I recently supervised, for example, the task that became centrally engaged in the analysis was the abandonment of an idealizing attachment to a severely disturbed father and the renewed search for psychic structure via a return to the weak but less disturbed mirroring mother.

8. I should like to mention here that Mr. Z.'s (Kohut 1979) pivotal dream of the return of the father depicted an analogous psychic situation, both in childhood and in analysis. Mr. Z.'s attempt to stem the tide of paternal gifts related to the threatened destruction of the remnants of his self by the intrusion of another's personality. He tried to modulate the influx in order to safeguard the remnants of his self, to maintain them for the activity—the *active* task—of gradual transmuting internalization that could only take place over a prolonged period of time. Only in this way would his weak and fragmented self become firm and cohesive; only in this way would it retain continuity in time and nuclear sameness. In childhood it had been the father's sudden reappearance after a prolonged absence during a crucial period of self development that had constituted the threat; in analysis it was the forthcoming termination of the first analysis with its implication that too much had to be done in too brief a span of time that threatened Mr. Z. in a similar fashion.

9. When they transgressed, they not only had to "say" they were sorry, they had to "mean" it.

10. My decision here is fully justified by the avowed purpose of this presentation: to present the self psychological viewpoint and to present it, with the aid of clinical illustrations, as clearly as I can within a comparatively limited space. I will not hide my opinion, however—I have, indeed, already expressed it before (cf. Kohut 1977, the chapter entitled "On the Nature of Evidence in Psychoanalysis")—that I am very skeptical about the validity of a proof of theory via clinical data. I believe that the profusion of clinical data that could be called by a psychologically gifted analyst even from the content of a single analytic session is so great and allows itself to be assembled in so many combinations that any proof through clinical evidence is more a testimony to the ingenuity and resourcefulness of the presenter's mind than a reflection of an intrinsic order in the world of experiences (for the only way out of this, to many I daresay disconcerting, fact, see again Kohut 1977, same chapter).

11. To spell out the order of the severity of the resistances: the brother theme evoked the least intense resistances, the attachment to the mother was resisted more, and the emergence of the father-grandfather theme evoked the greatest anxiety, the anxiety of exposing himself once more to a nonresponsive selfobject milieu, and, as I said, appeared last in the treatment.

12. I am speaking here of a difference *in principle* and am fully aware of the fact that the modern ego psychologist's adherence to the concept of resistance does not imply technical crudity or callousness toward his patients. Thus, when the ego psychologist attempts to show his patient that the situation in childhood and the situation in the transference are not the same, i.e., that the analyst is not like the father (distant, unavailable; subdued by the mother) and that the patient's adult personality is more capable of withstanding frustration and delays than the personality of the child, he will do so with understanding and respect. But while he thereby frees himself from the traces of intolerance and dogmatism that Reich's otherwise valuable and appropriately influential *Character Analysis* (1933) left in its wake, it can only be hoped that his inter-

pretations will contain no disapproval based on the conviction that the attitude in question warrants reevaluation and change.

Chapter Eight

1. We may fruitfully compare the assistance obtained via the use of the self-analytic function with the assistance that every healthy adult obtains via the occasionally solicited support of friends or family members who, during especially trying times, are willing to perform the functions that archaic selfobjects had performed when he was a small child. Although there are similarities here, there are also differences: the post-analytic function is performed by the former analysand himself; the use of archaic selfobjects in adult crisis situations requires the cooperation of others; the post-analytic activity characteristically deals with intellectual—in fact, I believe, frequently with intellectualizing—functions whereas the use of archaic selfobjects clearly aims at the fulfillment of archaic needs. Still, I believe that appearances may sometimes be misleading—the occurrence of self-analytic activity may not be as mature as it seems whereas the need for archaic selfobject functions may not be as immature as it appears to be.

2. I am here disregarding a suggestion I made elsewhere (Kohut 1978b, 2:675) that, expressed within the framework of mental-apparatus psychology, we must consider not only the shift that takes place via internalization, i.e., the laying down of features of the world within the mental apparatus, but also a possible further shift within the mental apparatus itself. Thus parental values, after first being half external, finally become fully internalized and form part of the superego. With the passage of time, however, generally over a number of generations, these internalized values may further shift from the superego to the ego: values cease to be values because they are gradually transformed into ego functions.

3. It was similar in this respect to the visual vividness of Mr. Z.'s first dream during his second analysis (see Kohut 1979, p. 11).

4. During this activity, the chewed material was kept in the mouth for long periods while the child, with eyes closed, tried to live through the long hours of the day.

5. The topic under scrutiny here deserves extensive investigation. Does the diminution of conscious self-analysis that takes place in some analysts as they mature in their profession necessarily represent a deleterious development? Should it, at least in some instances, be evaluated as a positive sign, indicating that the total functioning of the analyst qua analyst has improved? Has he replaced plain self-analysis, consciously undertaken, with more nuanced reactions that proceed silently?

6. For Kuhn, whatever the other shortcomings of his approach, change in what he initially called a paradigm does not, after all, mean the end of one science and the beginning of another. The science is the same, its definition given by the field of observation and the basic stance of the observer toward that field. Theory change, the introduction of a new paradigm, does not abolish the science; it is a step in its development. (In this context see Kohut 1977, pp. 298–312.) Analysts, however, have used Kuhn's thesis in defense of the status quo in psychoanalysis via the agreement that a relinquishment of Freud's basic theories, e.g., of transference and resistance, of drive primacy, of structural conflict, would be tantamount to the abandonment of psychoanalysis per se.

7. It is the nature of the subject matter of psychoanalysis, the science of complex mental states accessible to observation only via introspection and empathy, that more or less precludes the use of the experimental method and the application of statistical proof. These deficits—psychoanalysis shares them with other social sciences and the humanities—should be mentioned in the present context, even though they cannot be held responsible for the persistence of the several clannish groups in analysis which,

on the basis of different theoretical views, are inimical to one another. The experimental method and proof via statistical evidence, which are not in any event absolutely reliable prophylactics against the kind of group self pathology under scrutiny here, would still, if available to us, be a powerful antidote against the persistence and the spreading of the disease.

8. On the whole, I believe that we tend to idealize and, therefore, to overestimate the power of the innate creative urge and to underestimate the influence of external forces. As I have pointed out a number of times before, the clustering of outstanding creativity at certain points in history (the Athens of Pericles is an especially compelling example) clearly indicates the important role played by the cultural environment—whether it functions through its ability to encourage creativity through the absence of creativity-stifling factors, or both. That the cultural forces encouraging or discouraging creativity cannot be formulated in simple terms—e.g., in terms of permissiveness versus prohibition—is demonstrated not only by the example of Socrates being sentenced to death during the era of the flowering of creativity in ancient Greece, but also by the analogous examples of Giordano Bruno and Galileo Galilei at the end of the Renaissance.

9. If analysts subscribe to the belief that the capacity to mobilize a self-analytic function and the ability to use it at times of inner disturbance represent the ne plus ultra of mental health, I am inclined to respond by saying that such a claim represents the ne plus ultra of the "tool-and-method pride" I have discussed elsewhere (Kohut 1978b, 2:690 and 678).

Chapter Nine

1. In order to forestall the reproach of historical inexactness, I will add here that I am aware of the fact that Brunelleschi, like all great innovators, had precursors. At the time of his discovery (1490), he had contemporaries who were almost at the point of making the same discovery and who, at any rate, were able to broaden the insight he had provided in significant ways (Alberti 1435).

2. EDITOR'S NOTE. In this paragraph, Kohut is describing a *necessary* perception of misunderstanding on the analysand's part. In the case vignette that follows, he will elucidate such misunderstanding as a transference phenomenon that recapitulates certain events of childhood. It should be clarified at this point that misunderstanding of this sort is to be distinguished from the potentially *avoidable* misunderstanding on the analyst's part that Kohut previously described in the exposition of cure.

3. For another example of a similarly alarming, if less protracted therapeutic impasse, see Kohut 1971, p. 136. The patient reported on there once had the further delusional experience that a fish he was eating was actually looking at him.

4. The female counterpart of this patient, in a number of respects, was Miss F., described in Kohut 1971, pp. 283–93. Her tirades had a quite similar ring, a mixture of despair and reproach, as did those of Mr. A. B., whose treatment began only about two years after I started the analysis of Miss F. Cases of this type are not frequent in the average analyst's practice, but they are by no means rare, provided they are not weeded out by a, to my mind, overly cautious selectiveness. I recently treated a woman, for example, in whom the transference developed in a way that parallels the events that took place many years earlier in the analyses of Miss F. and of Mr. A. B. Although this woman was much less disturbed than Miss F. or Mr. A. B.—she was, in contrast to these analysands, a person with many assets and socially significant achievements—the transference impasse, the reproaches, and my limited ability to see things fully through her eyes, were all the same. Do these facts mean that the cause of these events is so much on the side of the transference repetition of the patient's past that all my learning and accrued experience cannot stem the tide as the traditional viewpoint would be

wont to see the situation? Or am I indeed subject at such times, as these particular patients tell me, to a bluntness of perception that makes their reproaches realistic? I am inclined to believe that both these conjectures contain an element of truth: that I have some remaining difficulty in giving myself over 100 percent to the empathic resonance required by such patients at these periods, and that a more than normal transference distortion of reality forces these patients to insist, on minimal clues, that the analyst is behaving in exactly the same way as the pathogenic selfobject of childhood.

5. I should point out that my use of value-neutral terms such as "event," "moving away," and "holding views that are foreign," is deliberate. I intentionally avoid such, by now, value-laden terms as "separation," "move toward autonomy," and "independence."

6. It should be noted that I am here describing the action under scrutiny in positive terms, i.e., I do not speak of the child's "walking away" from his mother. I might mention in this context that Balint, in his excellent paper contrasting two basic personality types (1955), not only marred his significant message by the use of two indigestible terms ("philobation" and "ocnophilia"), but, more significantly, failed to recognize that the two attitudes he was describing are, psychologically speaking, on different conceptual planes. Thus, in the context of a definition of normality as "that which functions in accordance with its design," the philobat, "the roamer," is normal, whereas the ocnophiliac, "the clinger," is not, independent of statistical frequency of occurrence, i.e., even if we should determine that more children in our culture are ocnophiliac than philobatic.

7. I am here focusing on the analyst qua selfobject in the analytic situation. The points I am making, however, apply, ceteris paribus, to the circumstances of childhood and my conclusions can easily be transposed to early development.

8. EDITOR'S NOTE. Kohut's present use of the expression "experience-distant" is different from its original one (Kohut 1971). In the preceding remarks, he seems to be arguing that the experience-distant appellation pertains to observations that are made (1) from the viewpoint of an outside observer; (2) from the standpoint of our assumptions about normal growth and development; (3) at a higher level of abstraction than "experience-near" observations; and (4) from a morally tinged posture. Yet, under certain circumstances, one can also see the child's anxiety from the outside as well as consider it an adaptive phenomenon that is part of normal development. In differentiating between experience-distant and experience-near perspectives, Kohut really seems to be comparing two theoretical approaches, one of which proceeds to closure without the necessary data whereas the other waits for the confirming data to emerge.

Chapter Ten

1. For an example of the application of this need, formulated in pre–self psychological days, see Kohut 1964.

2. This statement, needless to say, is simply a variant of the self psychological dictum that narcissism has a separate line of development.

3. For a poignant illustration of the sudden awareness of the significance of returning to a human world when the return is suddenly in jeopardy, see Kohut 1978b, 1:441. For a general, anticipatory discussion of the whole area I am dealing with here, see Kohut 1978b, 2:905–7.

4. A different kind of selfobject need influences sexual practice in those homosexual relationships in which the "child" tries to imbibe in homosexual intercourse (via the anus or the mouth) the parental strength he did not receive in childhood.

5. An excellent example of this pattern, worthy of careful self psychologically informed study, is the changing relationship of Nietzsche to Richard Wagner (see Fischer-Dieskau 1975).

6. It should be underlined here that the self psychological outlook tends to emphasize the developmental potential—rather than the lack of realism as adjudged by adult standards—inherent in the archaic psychic organization of early life, particularly in the archaic self. The fact that we can take this position allows us to avoid depreciatory judgments that would not promote the analysand's self development. Sharing with the analysand our sense of the legitimacy of the specific needs of his disordered self, we make it easier for him to integrate these needs with the mature segments of his personality and thus to transmute archaic self needs into their mature counterparts.

7. Vis-à-vis the example of returning home from a foreign country, the experience of feeling strengthened by the presence of alter egos has a quality that can be clearly distinguished from the sense of security we feel by virtue of the fact that, on our return, we are more relaxed because we know our way around, effortlessly understand the language in all its nuances, etc. The support that our self derives from being in a milieu of alter egos, from the nonverbalizable experiences of sameness, of identity, arises whether or not we get any actual help from those whom we feel are like us. It may occasionally occur even under circumstances when we return from a milieu of benevolent non–alter egos to a milieu of alter egos who are inimical.

8. My use of the word "someone" should not preclude the recognition that this "someone" may be a different aspect of the traumatic selfobject; it may also be that the very person who constituted the traumatic selfobject during most of the analysand's childhood became at least a marginally supportive selfobject during another period. I might mention, in this context, that the presence of grandparents in the parental house, or contingencies such as the mother and child living with the maternal grandparents while the father is away for prolonged periods, may be lifesaving for certain children not only because of the vitality of the grandparents, but also because of the mother's greater vigor when she is living with her own parents.

9. We cannot *always* put it this way since, as I pointed out above, it may not be the responses of the other parent but different *aspects* of a single parent's responses that are at stake.

10. I will stress once more that whereas the establishment of a selfobject transference focusing on the less traumatic selfobject and on the rehabilitation of the compensatory structures occurs frequently, there are instances in which the central transference (from the beginning of the analysis or at a later stage of the analysis that follows the unrolling sequence of transferences) focuses on the repair of structures that had been damaged ab initio. In these cases, the developmental needs mobilized in the selfobject transference are not focused on the less damaging of the two (or three) selfobjects to whom the child turned after the failure of the primary selfobject, but on the primary selfobject itself. The transference, in other words, is a renewed and protracted attempt to reactivate the development-enhancing but insufficient or unreliable selfobject responses of the primary selfobject.

11. I am convinced of the fact that Freud's frequently quoted phrase "a clear consciousness of inner identity" (1926, 1953, 20:274) must be understood as a reference to alter-ego support in the sense of modern self psychology. That "identity" here means sameness or alikeness, and not, as Erikson seemingly implied (cf. 1956, especially p. 57, where he says that the term connotes "a persistent sameness within oneself"), a precursor of the concept of a self, becomes clear beyond doubt when we consider Freud's own explanation (in mental-apparatus terms) that what he had in mind was "a common mental construction." No, clearly, the "safe privacy of a common mental construction" (p. 274) to which Freud refers was nothing else but the security of being aware of the presence of alter egos of which I spoke above.

References

Alberti, L. B. 1435. *On Painting*. Translated with introduction and notes by J. R. Spencer. New Haven: Yale University Press, 1956; rev. ed. 1966.

Balint, M. 1955. "Friendly Expanses—Horrid Empty Spaces." *International Journal of Psychoanalysis* 36:225.

Binswanger, L. 1956. *Erinnerungen an Sigmund Freud*. Bern: Frantze Verlag.

Brandchaft, B., and Stolorow, R. 1983. "The Borderline Concept: Pathological Character or Iatrogenic Myth." In J. Lichtenberg, ed., *Empathy*. Hillsdale, N.J.: Analytic Press, [1984].

Chamberlain, H. S. 1899. *Die Grundlagen des neunzehnten Jahrhunderts*. Munich: F. Bruckmann.

de Gobineau, J. A., Comte. 1884. *Essai sur l'inégalité des races humaines*. 2 vols. Paris: Firmin-Didot.

Eissler, K. R. 1953. "The Effect of the Structure of the Ego on Psychoanalytic Technique." *Journal of the American Psychoanalytic Association* 1:104–43.

———. 1963. *Goethe: A Psychoanalytic Study, 1775–1786*. 2 vols. Detroit: Wayne State University Press.

Erikson, E. H. 1956. "The Problem of Ego Identity." *Journal of the American Psychoanalytic Association* 4:56–121.

Fenichel, O. 1945. "Anxiety as Neurotic Symptom: Anxiety Hysteria." *The Psychoanalytic Theory of Neuroses*, pp. 193–215. New York: W. W. Norton.

Ferenczi, S. 1916. "Stages in the Development of the Sense of Reality." *Contributions to Psychoanalysis.* Boston: Badger.

Ferguson, M. 1981. "Progress and Theory Change: The Two Analyses of Mr. Z." *Annual of Psychoanalysis* 9:133–60.

Feyerabend, P. K. 1975. *Against Method: Outline of an Anarchistic Theory of Knowledge.* London: NLB.

Fischer-Dieskau, D. 1975. *Wagner and Nietzsche.* New York: Seabury Press.

Freud, A. 1937. *The Ego and the Mechanisms of Defense.* London: Hogarth Press.

Freud, S. 1953. *The Standard Edition of the Complete Psychological Works of Sigmund Freud.* James Strachey, ed. 24 vols. London: Hogarth Press, 1953–74.

Gedo, M. 1980. *Picasso: Art as Autobiography.* Chicago: University of Chicago Press.

Gitelson, M. 1964. "On the Identity Crisis in American Psychoanalysis." *Journal of the American Psychoanalytic Association* 12:451–76.

Glover, E. 1931. "The Therapeutic Effect of Inexact Interpretation: A Contribution to the Theory of Suggestion." *The Technique of Psychoanalysis,* pp. 353–66. New York: International Universities Press, 1955.

Goldberg, A. 1980. Letter to the Editor. *International Journal of Psychoanalysis.* 61:91–92.

———. 1981. "One Theory or More." *Contemporary Psychoanalysis* 17:4.

Goldberg, A., ed. 1978. *The Psychology of the Self: A Case Book.* New York: International Universities Press.

———. 1980. *Advances in Self Psychology.* New York: International Universities Press.

Hartmann, H. 1964. *Essays on Ego Psychology.* New York: International Universities Press.

King, C. D. 1945. "The Meaning of Normal." *Yale Journal of Biology and Medicine* 17, no. 3:493–501.

Klein, M. 1932. *Psychoanalysis of Children.* London: Hogarth Press.

Kohut, H. 1964. Letter to the Editor. *Christian Century,* 21 October.

———. 1971. *The Analysis of the Self.* New York: International Universities Press.

———. 1977. *The Restoration of the Self.* New York: International Universities Press.

———. 1978a. "Psychoanalysis and the Interpretation of Literature: A Correspondence with Erich Heller." *Critical Inquiry* 4, no. 3:433–51.

———. 1978b. *The Search for the Self.* Vols. 1 and 2. P. Ornstein, ed. New York: International Universities Press.

———. 1979. "The Two Analyses of Mr. Z." *International Journal of Psychoanalysis* 60:3–27.

————. 1980. "Reflections." In *Advances in Self Psychology.* A. Goldberg, ed. New York: International Universities Press.

————. In preparation. *The Search for the Self.* Vol. 3. P. Ornstein, ed.

Kohut, H., Anderson, R., and Moore, B. 1965. "Statement on the Use of Psychiatric Opinions in the Political Realm." *Journal of the American Psychoanalytic Association* 13:450–51.

Kohut, H., and Wolf, E. 1978. "The Disorders of the Self and Their Treatment: An Outline." *International Journal of Psychoanalysis* 59:413–25.

Kramer, M. 1959. "On the Continuation of the Analytic Process after Psychoanalysis: A Self Observation." *International Journal of Psychoanalysis* 40:17–25.

Kuhn, T. S. 1962. *The Structure of Scientific Revolutions.* Chicago: University of Chicago Press.

Laudan, L. 1977. *Progress and Its Problems: Toward a Theory of Scientific Growth.* Berkeley: University of California Press.

Lewin, B. 1958. "Education, or the Quest for Omniscience." *Journal of the American Psychoanalytic Association* 6:389–412.

Lewin, B., and Ross, H. 1960. *Psychoanalytic Education in the United States.* New York: Norton.

Loewald, H. W. 1960. "On the Therapeutic Action of Psychoanalysis." *International Journal of Psychoanalysis* 41:16–33.

Lovejoy, A. O. 1936. *The Great Chain of Being.* Cambridge: Harvard University Press.

Miller, S. C. 1962. "Ego Autonomy in Sensory Deprivation, Isolation, and Stress." *International Journal of Psychoanalysis* 43:1–20.

Modell, A. H. 1958. "The Theoretical Implications of Hallucinatory Experiences in Schizophrenia." *Journal of the American Psychoanalytic Association* 6:442–80.

Ornstein, A. 1981. "The Effects of the Holocaust on Life Cycle Experiences: The Creation and Recreation of Families." *Journal of Geriatric Psychiatry* 14:135–54.

Ornstein, P. H. 1979. "Remarks on the Central Position of Empathy in Psychoanalysis." *Bulletin of the Association for Psychoanalytic Medicine* 18:95–108.

Pflanze, O. 1972. "Toward a Psychoanalytic Interpretation of Bismarck." *American Historical Review* 77:419–44.

Schlessinger, N., and Robbins, F. 1974. "Assessment and Follow-up in Psychoanalysis." *Journal of the American Psychoanalytic Association* 22:542–67.

Schorske, C. 1980. *Fin de Siècle Vienna.* New York: Alfred A. Knopf.

Schwaber, E. 1979. "On the 'Self' within the Matrix of Analytic Theory: Some Clinical Reflections and Reconsiderations." *International Journal of Psychoanalysis* 60:467–79.

————. 1981. "Narcissism, Self Psychology, and the Listening Perspective." *Annual of Psychoanalysis* 9:115–32.

Stone, L. 1962. *The Psychoanalytic Situation: An Examination of Its Development and Essential Nature.* New York: International Universities Press.

Strachey, J. 1934. "The Nature of the Therapeutic Action of Psychoanalysis." *International Journal of Psychoanalysis* 15:127–59.

Terman, D. 1972. "Dependency and Autonomy in the Student Situation: Summary of the Candidates Pre-Congress Conference, Vienna, 1971." *International Journal of Psychoanalysis* 53:47–48.

Watson, J. B. 1925. *Behaviorism.* New York: W. W. Norton & Co.

Winnicott, D. W. 1965. *The Maturational Processes and the Facilitating Environment.* New York: International Universities Press.

Wolf, E. 1976. "Ambience and Abstinence." *Annual of Psychoanalysis* 4:101–15.

———. 1980. "On the Developmental Line of Self Object Relations." In A. Goldberg, ed., *Advances in Self Psychology*, pp. 117–35. New York: International Universities Press.

Zahn, G. 1964. *In Solitary Witness.* Boston: Beacon Press.

Index